ANAMNESIS

Eric Voegelin

ANAMNESIS

TRANSLATED AND EDITED BY

GERHART NIEMEYER

UNIVERSITY OF NOTRE DAME PRESS
NOTRE DAME   LONDON

Translated and edited from *Anamnesis: Zur Theorie de Geschichte und Politik* © 1966 R. Piper & Co. Verlag, Munich. A detailed account of the editorial procedure is available at the "Editor's Preface."

Chapter 6, "Reason: The Classic Experience" originally appeared in *The Southern Review* X, no. 2 (Spring 1974), pp. 237-64 © 1974 by *The Southern Review*.

Library of Congress Cataloging in Publication Data

Voegelin, Eric, 1901–
    Anamnesis.

    Rev. translation of Anamnesis.
    1. History—Philosophy.   I.   Title
D16.9.V5913   1978   901   77-89759
ISBN 0-268-00583-4

Manufactured in the U. S. A.

Grateful Acknowledgment
IS MADE TO
THE EARHART FOUNDATION
AND TO
MR. JOHN C. JACOBS, JR.
FOR GENEROUS SUPPORT IN BEHALF OF
THE TRANSLATION AND PUBLICATION
OF THIS BOOK

Table of Contents

Analytical
Table of Contents

The default of the contemporary school philosophies in the face of perplexing political movements—why do ideological thinkers prohibit the important questions?—the default due to a similar restriction—a desirable analysis of consciousness could refer only to the concrete consciousness of the analyst—the concrete consciousness as the specifically human mode of participation in reality—the content of consciousness could be recovered through historical restoration and original perception—also to be explored: the problem of the resistance to truth.

The conflict between open and restrictively deformed existence dominates our time—the violence of mentally diseased ruling cliques—academically, the restrictive school-philosophies and methodologies, refusing rational discourse—on the other hand: the study of man's normal life in open existence, as a revolt against the dominating forces—the philosopher's task: to find a theory of consciousness that fits these facts—the answer emerging from the study of Husserl's phenomenology—Husserl's concepts of "apodictic beginning" and "horizon of apodictic continuation" as a restrictive vision of existence, abolishing history—the alternative had to reintroduce the historical dimension—history is the permanent presence of the process of reality in which man participates with his conscious existence—man's conscious existence is an event within that reality—such statements could be accepted only if true in the concrete—verification had to penetrate from the engendered symbols to the engendering experiences—why was a consciousness constituted by reality preferable to a reality constituted by a transcendental ego?—the answers had to be sought in anamnetic analysis of a concrete consciousness, my own.

Chapter 2: On the Theory of Consciousness

Philosophizing about time and existence as a residue of Christian meditation—there is no experience of a stream of consciousness except in observing a particular process of perception—the flow of time experienced as sensual awareness of breathing or noises—the "fleetingness" of sense perception contrasted with the nonflowing consciousness—modern attention to the body had balanced our views of consciousness—it tends, however, to an exaggeration that makes a wasteland of consciousness—consciousness cannot be constituted thusly.

The starting point for a description of consciousness is attention—consciousness as the experience of a finite process between birth and death—tensions between the finite process and other, "infinite" processes—Kant's antinomies—since available symbols stem from the experiences of finite processes, the experience of the infinite leads to conflicts of expression—the phenomenon of myths—the problem of the "adequacy" of myths—the "deliberate" myth in Plato—the transcending process called "the others"—unsatisfactory treatment of this by Husserl—the capacity for transcendence is a fundamental character of consciousness—the problem of acknowledging the other as one like myself, as an equal—historical myths of equality— the function of the myth: to finitize transcendence—Vico's understanding of politics as struggles for the myth—the "de-sensualization" of myths in the West and the resulting loss of orientation—their replacement by "the movements."

Process-theology, the third problem area, seeks to express the tensions between human consciousness and transcendence in the language of an immanent process—Schelling's question: "Why is Something?"—the dismissal of this question is a restriction of transcendental reflection to the structure of subjectivity constituting the objective world—resistance to such restriction issues from two experiential complexes—man's structure as animalic, vegetative, and inorganic being is the ontic structure for his transcending into the world—the experience of meditation, at the climax of which consciousness apprehends the contents of the world nonobjectively—from this is inferred the substantive identity of the levels of being—Schelling's "Something" is a justified symbol of the experienced real ground of being.

Past and future as illuminations of a process—is the present a mere point?—while the moment is radically immanent, its ordering requires process-transcending consciousness—human consciousness as "pure" is an illusion—we can "grasp" only a consciousness in a body and in the world—experienceable only as a process—Kant's thing-in-itself overlooks that we experience only consciousness itself—being as a ground is not a datum but approachable only through meditation—neither idealistic nor materialistic metaphysics is possible.

There is no absolute starting point for a philosophy of consciousness—neither can consciousness be made into an "object"—why did there arise an attempt to construct the world out of the subjectivity of the I?—it seems to have sprung from a desire for a new beginning—not all "new beginnings" are of equal value—Plato's "new beginning" was based on the fundamental experiences of *thanatos, eros,* and *dike*—the creation of the transcendental I, however, implied the destruction of the cosmic whole in the subjectivity of the egological sphere.

Chapter 3: Anamnetic Experiments

PREFATORY REMARKS

The variety of transcendences of consciousness—the reflection of them is a biographical event—recalling experiences which have excited consciousness to the "awe" of existence:

1. Months, 2. Years, 3. The Fools' Parade, 4. The Monk of Heisterbach, 5. The Oelberg, 6. The Old Seamstress, 7. The Cloud Castle, 8. The Petersberg, 9. The Freighter, 10. The Koeln-Duesseldorfer, 11. The Netherlanders, 12. The Dutchmen, 13. The Comet, 14. The Loaf of Bread, 15. The Book of Realities, 16. The Kaiser, 17. The Song of the Flag, 18. The Emperor's Nightingale, 19. The Cannons of Kronburg, 20. First Emigration.

PART II. EXPERIENCE AND HISTORY

Chapter 4: What Is Right by Nature?

I. *PHYSEI DIKAION*

"Natural law" and Aristotle's "right by nature"—the connection of justice with the polis—the divisions of justice—the layers of meaning: life in the polis and beyond the polis—justice of the polis as essential law—essential law changeable among men, though not among gods—Aristotle's various meanings of *physika* and *nomika*—the question of the right order of society—tensions between what is right by nature and the changing modes of its realization.

II. *PHRONESIS*

Phronesis as the mediation between the poles of tension—the ontology of ethics—concrete actions as having higher truth than generalizations—the truth of existence in the reality of action— the wise man and the unwise "fortunate one"—ethics as *"kineton,"* being moved cosmically by the cause of all movement— the *spoudaios,* the man who is permeable for the movement— what is right by nature cannot become a set of immutable propositions—phronesis as the virtue of right action and right speech about action—Plato's *phronesis* as the virtue of the man who exists in the vision of the good—*phronesis,* like *philia,* is neither a moral nor an intellectual virtue but rather an existential virtue—summary of Aristotle's investigation of *phronesis:* it possesses the same character as political science but differs from wisdom—in Aristotle's cosmos man is not the highest ranking being—*phronesis* as distinct from knowledge of right action.

Chapter 5: What Is Nature?

Aristotle used "nature" in a traditional meaning that comprised constant structures in the movement of being, gods, and men—the definitions in *Metaphysics* delta—"form" and "matter" are not directly applicable to man in society—similar difficulties with the soul as form and the body as matter—other

philosophers experienced the body as an imprisoning form—
the saints experienced the transformation of their form, or a
new creation within the same identity—a wider philosophical
concept of nature thus is opposed to a narrower metaphysical
one—why was the concept narrowed?

The background of Ionic speculation, between myth and
philosophy—comparison of the Ionic speculation with Egyptian
myths—the Ionic *arche* is a concept that functions like a god but
already contains the experience of the soul-before-god—the
problem of the relation between the divine and being—the
world-transcendent God must be included in the order of
being—dangers of separating God and the world—the relation
between the order of being and the knowing human—the experience of the correspondence of mind and being—the
philosophic concept of nature still preserves the nature of being
as coming-to-be, as given in the primary experience of the
cosmos—this aspect was shoved aside in favor of the form—
because of the emotional block stemming from the fact that the
experience of being is also an experience of God.

When the experience of being differentiates itself from the
primary experience of the cosmos, there emerges the image of
the demiurge—Plato, Aristotle, and Anaxagoras on the
demiurge—the experience of being has attained clarity about
the relation of being and knowledge—still, the wider
philosophical horizon remains open in Aristotle—his discussion
of the *aitia*—three meanings of *aitia*—the subject is the disposition of human order through the accord of the human *nous* with
the divine *nous*—the disappearance of limit from action—
questioning knowledge and knowing question—the limit of
causalities concerns the coming-to-be from the ground of
being—the experience of being not grounded-in-itself does not
require proof—the proofs of the existence of God are myths *sui
generis* arising when the *nous* is demoted to world-immanent
ratio.

Chapter 6: Reason: The Classic Experience

Reason as a historical event—the epochal consciousness of the
philosophers—Plato's and Aristotle's balance—classic reason
sees no apocalyptic end—the newly experienced force of the *nous*.

I. THE TENSION OF EXISTENCE

The definition of man as a *zoon noetikon* referred to the reality of order in man's psyche—to it corresponded the definition *zoon politikon*—the definitions should have included *zoon historikon*—man is not a divine *causa sui*—characteristic of man is the unrest of wondering, the beginning of philosophy—feeling moved or drawn—the desire to escape ignorance.

The underlying experience is the key to an understanding of the *nous* in the classic sense—the experiences of Parmenides and Anaxagoras—the exploration of the soul contributes the dimension of critical consciousness—the ground is a divine presence that becomes manifest in human unrest—the unrest becomes luminous to itself in Plato and Aristotle—this unit of meaning is man's tension toward the divine ground.

II. PSYCHOPATHOLOGY

The *nous* symbols express the reality of man attuned to the divine order in the cosmos—reason has the existential content of openness toward reality—closure toward the ground of reality affects the rational structure of the soul—the analyses of Heraclitus, Aeschylus, the Stoics, and Cicero—anxiety as a variety of ignorance—in the states of both health and unhealth—mental disease as a disturbance of noetically ordered existence—there is no Aristotelian term for "anxiety"—Heidegger, Hobbes, Hegel, Marx built alienation into their system, and Freud and Sartre reject the openness to the ground—modern writers claim for their mental disease the status of mental health—Schelling's modern characterization of this condition as "pneumopathology," and Doderer's term "refusal of apperception."

III. LIFE AND DEATH

The "in-between"character of human existence—a construction of man as a world-immanent autonomous entity destroys the meaning of existence—distortion of the classic analysis through a restrictive concentration on the conflict between reason and the passions—a corresponding differentiation of Life and Death—a fully developed rejection of reason requires the form of an apparently rational system—Hegel, Schiller as examples—the distinction between dialectics and eristics by Plato—modern deformations as object-lessons of eristics—Hegel's misuse of an Aristotelian passage—and of a Pauline passage—the modern egophanic revolt against reason—Hegel's construction of "dialectical process" belonging to an imaginary "consciousness"—the contemporary preoccupation with depth, death, anxiety.

IV. APPENDIX

The classic insights were gained as the exegesis of the philosophers' resistance against the climate of opinion—reason is not a treasure to be stored away—principles to be considered in the study of human affairs: principles of completeness, of formation and foundation, of *metaxy* reality.

Chapter 7: Eternal Being in Time

History is not a given object of analysis—the reality of being divisible into four relations: philosophy as a phenomenon in time, philosophy as a constituent of history, history as a constituent of philosophy, history as a field of philosophically analyzable phenomena.

I. PHILOSOPHY AS A PHENOMENON IN THE FIELD OF HISTORY

Philosophy appears as a phenomenon in a context of other structuring phenomena—the minimum range consists of: spiritual outburst, ecumenic empire, historiography—Jasper's concept of the "axis time of mankind"—the Daniel Apocalypse and speculations about the *translatio imperii*—the accumulation of empires from China to Rome not to be construed as an autonomous determinant of history—historiography in Hellas, Israel, China, connected with imperial conflicts—spiritual outbursts preceding historiography, and exceptions.

II. PHILOSOPHY AS A CONSTITUENT OF HISTORY

Philosophy as an ontic event and a noetic experience—the resulting two tensions of the soul—the soul as the place where

interpretation—Augustine's symbol of *exodus* as the principle for a material philosophy of history.

PART III. WHAT IS POLITICAL REALITY?

Prefatory Remarks: Science and Reality

Mathematics is a science based on fundamental principles (axioms)—political science is not because of the special relation between science and political reality—the noetic knowledge of political order deals with an object already structured by another kind of knowledge—nonnoetic knowledge precedes noetic knowledge—noetic knowledge arises in a relation of tension with society—this relation can be made transparent—today this is difficult because of nonnoetic, ideological interpretations of society—which is why political science cannot be defined as a corpus of propositions and principles.

Chapter 8: The Consciousness of the Ground

No objective propositions are possible with regard to the experience of order in consciousness—noetic and nonnoetic interpretations conceive order in terms of their ground—noetic interpretations arise when consciousness seeks to become explicit to itself—Aristotle's vocabulary—the direction of consciousness: desire for knowledge, questioning in confusion, awareness of ignorance—this directional factor called *ratio*—the mutual participation of two entities called *nous*—here myth enters into the exegesis—"human nature" the symbol of an experience of the ground—the myth and its symbols a residue of prenoetic knowledge.

Four aporias arising in the objectivization by noesis—"objectivization" referring to the difference of truth arising in the search for the ground—there is no "objective" beyond—there is a "past" phase of the quest—the personal field of history generates a social one.

Three dimensions: the direction-giving *ratio,* the luminosity

Chapter 9: Linguistic Indices and Type-Concepts

methods compatible with the *ratio* of noesis—"history" as an index of a field of rational structure.

Plato's type-concepts stemming from the "objectivization" of other interpretations of order—various meanings of "object"— consciousness, though discrete, creates an intelligible field of history—its structure is the structure of reality—the sole meaning of the "field of history" is that discovered through the *ratio* of noesis—the material and the historical dimensions of consciousness interacting with a tendency toward objectivization— type-concepts formed around all kinds of "positions."

Chapter 10: The Tensions in the Reality of Knowledge

Noetic knowledge is concrete knowledge of participation illuminating the divine ground of being as the ground of man and world—thus the reality of participation is knowledge— which goes beyond the knowledge of reason to the knowledge of faith, hope, and love—the complex of knowledge being effective as a whole—man's existence ordered by knowledge prior to noesis—*ratio* both a component and an instrument of criticism.

Three phases in the process of tension: the hellenic one, the dogmatism of the philosophic schools and of theology, and the dogmatic ideologies—ideologies block man's access to reality— the solution consists in a turning again toward reality—which is rendered difficult by the historical background of theological and metaphysical dogmatisms—one must push on to the predogmatic reality of knowledge—the example of Camus—the study of predogmatic realities a strong recent movement— alternatively, there is resort to works of literature—the paradigm of mysticism.

Necessary distinctions: metaphysics in Thomas, Descartes, Voltaire, Baumgarten, Wolff—mysticism in Bodin and Bergson—Pico della Mirandola, Ficino, Pseudo-Dionysius—the dimension of the ineffable.

Chapter 11: The Concrete Consciousness

Human consciousness is always concretely personal—man's synthetic nature—his corporeality the basis of social existence—political theory must cover man's entire existence—

Editor's Preface

The present volume, appearing under the same title as the book Eric Voegelin published in German in 1966, is nevertheless not exactly a rendition of the original into English. Some of the chapters of the German book have been omitted, and one other chapter has been added. It happened that from time to time I received inquiries whether the German Anamnesis *was being, or would be, translated into English. Some of these inquiries seemed particularly anxious to have an English version of the third part, "What Is Political Reality?" This indicated a strong interest in learning more about Eric Voegelin's philosophy of consciousness, which the author himself also saw as the gist of his German book of 1966. When the editors of University of Notre Dame Press began to discuss with me the possibilities of translating* Anamnesis, *one of the most important chapters of the German original, "Historiogenesis," had already been included in Voegelin's fourth volume of the Order and History Series* The Ecumenic Age *(1974). This suggested a regroupment of the material. It was decided that a book pulling together the chapters most directly developing Voegelin's philosophy of consciousness would respond to the expressed needs of the public. Since "Historiogenesis" had already been taken out by its inclusion into another volume, it seemed advisable to drop from the translated version the chapters on "The Humanists' Image of Timur," "The Command of God," "Bakunin's Confession," and "John Stuart Mill," chapters containing analyses of historical materials which, while related to the main thesis, were not functional supports of its main weight.*

Regarding Part I of the German original, it seemed that the chapters "On the Theory of Consciousness," and "Anamnetic Experiments" would be put into sharper relief if detached from the preceding "Letter to Alfred Schuetz about Edmund Husserl," and the "In Memoriam Alfred Schuetz." Dropping these two items from the translation left a gap in the first part that Eric Voegelin himself generously offered to close, by writing what is now the first chapter in the American version of Anamnesis.

On the other hand, it seemed most desirable to include into the translation Voegelin's article "Reason: The Classic Experience," published in The Southern Review (*X, no. 2 [Spring 1974]*). *The article contained important further developments of the analysis contained in other chapters of the original Part II.*

These decisions were taken in continuous contact with the author. It is hoped that the result is a compact book on Voegelin's philosophy of consciousness, a book containing the answer to the question asked by many of Voegelin's readers: "What is the 'theory' behind the 'process of retheoretization' that Voegelin has brought to the treatment of historical patterns, events, creation of symbols, ideas, and institutions?" The book shows the continuity of the hypothesis present from the moment in 1943 when Eric Voegelin, abandoning his project of a history of political ideas, turned to that work on consciousness as history and history as consciousness, the nexus construed ontologically rather than subjectively, idealistically, or psychologically, a work in which he is still vigorously forging ahead.

April 1977

GERHART NIEMEYER

PART I

Anamnesis

CHAPTER ONE

Remembrance of Things Past

In 1943 I had arrived at a dead-end in my attempts to find a theory of man, society, and history that would permit an adequate interpretation of the phenomena in my chosen field of studies. The analysis of the movements of Communism, Fascism, National Socialism, and racism, of constitutionalism, liberalism, and authoritarianism had made it clear beyond a doubt that the center of a philosophy of politics had to be a theory of consciousness: but the academic institutions of the Western world, the various schools of philosophy, the rich manifold of methodologies, did not offer the intellectual instruments that would make the political events and movements intelligible.

This curious default of the school philosophies in the face of an overwhelming political reality had attracted my attention ever since I was a graduate student in the 1920s. The default was curious because it assumed the form not of a lack but of a superabundance of theories of consciousness and methodologies of the sciences. And I had to work through quite a few of them as part of my formal training, such as the neo-Kantianism of the Marburg school, the value philosophy of the Southwest German school, the value-free science of Max Weber, the positivism of the Viennese school, of Wittgenstein, and of Bertrand Russell, the legal positivism of Kelsen's Pure Theory of Law, the phenomenology of Husserl, and, of course, Marx and Freud. But when in the course of my readings in the history of ideas I had to raise the question why do important thinkers like Comte or Marx refuse to apperceive what they apperceive quite well? why do they expressly prohibit anybody to ask questions concerning the sectors of reality they have excluded from their personal horizon? why do they want to imprison themselves in their restricted horizon and to dogmatize their prison reality as the universal truth? and why do they want to lock up all mankind in the prison of their making?—my formidable school equipment did not provide an answer, though obviously an answer was needed if one wanted to understand the mass movements that threatened, and still threaten, to engulf Western civilization in their political prison culture.

A school is a formidable force indeed. Considerable time had to lapse before I understood the situation and its implications:

The default of the school-philosophies was caused by a restriction of the horizon similar to the restrictions of consciousness that I could observe in the political mass movements. But if that was true, I had observed the restriction, and recognized it as such, with the criteria of the observation coming from a consciousness with a larger horizon, which in this case happened to be my own. And if that was true, then the school-construction of an "intersubjective" ego as the subject of cognition did not apply to an analysis of consciousness; for the truth of my observation did not depend on the proper functioning of a "subject of cognition" in the Kantian, or neo-Kantian, sense when confronted with empirical materials, but on the "objectivity" of the concrete consciousness of a concrete human being when confronted with certain "subjective" deformations. An analysis of consciousness, I had to conclude, has no instrument other than the concrete consciousness of the analyst. The quality of this instrument, then, and consequently the quality of the results, will depend on what I have called the horizon of consciousness; and the quality of the horizon will depend on the analyst's willingness to reach out into all the dimensions of the reality in which his conscious existence is an event, it will depend on his desire to know. A consciousness of this kind is not an a priori structure, nor does it just happen, nor is its horizon a given. It rather is a ceaseless action of expanding, ordering, articulating, and correcting itself; it is an event in the reality of which as a part it partakes. It is a permanent effort at responsive openness to the appeal of reality, at bewaring of premature satisfaction, and above all at avoiding the self-destructive phantasy of believing the reality of which it is a part to be an object external to itself that can be mastered by bringing it into the form of a system.

What I had discovered was consciousness in the concrete, in the personal, social, and historical existence of man, as the specifically human mode of participation in reality. At the time, however, I was far from clear about the full bearing of the

discovery because I did not know enough about the great pre-
cedents of existential analysis in antiquity, by far surpassing, in
exactness and luminosity of symbolization, the contemporary
efforts. I was not aware, for instance, of the Heraclitian analysis
of public and private consciousness, in terms of the *xynon* and
the *idiotes,* or of a Jeremiah's analysis of prophetic existence,
before I learned Greek and Hebrew in the 1930s.

Nevertheless, I was very much aware that my "larger horizon" was not a personal idiosyncrasy but surrounded me from
all sides as a social and historical fact from which I could draw
nourishment for my own consciousness. In the early decade of
the twentieth century, the revolt against the restrictive deformations and the recovery of the content of consciousness
through historical restoration and original perception was a
massive, if diffuse, movement. My own horizon was strongly
formed, and informed, by the restoration of the German language through Stefan George and his circle, the renewed
understanding of German classic literature through Gundolf
and Kommerell, the understanding of Platonic philosophizing,
and especially of the Platonic myth, through Friedlaender, Sa-
lin, and Hildebrandt, by the impact of Marcel Proust, Paul Valéry, and James Joyce, by Gilson and Sertillanges, whose work
introduced me to medieval philosophy, by Jaspers's existen-
tialism and, through Jaspers, by Kierkegaard, and by Speng-
ler's *Decline of the West* that was based on the conception of
civilizational cycles developed by Eduard Meyer whose lectures
I still heard as a student in Berlin. The list is by far not exhaustive,
but I have made it long enough to suggest the range of the
revolt as well as the difficulty of coping with such richness. I
sensed the revolt, but I sensed it also as a beginning that could
be short-circuited into new restrictive school formations. And if
I certainly did not care to become a neo-Kantian subject of
cognition, not even an intersubjective one, neither did I particularly care to become a neo-Platonist, or a neo-Thomist
metaphysician, or an existentialist, Christian or otherwise. I was
grateful, and still am, for every appeal to expand the horizon,
from whatever direction it may come; but I also knew that the
revolt had to be considerably more radical to match the problems raised by the disorder of the age.

Above all, there was the profound problem of resistance to
truth, and the various forms it assumed, that required explora-

tion. The reasons why the various ideologies were wrong were sufficiently well known in the 1920s, but no ideologist could be persuaded to change his position under the pressure of argument. Obviously, rational discourse, or the resistance to it, had existential roots far deeper than the debate conducted on the surface. In the interwar years, truth was definitely what did not prevail. The restrictive deformation of existence was a social force that had, and still has, a long course to run. Some forms of this resistance I could observe in my more limited environment of neo-Kantian and positivist methodologies. A man who aspired to recognition as a philosopher had to base his work on Kant and the neo-Kantian thinkers; anybody who wanted to learn from a work written before Kant was a historian. Consequently, I was classified as a historian; and inevitably I was under some suspicion as a true school member because of my "tolerance"; a methodologically reliable scholar had intolerantly to maintain the truth as represented by his school and not to flirt with larger horizons.

At the time, I could not yet develop such observations into well-founded insights concerning their meaning. Precisely for that reason, however, they are worth recalling; for in their manner of primitive puzzlement they correctly sensed a configuration of forces that has grown, from its modest beginnings, into the characteristic of the present century. During the last fifty years, the conflict between open and restrictively deformed existence has hardened into the great *stasis* (in the Aristotelian sense) that we witness in our time. A few summary remarks on the rapid growth of this configuration into an ecumenic disruption of rational discourse will be in order:

(1) On the level of pragmatic history, of the mass movements, totalitarian governments, world wars, liberations, and mass slaughters, the deformation of existence has produced "a tale told by an idiot, full of sound and fury, signifying nothing"; it has revealed itself as a febrile impotence that cancers out in bloody dreams of greatness and has brought the majority of mankind into subjection under mentally diseased ruling cliques. I am using the term "mentally diseased" in the Ciceronian sense of the *morbus animi,* caused by the *aspernatio rationis,* the contempt of reason.

(2) On the academic level of the sciences of man, the aggravation of the conflict I experienced in the 1920s is particularly striking. The restrictive school-philosophies and methodologies are more dominant than ever; and I even have to observe a boring repetition of the very situation in which I grew up inasmuch as the contemporary methodological debate in America lives to a large extent on the revival of the earlier German ideologies, methodologies, value theories, Marxisms, Freudianisms, psychologies, phenomenologies, hermeneutic profundities, and so on. This peculiar repetition, as if there were no Americans who can think, is partly due to the influence of the German intellectuals who emigrated to America, but the social force it has gained stems from the populist expansion of the universities, accompanied by the inevitable inrush of functional illiterates into academic positions in the 1950s and 60s. The intellectual quality of the debate has not been improved by its repetition. Today, the academic world is plagued with figures who could not have gained public attention in the environment of the Weimar Republic, dubious as it was, with neo-Hegelians who combine Marx and Freud in a theory of repression that assures a monopoly of repression to themselves; with megalomaniac behaviorists who want to manipulate mankind out of freedom and human dignity; and with egalitarian Holyrollers who want to redistribute distributive justice. It is only fair to add, however, that in the country of its origin, in Germany, the quality of the methodological debate has declined even worse, if that is possible. But it has become increasingly difficult to describe this sector of the academic world, with its peculiar mixture of *libido dominandi,* philosophical illiteracy, and adamant refusal to enter into rational discourse, because the adequate form would have to be satire and, as Karl Kraus noted already in the 1920s, it is next to impossible to write satire when a situation has become so grotesque that reality surpasses the flight of a satirist's imagination.

(3) Depressing as these remarks may sound, the end of the world has not come. For the third factor in the configuration, the revolt, has also gained momentum, beyond any expectations one could entertain in the 1920s. In the nature of the case, the revolt has its academic site in the study of man's normal life in open existence, and that study comprises the whole history of mankind with the exception of the restrictivist enclaves. A stu-

dent of Homer or Aeschylus, of Dante or Shakespeare, of the
Old or the New Testament, of early creation myths or of Up-
anishadic meditations, or of any of the great figures in the
history of philosophy cannot arrive at an understanding of the
literary work that lies before him on the table, if he insists on
interpreting it by one or the other of the restrictivist
methodologies or ideologies, because the author he tries to
understand has a self-reflective, open consciousness whose language is incompatible with the language of restricted consciousness. And the same is true for the student of ancient
history, of Western medievalism, of Chinese, Indian, Persian,
or pre-Columbian civilizations, of their rites and myths. He too
will soon discover that he cannot interpret tribal or imperial
societies, cosmological, ecumenic, or orthodox empires in the
language of the ideological "philosophies of history" without
making nonsense of his materials. Not that of necessity the
revolt would always have to become self-reflective and articulate. Though it is inherent in the enormous enlargement of the
historical horizon, spatially covering the global ecumene and
temporally extending into the archaeological millennia that has
occurred in the present century, the form it will assume in the
individual case will depend on the circumstances. The departments in our universities are sometimes so rigidly segregated
that a student of history, of art or literature, of comparative
religion or mythology can quite well spend a life of scholarship
without being forced to take formal notice of what he perhaps
will consider the inevitable lunatic fringe in his university. And
even if he is forced to take notice, he need not make an issue of
it.* A true scholar has better things to do than to engage in

*An amusing incident occurred in the UNESCO *History of Mankind* (1963),
in the section on *The Beginnings of Civilization,* written by Sir Leonard Woolley.
Everything went fine in a work devoted to the material and organizational
progress of man on the level of the *homo faber* until Sir Leonard reached the
chapter on the fine arts. As he was a connoisseur in matters of art, he was
struck by the fact that the works of art he had to deal with ranked in their
quality at least as high as certain modern achievements which he named. But
if there was no advance of quality what then became of the restrictivist "development" of mankind into which he had to fit his own study? Being a
conscientious scholar, he had to bring the issue to attention, but he did not
care to pursue it further into its theoretical ramifications. I am mentioning
the incident as an example of the subdued form the conflict will usually
assume.

futile debate with men who are guilty of the *aspernatio rationis*. The revolt at large has not become vociferous enough, and perhaps never will, to match the paranoiac aggressiveness of the mental cases, but it has become extensive enough to leave no doubt that the restrictivist movements have maneuvered themselves out of the empirical advance of the historical and philosophical sciences.

But however extensive the revolt may become and however successfully it may force the restrictive deformation of existence on the defensive by the sheer weight of empirical evidence, there remains the philosopher's task of finding a theory of consciousness that will fit the facts of the great stasis that has grown, ever since the eighteenth century, to its present proportions.

The answer I attempted in 1943 emerged from long years of occupation with Husserl's phenomenology, and equally long years of discussion with Alfred Schuetz about its merits and limitations. We both agreed on the work of Husserl as the most thorough and competent analysis of certain phenomena of consciousness that was available at the time; but we also agreed on the insufficiencies of his analysis that had become all too obvious in the *Méditations Cartésiennes* of 1931 and made it impossible to apply the phenomenological method, without further development, to the social phenomena that were our primary concern.

Our discussions came to a head when, in the summer of 1943, I was at last able to obtain a copy of Husserl's *Krisis der Europaeischen Wissenschaften,* published in *Philosophia I* (Belgrade, 1936). In this essay, planned as an "Introduction to Phenomenological Philosophy," Husserl elaborated on the motivations of his own work by placing it in the context of a philosophical history. In his conception, the history of man's reason had three phases: (1) a prehistory, of no particular interest to the philosopher, ending with the Greek foundation of philosophy; (2) a phase beginning with the Greek *Urstiftung,* the primordial foundation of philosophy, that was interrupted by the Christian thinkers but then renewed by Descartes, and reached up to Husserl; and (3) a last phase, beginning with the *apodiktische Anfang,* the "apodictic beginning" set by his own work, and going on forever into the future, within the "horizon of apodictic continuation" of his phenomenology. I still remember the shock when I read this "philosophy of history." I was horrified because I could not help recognizing the all-too-familiar type of phase constructions in which had indulged the Enlightenment philosophes and, after them, Comte, Hegel, and Marx. It was one more of the symbolisms created by apocalyptic-gnostic thinkers, with the purpose of abolishing a "past history" of mankind and letting its "true history" begin with the respective author's own work. I had to recognize it as one of the violently restrictive visions of existence that, on the level of pragmatic action, surrounded me from all sides with its tale told by an idiot, in the form of Communism, National Socialism, Fascism, and the Second World War.

Something had to be done. I had to get out of that "apodictic horizon" as fast as possible.

The immediate action went into the correspondence with Alfred Schuetz, continuing our discussion and clarifying the situation. The first piece I wrote and sent him was a critical analysis of Husserl's *Krisis* essay. The reader who is interested in the details of my criticism will find it published in the German edition of my *Anamnesis* (Munich: R. Piper & Co. Verlag, 1966).

But that was not enough. I had to formulate the alternative to Husserl's conception of an egologically constituted consciousness; and a formulation suggested itself as possible now, at least on principle, because his conscientious construction of the defense mechanism against all potential criticism of his apodicticity had given the cue. Husserl's apocalyptic construct had the purpose of abolishing history and thereby to justify the exclusion of the historical dimension from the constitution of man's consciousness; the alternative, therefore, had to reintroduce the historical dimension Husserl wanted to exclude. Such a reintroduction could, of course, not be achieved by dabbling with problems in the so-called history of ideas as a substitute for philosophizing; nor would it make sense to reject the magnificent work Husserl had done in clarifying the intentionality of consciousness. The historical dimension at issue was not a piece of "past history" but the permanent presence of the process of reality in which man participates with his conscious existence. Reality, it is true, can move into the position of an object-of-thought intended by a subject-of-cognition, but before this can happen there must be a reality in which human beings with a consciousness occur. Moreover, by virtue of their consciousness these human beings are quite conscious of being parts of a comprehensive reality and express their awareness by the symbols of birth and death, of a cosmic whole structured by realms of being, of a world of external objects and of the presence of divine reality in the cosmos, of mortality and immortality, of creation into the cosmic order and of salvation from its disorder, of descent into the depth of the *psyche* and meditative ascent toward its beyond. Within this rich field of reality-consciousness, finally, there occur the processes of wondering, questing, and seeking, of being moved and drawn into the search by a consciousness of ignorance, which, in order to be sensed as ignorance, requires an apprehension of something worth to be known; of an appeal to which man can lovingly respond or not so lovingly deny himself; of the joy of finding and the despair of having lost the direction; of the advance of truth from the compact to differentiated experiences and symbols; and of the great breakthroughs of insight through visions of the prophetic, the philosophic, and the Christian-apostolic type. In brief, Man's conscious existence is an event within reality, and man's consciousness is quite conscious of being constituted by the reality of which it is conscious. The intentionality is a substructure within the comprehensive consciousness of a reality that becomes luminous for its truth in the consciousness of man.

Recognizing this comprehensive structure of consciousness, however, raised a fundamental issue in philosophical epistemology. If the abstract statements about the structure of consciousness were to be accepted as true, they had first to be recognized as true in the concrete. Their truth rested on the concrete experiences of reality by concrete human beings who were able to articulate their experience of reality and of their own role as participants in it, and thus engender the language of consciousness. The truth of consciousness was both abstract and concrete. The process of verification had to penetrate, therefore, through the engendered symbols to the engendering experience; and the truth of the experience had to be ascertained by a responsive experience that could verify or falsify the engendering experience. Even worse, the process was further burdened with the impossibility of separating language and experience as independent entities. There was no engendering experience as an autonomous entity but only the experience as articulated by symbols; and at the other end of the process of verification, there was no responsive experience as an autonomous entity either but only an experience that could articulate itself in language symbols and, if necessary, modify the symbols of the engendering experience in order to let the truth of symbols more adequately render the truth of reality experienced. The truth of consciousness, its verification and advance, could not be identified with either the truth of statements or the truth of experience; it was a process that let its truth become luminous in the procedural tension between experience and symbolization. Neither the experiences nor the symbols could become autonomous objects of investigation for an outside observer. The truth of consciousness revealed itself through participation in the process of reality; it was essentially historical.

The insight into a process of reality that let its truth emerge into the luminosity of consciousness and its processes affected my work in years to come considerably inasmuch as I had to abandon an almost-completed, multivolume history of political ideas as philosophically untenable and to replace it by a study of the order that emerges in history from the experiences of reality and their symbolization, from the processes of differentiation and deformation of consciousness. But the far-reaching consequences, for instance for a philosophy of language, did not become visible all at once. What imposed itself as immediately necessary was the achievement of some clarity about the reason why a consciousness constituted by reality seemed to me preferable to a reality cognitively constituted by a transcendental ego. I was confronted with the question of why I was attracted by "larger horizons" and repelled, if not nauseated, by restrictive deformations. The answer to this question could not be found by pitting truth against falsehood on the level of "ideas." For that procedure would only have introduced the libidinous apodicticity of the restriction into the "larger horizon." The reasons had to be sought, not in a theory of consciousness, but concretely in the constitution of the responding and verifying consciousness. And that concrete consciousness was my own. A philosopher, it appeared, had to engage in an anamnetic exploration of his own consciousness in order to discover its constitution by his own experiences of reality, if he wanted to be critically aware of what he was doing. This exploration, furthermore, could not stop short at the more recent enrichments of his horizon by learning and the observation of political events because his manner of response to learning and events was precisely the question to be clarified. It had to go as far back as his remembrance of things past would allow in order to reach the strata of reality-consciousness that were the least overlaid by later accretions. The *anamnesis* had to recapture the childhood experiences that let themselves be recaptured because they were living forces in the present constitution of his consciousness.

The results of my anamnetic analysis constituted the second piece sent to Alfred Schuetz. In the present English edition, this is reprinted as Chapter 3 under the title "Anamnetic Experiments." Immediately afterwards I wrote, again as part of my correspondence with Schuetz, the reflections "Concerning a Theory of Consciousness," published here as Chapter 2, explaining the theoretical situation as I understood it at the time.

The reader should be aware that these pieces were part of a correspondence between friends. They were not written for publication and will, therefore, sometimes appear abrupt in style. I have left them unchanged in order to preserve their documentary value as an analysis of consciousness.

Stanford, California
March 1977

CHAPTER TWO

On the Theory of Consciousness

The following remarks contain biographical materials but are not intended to tell the history of life. To use a brief formula, they report on the results of anamnetic experiences.

The motive for pursuing them came from a feeling of discontent with the results of those philosophical investigations that have as their object an analysis of the inner consciousness of time. As far as I can survey the historical situation, the problem of the consciousness of time became a central theme of philosophy only in the nineteenth century. Philosophizing about time and existence today occupies the place that was held by meditation before thinking in Christian categories dissolved. The analysis of the time-consciousness of world-immanent man is the laicist residue of the Christian ascertainment of existence in meditation with its spiritual climax of the *intentio animi* toward God.

My first specific interest in these questions goes back to my first stay in America. In the chapter "Time and Existence" of my book on America [*Über die Form des Amerikanischen Geistes* (Tuebingen: Mohr, 1928)], I performed a comparative analysis of the concepts of perception and time-consciousness in Hodgson, Brentano, Husserl, Peirce, William James, and Santayana. In its course, the supposed description of perception and consciousness—with its categories of thatness and whatness, pure experience, act and reflection etc.—was shown to be the speculative construction of an experience that obviously could not be grasped with the conceptual apparatus of description. The same result emerged from the examination of the later published work of Husserl about the inner consciousness of time: Husserl's refined terminology of *retention* and *protention*, already reflecting the failure of Brentano's description of act and reflection, also describes nothing; Husserl, too, did not get beyond the construction of a subtle apparatus of equivocations.

The feeling that the analysis of consciousness is a dead end was reinforced through the consideration that in experience there is no given stream of consciousness except in the experience of turning to a specific process of perception on the occasion of selected, simple perceptions. It seems to be no accident that the analysts of time-consciousness use preferably the model of an auditory perception of a tone that is heard and still heard while the beginning of the tone-perception slides into the past but nevertheless is still continually remembered. A time-consciousness without an object-consciousness can hardly be described. One is pushed to infer that that which is described on the occasion of an auditory perception is not the consciousness of time but precisely the consciousness of the perception of a tone, a tone that has an objective structure determined in turn by the structure of man's faculty of perception, the noetic structure in Husserl's sense. I have never found a philosopher trying to demonstrate the structure of time-consciousness using as his model "the comprehension of a painting." One cannot comprehend a painting by simply staring at it and turning one's attention to the flow of time while staring. One's attention is absorbed by problems of the subject, composition, color values and their balance, the artist's technique, comparison with other paintings, and so on. In this process, in which the "meaning" of the painting is constituted, time "flies" without being noticed. The "apperception" of a painting, while the eye canvasses it, occurs in the function of a sensual entering into a spiritual realm, which has, at least directly, nothing to do with the flow of time. The phenomenon of "flow" can be made present under very specific and favorable conditions, to wit, when the object of perception is so sensually simple that in turning to the object the I can still economize enough attention to become conscious of its consciousness. On the occasion of "understanding a painting", one can disengage the attention that is absorbed in constituting the meaning, to concentrate it on the sensuous perception of a color spot, and in such concentration one can become conscious of one's own perception. But when one performs this experiment, something remarkable results. The more one succeeds in becoming conscious of perception as a time-process, the more the perception of the color spot is mingled with other perceptions that obviously are better suited to render conscious "the flow": physical perceptions like the pressure of one's feet on the ground before the picture, one's heartbeat and breath, auditory perceptions of the walking by of another person or of other noises. Based on these experiences, it seems to me that time-consciousness has a specific affinity to the sphere of the senses, especially to that of the body and acoustics.

Selecting a simple, sensuous perception as a model through which the flow of consciousness is to be made clear does not seem to be the elementary way to an understanding of the time problem. On the contrary, we have here a most complicated and artificial abstraction of the "normal" experiences and a quite special direction of attention to a class of phenomena that have not always served as a model for this purpose. There arises the question of what is the meaning of such selection. It does not fulfill its purpose to describe the flow of consciousness, for, as we have seen, the so-called descriptions turn out to be speculative constructions. How is one to explain the fascination with just this class of experiences, a fascination so strong that it blinds excellent thinkers to the failure of their understanding? I cannot find any other reason than that the "flow" as such—the gliding and sliding away—is what fascinates, the flow that can be grasped most purely precisely in simple, sensuous percep- tion, especially the auditory perception of a tone. Now this class of experiences certainly is worthy of our attention, for they reveal most clearly the "fleetingness" of sensuous awareness. But, conversely, the selection of this class of experiences seems to reveal that one must rely on the sphere of the senses in order to make us conscious of the "fleetingness" of consciousness, in which, by the way, not everything is fleeting. The interest in "the flow" is primary. Only in the light of this determining sentiment can one understand why the analysis of conscious- ness is thematically focused on the problem of the "vanishing point" of fleetingness, even though it is the function of human consciousness *not* to flow but rather to constitute the spaceless and timeless world of meaning, sense, and the soul's order. Turning to a vanishing point of "fleetingness" does not con- duce to a better understanding of the problem of consciousness and time as a whole but only to an understanding of the roots of consciousness in the sphere of the body. William James, who very closely observed his introspective attempts in this direc- tion, concluded that with the greatest care he could not find in the I, as it appears in the stream of consciousness, anything but the rhythm of breathing. The phenomenon of "flow" is eminently important but not as a key to the understanding of time-consciousness, rather it is important as an experience in which the bottleneck of the body can be felt as something through which the world is forced as it enters the order of consciousness.

Turning attention to the phenomenon of "flow" in the history of thought in the nineteenth century parallels others turnings toward the sphere of vital forces such as Darwinism, Marxism, and psychoanalysis. Each of these new focuses of attention was legitimate insofar as the world of consciousness is based on the sphere of vitality. The connection is to intimate that between birth and death the body determines what part of the world may enter consciousness through it, not merely as a sensorium but also is one of the most important determinants (even though not the only one) for the inner tensions and relations of relevance of the world of consciousness. Turning attention toward the body has the historical merit of having balanced our views of the world of consciousness. If these focuses of attention, however, are radicalized to the point of negating all structures of consciousness that are not directly determined by the body, if basing consciousness in the body hypertrophies into the causation of consciousness by the body, then the radicalization and hyperbolization reveals an attitude that is to be characterized as morbid in the pneumato-pathological sense of Plato's *nosos*. The world of consciousness becomes a wasteland (of different degrees in different thinkers), and the fascination with the vital sphere—sensuousness and vital forces, their growth and decline—dominates philosophical attitudes.

Narrowing down the problem of consciousness to the flow and its constitution is untenable if only because of its incompatibility with the phenomena of sleep, dreams, and the subconscious psychic processes. But even apart from this complex of problems, the reduction remains symptomatic of a doubtful hypertrophy of a correctly observed experience—that in which the physiological limit of consciousness comes into sight—into an elementary experience through which consciousness itself is constituted. This hypertrophy implies a radical perversion of the facts as given in experience. In experience, consciousness with its structures, whatever they may be, is an antecedent given. The limit experience of "flowing," as demonstrated through the model of the perception of a tone, is possible only in a specific act of turning attention to that limit. It is not the consciousness of time that is constituted by the flow but rather the experience of the flow is constituted by consciousness, which itself is not flowing. This fact seems to me to furnish the explanation for the failure of all analyses of simple perception, and particularly the perception of a tone. Analyzing sensuous perceptions implies a transition from the gestalt of the perception to its founding elements; these elements, however, are by themselves neither gestalt nor perceptions, but can arise within consciousness only as speculative structures (and as such quite legitimate) as formulas for the proposed subject of the simplest, still structured contents of consciousness. The conceptual apparatus that is used to cope with this problem is typical of every infinitesimal speculation. It is applied not only to the analysis of time-consciousness and auditory perception, but in the same way to the limit-problems of visual perception. In my book on America, I have shown the speculative construction in the case of Husserl's allegedly phenomenological description of *noema* and *hyle* through the model of the perception of color of a tree. His misunderstanding of speculation about the limit, as if it were a description of this limit and of what lies underneath, seems to me, as mentioned before, to have the function of an ascertainment of existence, which is no longer possible through other, spiritual sources. A speculation about the stream of consciousness may serve as a substitute for meditation because it, too, conduces to transcendence; both processes have the function to transcend consciousness, one into the body, the other into the ground of being; both processes lead to a "vanishing point", in that the transcendence itself cannot be a datum of consciousness. The processes carry one only to the limit and make possible an instantaneous experience of the limit, which empirically may last only a few seconds. Bergson's treatment of the eleatic paradoxes seems to me to solve these problems altogether correctly; it retains the miracle of a continuum that cannot be traversed in spatial segments, as a miracle for consciousness, transferring it into the *durée* of bodily movement beyond the operations of consciousness.

The problem of consciousness and its constitution thus seems to me *mal posé*. I do not deny that there is a phenomenon of "flow," but it is only as a limit experience under the specific conditions of giving oneself to a simple sensuous perception.

Not all perceptions are equally suitable to produce the experience of "flow." Visual perceptions require too much attention: the focusing of a stationary object fixes the object so powerfully that the flow is felt only weakly or not at all. The perception of an atmospheric spectacle, however, for instance the changing light over a landscape, produces the experience of gliding in the object, vis-à-vis which the consciousness remains in place, as it were. Perceptions of odor impose themselves and thus do not require much energy of attention, especially when the smell is strong, but they have a perculiarly static presence, which hardly permits the experience of flow to come up. Auditory perceptions seem qualitatively most suited to induce the experience of flow. A more precise analysis of the sensual values involved might perhaps clarify a number of aspects of the problem of music.

The "flow" is a phenomenon of limit; consciousness as a whole does not flow. There seems, then, to be no need to look for the constitution of a flow of consciousness. Furthermore it seems to me that there is no I that would be the agent of the constitution. It is doubtful whether consciousness has the form of the I, or whether the I is not rather a phenomenon in the consciousness. One does not have to accept the psychoanalytical investigations regarding the I and the Id in order to acknowledge that Freud has seen certain fundamental givens of psychic life generally quite well. I cannot even find the I on the occasion of certain acts of will. An example: I "will" to get up from my chair and observe how the "willing" and the "getting up" proceed. I can clearly recognize the project of my "getting up," but what occurs between my decision and my actual getting up remains quite obscure. I do not know why I get up just at this moment and not a second later. Closely though I may observe the process, I can find only that at the actual getting up something, from a source inaccessible to me, makes me get up and that nothing of an "I" is discoverable in the act. This observation does not tell me anything about the determination or indetermination of acting; it merely indicates that the actual getting up does not occur in the form of "I." The "I" seems to me to be no given at all but rather a highly complex symbol for certain perspectives in consciousness.

The positive starting point for describing the structure of consciousness is to be found in the phenomenon of attention and the focusing of attention. Consciousness seems to have a center of strength whose energy can be turned to the different dimensions of consciousness and thus initiate processes of constitution. This energy is obviously finite, for I can engage my attention at any one time only in a limited way. As I "concentrate" my attention, the horizon of constitution narrows; and when I keep it loose, I can span a wider area simultaneously. The degree of concentration conditions not merely a more or less, e.g., of the field of attention; it can also condition the degree in which, for instance, certain complex relations become transparent, or it may increase the richness of associations or recall forgotten things into memory. The control of this quantum of energy, possibly even the quantum of energy itself, seems to be of no fixed magnitude but rather varies from individual to individual, and it may even vary from time to time within the consciousness. Furthermore, the degree of control can be increased by training, or possibly even the quantum can be augmented by intensive effort. At any rate consistent practice of concentration results in increased capacity of concentration. This center of energy, whatever may be its nature, is engaged in a process, a process that cannot be observed from without, like the movement of a planet or the decomposition of a crystal. Rather, it has the character of an inner "illumination"; i.e., it is not blind but can be experienced in its inner dimensions of past and future. The problem of past and future as dimensions of consciousness must be distinguished from the "external" past and future. Knowing a fact of history on the basis of sources or predicting an event on the basis of laws of development are complex, derived phenomena. Above all, one must avoid the misconception that the dimensions of consciousness are something like empty stretches on which data can be entered, the misconception that there is something like a time-problem "as such", apart from the process of a substance. I do not remember something that lies "in the past," but I have a past because I can make present a completed process of consciousness—either through a deliberate effort of my attention or in less transparent processes of so-called "free associations." Past and future are the present illuminatory dimensions of the process in which the energy center is engaged.

In the illuminatory dimensions of past and present, one becomes aware not of empty spaces but of the structures of a finite process between birth and death. The experience of consciousness is the experience of a process—the only process which we know "from within." Because of this its property, the process of consciousness becomes the model of the process as such, the only experiential model to serve as the orientation point of the conceptual apparatus through which we must also grasp the processes that transcend consciousness. The conflict between the finiteness of the model of experience and the "infinite" character of other processes results in a number of fundamental problems. (The term "infinite" indicates already by its negativity that along with it we enter on an area transcending experience. To speak of a process as infinite is tantamount to saying that we have no experience of it "as a whole.") One of the most interesting of these problems is that of the antinomies of infinity in Kant's sense. We can subject the finite process to certain derivative transformations, the so-called "idealizations," which conduce to such concepts as the infinite series or the infinite regress. When such "idealizations" are related to finite series, there result the paradoxes of set theory; when they are related to such processes as the causal nexus, there result Kant's antinomies. The causal series cannot begin in time because we have no experience of a beginning "in time"; more precisely, one could say that because we have no experience whatsoever of a time in which something might begin—for the only time of which we do have experience is the inner experience of the illuminated dimension of consciousness, the process that drops away, at both ends, into inexperienceable darkness.

Since processes transcending consciousness are not experienceable from within and since for purposes of characterizing their structures we have no other symbols available than those developed on the occasion of other finite experiences, there result conflicts of expression. These are, if not the only one, still the most important root of the formation of myths. A mythical symbol is a finite symbol supposed to provide "transparence" for a tranfinite process. Examples: a myth of creation, which renders transparent the problem of the beginning of a transfinite process of the world; an immaculate conception, which mediates the experience of a transfinite spiritual beginning; an anthropomorphic image of God, which finitizes an experience of transcendence; speculations about the pre-existence or post-existence of the soul, which provide a finite formula for the beyond of birth and death; the fall and original sin, which illuminate the mystery of finite existence through procreation and death; and so on.

Historically a tendency to spiritualize sensual mythical symbols can be observed over longer periods. In Egyptian, Persian, and Hellenic civilization the movement proceeds from polytheistic to monotheistic symbolism, and within monotheistic symbolism from the concept of a deity with sensual attributes to one without attributes. Plato's creation of myths is particularly remarkable. As far as I know, there is no parallel to his attempt deliberately to insert the creation of myths into philosophy as its instrument. Once the phase of the dissolution of sensual myths has been reached, one of two things may happen. A good philosopher may "normally" rationalize the mythical problems by reducing them to formulas of speculation. A bad philosopher will try to juggle them away by an ontological reduction of the quantity of processes, the relations of which to human experience result in conflicts of expressions, to a single process so that we get one of the variants of physicalism, biologism, psychologism, or the like. Plato deliberately resorts to myths where another philosopher would use the instruments of speculation. One may well assume that he did this knowing that fundamentally it makes no difference in which system of symbols experiences of transcendence are expressed; possibly also because he felt that the myth is a more precise instrument for communicating the psychic excitement of the experience of transcendence, more precise than speculation, even though it is an instrument which not everybody can handle safely. This raises a problem that, as far as I can see, is usually not mentioned in the examination of naive myths: the problem of the "adequacy" of the respective myth, the question whether the myth actually renders "rightly" an experience of limit. This question is of special importance for Plato, since in a concrete case he has created two myths of which the later one is meant to be better. In the *Politeia*, having introduced the three types of the wise, the courageous, and the desirous that form the three classes of the rulers, the warriors, and the producers, Plato inserts the mythical story that the three human types are due to the gods having put either gold, or silver, or iron into their various souls. This is the only myth of Plato that must be classified as pragmatic. Plato himself does not "believe" it, but uses it as a fable in the polis to keep the lower classes quiet. In the *Nomoi*, this pragmatic myth is superseded by the "true" myth of the golden threads by which the gods hold and guide men like puppets, ruling all men in the same fashion. In place of the external-mechanistic distribution of good and lesser qualities to different human types, there is now a myth of the nature of man as such, whose character is determined by his willingness to yield himself to the pull of the various noble threads. The second myth, through the puppet symbol, "adequately" finitizes the experience of action at the nodal point of determinants which we call, respectively, the "I" and "world-transcendent being." The first myth was "false" because the *Politeia* system of myths as a whole is geared toward the mystical type of man and neglects the differing inner tensions of the "common man" so that the story of the metals was required as an external expedient to hold together a human community consisting not only of mystics. The different quality of the two myths makes itself also felt in that the first myth is emotionally well-nigh indifferent, while the puppet symbol in Plato's representation evokes the awe of transcendence, the "numinous" in the sense of Rudolf Otto.

The problem of the "deliberate" myth, and in particular the problem that drove Plato to revise his myths between the *Politeia* and the *Nomoi,* seem to throw some light on the history of the mind. Among the processes transcending consciousness a special position is held by the processes which we call "the others." The "other" as such is just as transcendent for consciousness as a process of nature, but the case is special in that we recognize in the "other" a process that is in principle akin to our own process of consciousness. The relation to the transcendence of the others, it seems to me, cannot be dealt with by the methods which Husserl, in his *Méditations Cartésiennes* has pushed to an extreme. Husserl's great question—How is the Thou constituted in the I as an *alter ego?*—takes care of itself in that the Thou is not constituted in the I at all. The problem of the Thou seems to me to resemble that of all other classes of transcendence. The fact that consciousness has an experience at all of the other, as a consciousness of the other, is not *a problem* but a given of experience from which one may start out but behind which one may not retreat. The capacity of transcendence is a fundamental character of consciousness just as much as is illumination; it is given. The fundamental question rather is this: In what symbolic language can the other human person be acknowledged as such? and how, in particular, can we understand him, of whom we have no inner experience, as "an equal"? The answer to these questions is one of the few in this complex area of problems that has been definitively given by the history of the myth. The acknowledgment of "equality" occurs along the same lines that are defined by the poles of the transcendence of the body and of the spirit. Historically we know of only two original myths of equality: the myth of the equality of the children by virtue of their origin in the same mother's womb and the myth of the equality of the children by virtue of the spiritual mold of the same father. All other ideas of equality are demonstrably historical derivatives of one or the other of these two myths. Only within the framework of these myths can one stake out the epistemological problems of the knowledge regarding the Thou. The myths in which the Thou is acknowledged as "equal," however, are by no means the only expressions for our experience of the transcendence of the other man. The speculative idealizations of the myth of equality, with their expansion of equality from a con-sanguinity—which in historical times probably was already fic-titious—to an equality encompassing "all men" is a late de-rivative. Even when they appear in history they do not always destroy the symbolic power of other myths. The basic function of the myth, to finitize the transcendence, proves itself histori-cally rather in the creation of finite human communities as mythically constituted units, which present man *as such* in *their own* image. This is no place to deal with the problems of con-flicts between such myths and the relations between com-munities. Only this much may be said: The tension between myths may be augmented to the point of a denial of a fully human character to the members of a foreign mythical com-munity; or it may, in polytheistic symbolism, appear as a rivalry between the gods of the respective communities, the com-munities abiding within the compass of humanity through the identical ontic origin of both deities; or it may soften down to the feeling that a conflict, when it occurs, has its root in a guilt common to both communities (e.g., the Christian idea of a community of sin).

At any rate, the thesis that the Thou is experienced as an alter ego can be accepted only with qualifications. The radical experience of the Thou as alter ego is probably a marginal case that is realized only in certain sectarian communities. The normal experience is a Thou that is transcendent in the direction of the body and the spirit, the space between these poles being open to a multitude of different experiences. We may say, then: The most comprehensive symbolism of process in which the Thou appears as the other man is the monosomatic and monopneumatic conception of humanity as typically represented by the Hebrew Genesis. Within this comprehensive symbolism, which secures the equality of men through the original creation of Man, we find the myths of the particular community, which differentiate man's image more or less sharply and which is again typically represented by the Hebrew *berith*, the finitization of community in partnership with God as a "chosen people." This is not the end of the finitizing myths. The series continues in the mythical tensions within the community. It is the merit of Giambattista Vico to have seen for the first time the *contese eroiche*, the heroic struggles of Roman patricians and plebians, as struggles for the myth. The main phases of this development were: (i) the monopoly of gods of the patricians, (ii) the creation of the plebeian gods, (iii) the recognition of the equality of cults and the rationalization of social relationships through ethics. Vico's thesis, I believe, touches on a fundamental problem of community structure that has been quite insufficiently explored as yet. As far as I know, for instance, nobody has investigated the interesting problem that Plato's and Aristotle's god is not only a god of the mystics but also a god for gentlemen, since a full-fledged relation with him requires leisure secured by an adequate income. The Platonic-Aristotelian theology, then, continues the gentlemen's polytheism, underneath which there is a social stratum of mystery cults and orgiastic cults of which we know but little. The problem is of first importance, since human consciousness, occurring in a multitude of successive and simultaneous exemplars, shows in a constant framework a wide range of variations of experiences of transcendence, and of possible expressions for them, which is what we call the history of the mind. Each human community under a myth implies a minimum— sometimes very considerable—of standardization of the prevailing image of man in the direction of that variant of transcendence that the respective myth could encompass. One cannot expect that all the particular exemplars of consciousness in a community would respond positively to the prevailing myth; thus there is a problem of mythical tension within the community. Polytheistic civilizations have an advantage with regard to this problem inasmuch as the plurality of gods without the complications of a system makes possible a fuller satisfaction of variants. A monotheistic community, like that of the Hebrews, has its constant troubles with the "idolatry" of people, i.e., members of the community who feel a need for orgiastic cults. A special aspect of this problem relates to the desensualization of the myth through Western rationalism. For ever-increasing masses of people, the sensual myths of the Christian tradition are being dissolved, while the spiritualized expressions of the experience of transcendence in intellectual mysticism and philosophical speculation are accessible only to a small minority. The inevitable result is the phenomenon of "being lost" in a world that has no more fixed points in the myth. People, of course, do not cease to have experiences of transcendence, but these experiences remain in the psychic strata of shudder and fear; they cannot productively contribute to the creation of an order of symbols through which the transfinite processes can be made comprehensible in the transparency of the myth. In the social dynamics of our time, the most important symptoms are the "movements" which in part have obvious orgiastic character, and the "great wars." The wars are symptomatic not only insofar as they possibly reveal a positive will to an orgiastic discharge but also insofar as they must be endorsed because actions that might prevent them have become impossible through the paralysis of the will to order, which can be active only where its meaning is secured in the community myth.

The third fundamental problem area, besides the cosmological antinomies and the myths, is the process theology, from the Pythagorean *tetraktys* to the process of the Trinity and the kabbalistic mysticism to Schelling's theory of potency. Process-theology is a matter of developing a symbolic system that seeks to express the relations between consciousness, the transcending intraworldly classes of being, and the world-transcending ground of being, in the language of a process constructed as an immanent one. I incline to believe that the process-theological attempt and its expansion, a metaphysics that interprets the transcendence system of the world as the immanent process of a divine substance, is the only meaningful systematic philosophy. It at least tries to interpret the world order transcending consciousness in a "comprehensible" language, while any ontologically different metaphysic not only cannot comprehend transcendence in immanence but also adds the nonsense of interpreting it in a language that is "incomprehensible" because it is not oriented to the only experience of consciousness which is accessible "from within".

The systematic starting point of this problem was classically formulated by Schelling in his question: "Why is Something, why is there not rather Nothing?" Every being implies the mystery of its existence over the abyss of a possible nonexistence. No doubt one can dismiss this problem by saying that the question is not legitimate because the "Something" in Schelling's question is a formalized or idealized formula for the only finite something that can be experienced so that the question "Why?" for this formalized something cannot be raised in any meaningful way, while for any finite something it can be answered by recourse to the causalities of nature. Philosophy is supposed to confine itself to the framework of finite, critical cognition. This position constitutes the strength of critical transcendental philosophy. Consciousness that is attentive to the content of the world including the givens of consciousness, can lift itself above finite experience only to a transcendental reflection on the structure of subjectivity, in which the objective order of things in the world is constituted.

While this position is immanently irrefutable, it seems to me to be just as true that human consciousness may accept this answer in a few cases but never in the general course of history. Resistance to it may in particular cases stem from various sources, but ultimately it issues from two experiential complexes.

The first complex is given through man's experience of his own ontic structure and its relation to the world-immanent order of being. Human consciousness is not a process that occurs in the world side by side with other processes without contact with these processes other than cognition; rather, it is based on animalic, vegetative, and inorganic being, and only on this basis is it consciousness of a human being. Man's structure seems to be the ontic premise for man's transcending into the world, for in none of its directions of transcending does consciousness find a level of being which is not also one on which it itself is based. Speaking ontologically, consciousness finds in the order of being of the world no level which it does not also experience as its own foundation. In the "basis-experience" of consciousness man presents himself as an epitome of the cosmos, as a microcosm. Now we do not know in what this basis "really" consists; all our finite experience is experience of levels of being in their differentiation; the nature of the cosmos is inexperienceable, whether the nexus of basis be the foundation of the vegetative on the inorganic, of the animalic on the vegetative, or of human consciousness on the animal body. There is no doubt, however, that this basis exists. Even though the levels of being are clearly distinguishable in their respective structures, there must be something common which makes possible the continuum of all of them in human existence. The basis-experience is further reinforced through the experience that this is not a matter of a static complex but of intimate interrelationships in a process. We know the phenomena of maturing and growing old with parallels in processes of the body as well as the consciousness. And we know—even though it is not transparent to us—the nexus of being by virtue of which it is possible to "date" the succession of inner illuminations of consciousness in symbols of external time. Finally we are related to the transcendent world in the mysterious relation of objective knowledge, a relation which phenomenology has by no means illumined but rather only described from without. (Nothing in these relations goes without saying; the various classes of being in the world might also be related to each other differently. It is in this possibility of different being that ontological imagination is rooted. For instance, could consciousness not continue its process after it has separated itself from the body? Compare, with regard to these questions the very serious "Dreams of a Metaphysicist," the first part of Kant's *Dreams of a Ghost-Seer*. This work is indispensable for an understanding of the psychic background of Kant's metaphysic of reason.)

The second experiential complex is the experience of meditation, at the climax of which the intention of consciousness is directed toward the contents of the world, not objectively, through the *cogitata,* but rather nonobjectively toward the transcendent ground of being.

In the area of these two experiential complexes arise the considerations which lead to process-theology. If the levels of being in human existence are based on each other, if there is a parallelism of processes, if human existence is incorporated in the world spatio-temporally and causally, if finally there is in consciousness a reflection of the world, then the ontologist infers a background of substantive identity of the levels of being. The differentiation of the experienced levels of being can be made understandable only by interpreting it through the category of process as a series of phases in the unfolding of the identical substance that attains its illumination phase in human consciousness. The mediative complex of experiences in which the reality of the ground of being reveals itself then leads to the necessity of seeing the world-immanent process of being conditioned by a process in the ground of being. The combination of these experiences and necessities conduces to the ontological images, the chief form of which is described, e.g., in Lovejoy's *Great Chain of Being,* and especially the theological speculations about the process in the ground of being, which induces the unfolding in world-immanent being.

In the frame of this complex of problems Schelling's basic question appears in a different light than that of a critical epistemological argument. Ontological speculation is a legitimate philosophical undertaking, founded in precisely describable experiences, which it interprets with the means of "understandable" categories of process. The formalized Something as an alternative to Nothing is a correctly formed ontological concept. It is antinomic in Kant's sense, but the idealization of reason that leads to the antinomies is not "nonsense," its problems are not "false problems." Schelling's "Something" is a symbol as much as is a logical or cosmological "infinite," a symbol justified inasmuch as it renders transparent the meditatively experienced real ground of being in finite language. The idealizations lead to "insoluble" problems only within the framework of word-immanent experience; they are, however, "significant" in the framework of ontological experiences. Schelling's question is significant insofar as it refers to the problem of process in the ground of being, the assumption of which seems to me to be an unavoidable requirement of system in a consistent interpretation of the ontological experience complex.

So far I have spoken of consciousness as a process that is illuminated within itself, which furthermore occurs side by side with other processes in a world and is connected with these other processes and the world as a whole in the relations of bases of knowing, and of the meditative *intentio*. The process of consciousness figured in this as the fundamental experience from which any philosophizing about consciousness must start out. A follower of the theory of a "stream of consciousness", and its constitution through the I, can object that the problem of the "flowing" has simply been shifted to the "process" and that introducing this word has not contributed anything to the comprehension of consciousness and its processive character. He would be right in raising this objection, if the analysis were to stop at this level as the last one. But it is only a provisional resting point; the analysis must be supplemented through a closer examination of the process-consciousness. So far nothing more has been said about it other than that it does not have the form of I, but that, however, it has a center of energy and it is illumined.

Let us start from the illumination dimensions of the past and the future. Past and future, we mentioned before, are not empty stretches in which a succession of phenomena could be entered, but illuminations of a process in its dimensions. Insofar as these dimensions can be made present by turning attention to them, consciousness is "illuminated," that is, experienceable from within. The problem, then, is in the concept of the "present". One may object to the concept that it is no fixed point from which the directions of a process would become visible, but that the process-dimension is already implied in the term "process," and that the dimensions therefore must be experienceable from other sources than the turning of attention from a point of present to the dimensions of the process. This objection seems to me to have merit. A radical philosophy of the moment between past and future would therefore have to do without the term "present" and to adopt a solipsism of the moment, the moment in which images becomes visible of which we cannot say with certainty that some of them precede others in a succession. The succession which becomes visible in the moment might be a phantasmagory behind which there is no reality. A process with dimensions seems indeed not to be a matter of experience. There is only one way out of the solipsism of the moment: Consciousness is not a monad that exists in the form of the momentary image but rather human consciousness, i.e., consciousness based on the body and on the external world. The only radically immanent phenomenon is the moment and its illumination; the *ordering* of the momentary image, in the dimension created by illumination, into the succession of a process requires experiences of processes transcending consciousness. The "present," thus, seems to be indeed not directly experienceable; rather, it is the result of the interpretation of the momentary image as we resort to the knowledge of the history of our bodily existence and the dating of this history through references to events in the external spatio-temporal world. The description of human consciousness as a "pure" consciousness roots in an illusion induced by the fact that we can experience the levels of being "objectively" only in their differentiation but not in their ontic connection. We have experience of our consciousness only qua consciousness, only as the process experienced from within, which is neither bodily nor material. The substantive unity of human existence, which must be accepted as ontological hypothesis for the understanding of consciousness's basis in body and matter, is objectively inexperienceable. That does not mean, however, that there is no such thing. At any rate, the hypothesis is indispensable for grasping the "ensemble" of consciousness and bodily process in the total process of human existence. We cannot descriptively grasp "pure" consciousness as process; rather we can only interpretatively grasp a "human" consciousness as consciousness in the body and the world. The illuminated, but really flat momentary image acquires the depth of a process, and thereby becomes presence, as the elements of the image, the memories, and projects are incorporated into the experiential nexus of the body's history and the external history. Reversely one may say that the being of inanimate nature "as such," i.e., without relation to a consciousness, strictly speaking is "nothing" and only turns into a dimensional process as its facts become historical dates for consciousness. The phenomena of dates for consciousness and the dating of consciousness are closely connected. In this dependence of the order of the natural process of its relatedness to consciousness, I see the root for the epistemological theory of the ideality and categoriality of time in the experience of nature. The reference to the natural process provides consciousness with the corpus of its process; the relatedness to the illumined dimensions of past and future in consciousness provides for natural being the order of time; the intersection of these relations is the "present" of consciousness.

These last remarks perhaps need to be protected against the misunderstanding that through them we have entered the relatively peaceful waters of epistemology. We still are in the areas of ontological problems that constitute the *premise* of epistemology. Kant has contributed to these questions his concept of the thing-in-itself. The thing-in-itself is a symbol through which Kant sought to grasp the correctly seen fact that our experience of nature is an experience "from without", while the "within" of matter remains inaccessible for us: our experience of natural being is, strictly speaking, phenomenal. Kant furthermore has seen correctly that consciousness, under the title *Vernunft* [reason], is a special case, inasmuch as in consciousness we have experience of a process "from within." He interpreted this situation through the assumption that in the metaphysics of *Vernunft* we are indeed dealing with the thing-in-itself. This assumption, however, seems to me to be rash. While it does see that, different from nature, we experience consciousness from within, it overlooks that in this experience-from-within we do not experience being as a whole, within which consciousness is a particular process, but experience only consciousness itself. The experience of consciousness thus is not phenomenal, but noumenal, but even the *noumena* of *Vernunft* are not the *noumena* of being as a whole. That being which is the ground of all experienceable particular being is an ontological hypothesis without which the experienced reality of the ontic nexus in human existence remains incomprehensible, but it is nowhere a datum in human existence rather it is always strictly transcendence that we can approach only through meditation. It cannot be drawn from that Beyond of finiteness into finiteness itself. Our human finiteness is always within being. At one place, namely consciousness, this being has the character of illumination, but the illumination clings to this particular level; it illuminates neither the basic being of nature nor the ground of being. Natural being remains external world in the double meaning of external to consciousness and external to one's self. With regard to ontological speculation, it follows that neither an idealistic nor a materialistic metaphysic is tenable, for both positions try to reduce the total being to the level of a particular being. One may at most recognize the difference of value in that the idealistic metaphysic sees a substance of the world that we know "from within," while a materialist metaphysic not only commits the mistake of *pars pro toto* but adds the additional one of choosing a *pars* that we know but phenomenally. All the same, even a materialist metaphysic is not without same value, especially when matter is not understood physically but rather as a substratum of the natural phenomena, as, e.g., in the metaphysics of Santayana or Paul Valéry, influenced, as they are, by Lucretius. In such cases the concept of matter approaches the unity of being, and the symbol "matter" represents the apprehension of sinking from the illumination of human consciousness into the infinite ground, from which it lifts itself enigmatically; the symbol "matter" is then hardly distinguishable from Nirvana. See especially Valéry's *Cimétiere Marin*.

From the preceding considerations certain general principles seem to follow for a philosophy of consciousness. First: there is no absolute starting point for a philosophy of consciousness. All philosophizing about consciousness is an event in the consciousness of philosophizing and presupposes this consciousness itself with its structures. Inasmuch as the consciousness of philosophizing is no "pure" consciousness but rather the consciousness of a human being, all philosophizing is an event in the philosopher's life history—further an event in the history of the community with its symbolic language; further in the history of mankind, and further in the history of the cosmos. No "human" in his reflection on consciousness and its nature can make consciousness an "object" over against him; the reflection rather is an orientation within the space of consciousness by which he can push to the limit of consciousness but never cross those limits. Consciousness is given in the elemental sense that the systematic reflection on consciousness is a late event in the biography of the philosopher. The philosopher always lives in the context of his own history, the history of a human existence in the community and in the world.

In the light of this ontological insight, the attempt of a "radical" philosophy of consciousness seems to stand in the need of explanation. An attempt to withdraw consciousness from its ontic context, to squash the world and its history and to reconstruct it out of the subjectivity of the I, and, finally, to have the flow of consciousness constitute itself in the I, is not a matter of course. We must ask about the conditions under which there arises the need for such a new foundation of the world out of consciousness and in consciousness. The reply doubtless is: the desire to make *tabula rasa* and to begin anew will be felt when the symbolical language, in which the ontic contexts are couched, has become questionable, or—historically speaking—when a civilization with its symbols has fallen into a crisis. In such a situation, an attempt to begin anew is not only legitimate in the sense that an old symbolism cannot be honestly used when its value of communication has declined, but it is also the indispensable requirement for the development of a new, more adequate symbolism. Protesting against such a new beginning in the name of a tradition is nothing more than a symptom of spiritual sterility. The legitimacy of a new beginning as a "reaction" against a crisis of the spirit, however, does not say anything about the value of the new beginning as a positive spiritual substance. There are good and bad reactions, and sometimes the reaction is worse than the tradition against which it critically reacts. If we look at the "new beginning" in this way as a reaction to a crisis, the various cases of reaction, of which there are many, can be compared; there results the possibility to discuss their relative value for the new orientation of the spirit by means of the creation of a new symbolism. The first great crisis to occur in the full light of history was that of the fifth century B.C., which led to the reaction of Plato's new creation. The historically enduring value of this reaction consists in Plato's breadth of spirit, which enabled him to supplant the dying world of the polis with a new spiritual world based on the fundamental experiences of *thanatos, eros,* and *dike,* and that he had the creative imagination to develop a symbolic language adequate for the expression of the new psychic experiences. The great defect of this creation roots in Plato's incapacity to make a radical break with the polis and to see the new spiritual man as member of a new type of community rather than of a regenerated polis. When Zeno came to Athens, he, after long deliberation, joined the school of the Cynics, which had made a radical break with the polis. If we now compare this reaction with that of the seventeenth century, which begins with Descartes and culminates in the radical philosophy of transcendence of our time, we have to say that the radicalism in negating the tradition leaves nothing to be desired, but we must also say that not much of a spiritually new creation and the development of a new symbolism can be noted. The development of the transcendental critique down to Husserl is characterized by the dissolution not only of traditional symbolic systems but also by the exclusion of the underlying areas of experiences and problems from the orbit of philosophical reflection. It is the fate of symbols in the history of the mind that transparence turns to "appearance." But that the reality that they illuminated comes to be, if not downrightly denied, at any rate rejected as a motive of philosophizing, is a desperate move, a bankruptcy of philosophy. Transcendentalism has had magnificent successes in the clarifications of consciousness-structures in which the objective order of the world is constituted; but these successes cannot gloss over the abandonment of philosophy as the creation of an order of symbols through which man's position in the world is understood. The creation of the transcendental I as the central symbol of philosophy implies the destruction of the cosmic whole within which philosophizing becomes at all possible. The basic subjectivity of the egological sphere, Husserl's philosophical and nondiscussable ultimatum, is the sympton of a spiritual nihilism that still has merit as a reaction, but no more than that.

CHAPTER THREE

Anamnetic Experiments

PREFATORY REMARKS

The following anamnetic experiments are based on the assumption: (1) that consciousness is not constituted as a stream within the I; (2) that in its intentional function consciousness, in finite experience, transcends into the world, and that this type of transcendence is only one among several and must not be made the central theme of a theory of consciousness; (3) that the experiences of the transcendence of consciousness into the body, the external world, the community, history, and the ground of being are givens in the biography of consciousness and thus antecede the systematic reflection on consciousness; (4) that the systematic reflection operates with these experiences or, at least, in its operations sets out from these experiences; that thus (5) the reflection is a further event in the biography of consciousness that may lead to clarification about its problems and, when reflection is turned in the direction of meditation, to the ascertainment of existence; but that it never is a radical beginning of philosophizing or can lead to such a beginning.

Supposing these assumptions as correct, I could further say that the radicalism of philosophizing can never be gauged either by the results or the critical framework of a system but rather, in a more literal sense, by the radices of philosophizing in the biography of philosophizing consciousness, i.e., by the experiences that impel toward reflection and do so because they have excited consciousness to the "awe" of existence. The nature of the irrupting experiences and of the excitements they induce, together with the result of an "attunement" of consciousness to its "problems," seem to me to be the determinants on which depend the radicalism and the breadth of philosophical reflection.

When these connections are recognized, it could be useful to make anamnetic experiments, i.e., to recall those experiences that have opened sources of excitement, from which issue the urge to further philosophical reflection. Obviously such anamnesis is a complicated process that is only partly transparent, so that its results are not at all sure. It would be an immense task to investigate the various grades of this complication. For the moment we must confine ourselves to those problems underlying the efforts which have led to the following set of notes.

A first section of these notes did not require a special effort: they were "always"—i.e., for an indefinite time— "present" as important memories, and it was also clear to me why they were important. This group comprises, e.g., numbers 1, 2, and 14. A second group contains experiences that I have always remembered without being *completely* clear about their meaning. That meaning became clear on the occasion of this writing. To this group belong numbers 5, 8, 15, 17. A third group had been long forgotten and reappeared only on this occasion, e.g., numbers 3, 4, 6, and 9. A further group "imposed itself" when I undertook these experiments of memory but only slowly became meaningful, e.g., number 18. The memory of number 16 is strong but its meaning only half transparent. Two cases, numbers 7 and 19, have been included because the memory is charged with strong excitement though without a clear meaning; the meaning of number 19 occurred to me after I had written it down; number 7 still does not allow me to relate it to any problem of consciousness that occupies me at present. This classification shows that anamnesis may on principle either move back from present problems and their excitements, in order to find the occasions on which the excitement erupted, or that it may move forward from the excitements and the memory of their occasion, toward present problems.

The selection of cases was made for reasons of time and content. Cases relevant in terms of content are those having to do with excitements from the experience of a transcendence in space, time, matter, history, wishful dreams, and wishful times (with the exception of number 7, the meaning of which, as I said, is not clear, but which "imposes itself"). In terms of time the experiences occurred in my first ten years of life. Later experiences were not selected, first of all, because they were complicated through the trauma of emigration and, second, because the experiences of later time no longer have the elementary character of earlier ones but rather occur on the basis of the earlier ones, which entails further complications for an analysis.

1. MONTHS

My earliest datable recollection takes me back to Cologne. My mother took me along on her shopping trips. In a bakery the saleslady expressed proper admiration for the little creature who could hardly walk and asked about my age. My mother informed her: fourteen months (*Monate*).

I recall a general feeling of pride about the attention paid to me, and a feeling of special significance on learning that I was such a thing as "*Monate*." The word had weight; the sonority of the O with the subsequent nasal consonant may account for the fascination of something mysterious.

This recollection is neither supported nor influenced by information on the part of my family. As far as I know, I myself told it when I was more than twenty years old, calling forth only the incredulity of my parents.

2. YEARS

My birthday is on the third of January. It must have been my sixth one, for I already was in school and had vacation. On this birthday I played in my room with tin soldiers, which had appeared on this day and on Christmas. Above the table, on which I arranged the battle, there was a calendar.

I began to take interest in the calendar and to lift the leaves in order to see what came next. Soon I returned, after the 31, to a 1. When my mother came into the room I informed her that soon we would have New Year again, surrounded, as it was, by the two exciting and present-filled days. She showed me my error; and I learned about the twelve months that had to pass before the year was full.

My mother observed that it would be nice if the year would pass that quickly, but unfortunately this was not the case.

The recollection is curious: At the age of six, I must have already heard a lot about months and their names; obviously this knowledge, until that moment, had remained in the realm of sensuous images; the order of the months I only discovered as I played with the calendar.

3. THE FOOLS' PARADE

Still in Cologne. I must have been about three years old. At the time of the carnival (Mardi Gras) the city is topsy-turvy. Fools' parades are formed; persons in carnival costumes roam the streets in groups; they are joined by passersby, while others, who have grown tired, drop away.

From our window I could see such parades. What fascinated me was the "dropping away." The parade was tightly formed, but the last few rows dissolved. Some "fools" fell behind and disappeared into side streets. Though the parade as a whole seemed intact, I was disturbed by this phenomenon of crumbling: What would become of the parade if it finally dissolved into fringes and then into nothing? I recall an oppressive feeling of a threat involved in this dropping away, an anxiety that the magic charm could fade away.

4. THE MONK OF HEISTERBACH

Oberkassel. Age: about five. A favorite object of Sunday afternoon walks were the ruins of Heisterbach, a romanesque monastery, with a neighboring restaurant. Pieces of the church apsis and fragments of stone benches were still standing. We children played on the grass in the ruins.

The most famous inmate of the monastery had been Caesarius of Heisterbach. With his name I became familiar only much later, nor did I then know anything about him as an historical figure. He was simply "the Monk," surrounded by legends.

The chief legend: The Monk went for a walk one day, lost in meditation. When he returned, he found new faces, and much had changed in the environment; he himself was unknown to the other monks. Lost in meditation, he had been in the wood for a hundred years, and to him the hundred years had passed as if they were the hours of an afternoon.

I do not remember having felt an urge to pursue the meaning of that legend further. The event seemed to me wholly natural. But I do recall the temptation of the thought to let time stand still and then to return from lostness-in-thought into the world.

5. THE OELBERG

Oberkassel and Koenigswinter, the places where we lived from my fourth to my ninth year, are situated on the Rhine between the river and the Seven Mountains in the relatively narrow valley ground. The Oelberg is the highest of the seven mountains. Climbing it was a major undertaking for a child, and I do not remember having been on its top more than twice. It was distinct from all other mountains by its height and the difficulty of the climb.

Its great and singular importance, however, came from the view which it afforded the climber: from the Oelberg one could see the three Breiberge, the big, the middle, and the small one, and behind the Breiberge is the Never-Never Land.

The Never-Never Land was well known to me in all its details, from my fairy-tale books and pictures. I also knew that in order to get there, one had to eat one's way through the Breiberg [lit.: pap mountain]. The view from the Oelberg stimulated deep thoughts in me.

To get to the Never-Never Land seemed to be worth some pain. But even climbing the Oelberg was hard, and the Breiberge were far away; how could one ever get there? And if one got there, the difficulties had just begun. How could one eat one's way through such a gigantic mountain of pap? A further aggravating fact was that I hated cream of wheat, and I never doubted that the Breiberge consisted of cream of wheat.

I negotiated with my father whether one had to eat through the Big Breiberg or whether the Small one might do. He was of the opinion that the Small one was sufficient. But that did not give me any peace; I had a dark feeling that it might have to be the Big one. Most of all I was afraid that in the middle of the mountain pap one might get stuck and suffocate.

The Never-Never Land remained a beautiful dream, but the nightmare of the *Breiberg* has remained indissolubly linked with it. This area of timeless happiness appeared as a pleasure that was not worth the price.

6. THE OLD SEAMSTRESS

Our old family seamstress in Oberkassel, Mrs. Balters, has much influenced me gently. She introduced me to the *Leather-Stocking Tales;* I still remember distinctly the much-used and greasy book that she brought. I must have been about six years old. Leather-Stocking constituted an inner kingdom of adventure; I do not remember having understood America to be the scene of the tales.

More important were our theological conversations. Mrs. Balters had excellent information about Paradise. All that I know about Paradise I learned from her. What occupied me most of all, just as with the Never-Never Land, was the question of how to get there. My imaginations were unclear: Placing it in heaven was unsatisfactory, for heaven was above, and I could see that there was nothing above. A trace of skepticism seems to have stirred in me. Mrs. Balters knew that Paradise was not "above" but quite firmly on the earth; one could get there and did not even have to die first. That was most reassuring, for I could not imagine what dying was. Unfortunately, Paradise was very far away, in the east, in "Sheena." The way there was long and difficult and dangerous; only very few had ever made it. Mrs. Balters herself had never attempted it and doubted that she could ever get there. The matter seemed hopeless also to me; I gave up Paradise.

7. THE CLOUD CASTLE

The Cloud Castle always remained in the clouds, as it should. I know almost nothing about it. The Cloud Peak [Wolkenstein] is one of the seven mountains. On it there is the Wolkenburg [Cloud Castle] and in it there dwells the Knight of the Wolkenburg. There was a legend about this knight. I have forgotten it and do not know whether it ever was important to me. The only thing important was that he "dwelt" up there.

The great attractiveness of the Cloud Peak was its inaccessibility. There were quarries at the mountain, and the ascent was not permitted. The castle itself could not be seen from below—if it existed at all. I, at any rate, did not doubt its existence.

The fuzziness of the details possibly accounted for the fact that the Cloud Castle and its knight were firmly ensconced in my soul. The place was dark and moist, surrounded by rags of clouds; the knight, a vague, sad, lost figure, traveling much on mysterious business, always returning in order to "dwell there" for a while.

8. THE PETERSBERG

The *Petersberg* (St. Peter's Mountain) was a serious problem. From our house one could see it well. There it was, not too far away, a high ridge with rounded shoulders; on top, in the middle, a little house, a toy house like the several toy houses I possessed.

One day I learned that a passing-through friend of my parents lived up there. I could not believe it. The toy house was a real house, a hotel in which one could eat and sleep! By insistent questioning I made sure that the house was as big as ours, that it contained real rooms, that the door was as large as a real door and that one could enter in through it.

Something new broke in on me. I learned that the house up there was small when I was below; that it was big when I went there and stood in front of it; that our house, which was big, was also small when I stood above on the mountain and looked down on it.

The experience was disturbing and has remained so until today. At that time I could not cope with it. There remained the discovery that space is a weird matter and that the world which I knew looked differently if one stood at a different place in it.

Later this first shaking of my world center was followed by other experiences that concerned the relations of spatial position to psychic and spiritual perspectives. These experiences, however, occurred after the years in the Rhineland; they did not begin until after my own revolutionary change of location to Austria. At any rate, space was never something neutral, a quantitative extension; it always remained for me a problem of the soul.

9. THE FREIGHTERS

In Koenigswinter we lived in a house on the waterfront. It stood on a little bluff, which had a stonewall; in front of the wall was the river-lane. When the Rhine carried high water, it flooded the path and the water rose on the wall. At that time, in order to leave the house, we had to pass through a neighbor's garden behind our own. Unfortunately, this exciting change occurred only a few days once a year.

From our front yard we looked down on the river where the steamboats were passing. There were three kinds: most numerous were the tugboats with barges behind them; then there were the passenger boats of the Koeln-Duesseldorf Line coming by every one or two hours; and finally the Netherland Line passenger ships, twice or thrice a day.

The freighters were the source of a physical discovery, and the nature of this discovery taught me for the first time caution in the delicate questions of interpretation. They emitted thick clouds of smoke. I followed these clouds—partly with pleasure, partly with uneasiness—for when clouds appeared then rain would follow, and I would have to stay in the house.

One day, in the circle of the family, I summed up the result of my observations: that tomorrow it would rain because today the freighters had produced many clouds. My parents laughed, and I learned that clouds of smoke and rain-producing clouds are not the same thing. I was ashamed about my ignorance and because I had made a fool of myself.

I still love to see interesting relationships—but just when I see them in the most satisfactory and beautiful way, the smoke of the freighters rises and clouds my pleasure.

10. THE KOELN-DUESSELDORFER

The Koeln-Duesseldorfer boats were the great and festive world. They were colored white and light yellow; and on their decks were many people who did nothing but have themselves carried by the boats along the river. Waiting at the pier, there always was a body of hotel bellboys; on their high, round caps they wore the names of their hotels. An especially good-looking man had a cap inscribed *Europaeischer Hof*. When the boats made fast at the piers, there was much wonderful noise, for the bellboys hollered the names of their hotels in order to attract the emerging passengers. These people were "strangers."

During the summer, organized groups rented such boats. One then saw them coming up the river at night, turn around at Bonn, and then coming down again. On the decks there were Chinese lanterns, music, and dancing people. It was a magic world sliding past, strange and mysterious; vibrations of something intoxicating but unknown reached me.

On Sundays we ourselves used these boats for excursions into the Rhine Valley. The occasions were festive; and when I found a quiet corner, I could watch the scenery by the hour, as it slowly and steadily changed, the various views merging into each other. I was especially fond of a ruined arch on a mountain. One could see the sky through it. As the boat glided on, the light section of sky gradually became narrower, was reduced to a mere slit, and then disappeared. One could clearly observe the gliding by.

Sometimes I closed my eyes in order to interrupt the gliding and to see how after a minute the views had changed. But then I regretted having done that; something precious seemed to have been lost in the not-observed gliding by of this minute.

11. THE NETHERLANDERS

The Netherland Line boats were blue-grey and dark-goldish yellow. They came more infrequently; and only few people traveled on them. They also appeared somewhat dirty, and on the rear deck they carried freight. We never made use of them.

The realistic details were fully conscious to me, but they did not get into the way of the secret meaning that for me attached to these boats. They steamed toward the Netherlands, and in golden letters they carried names like *Kriemhild, Siegfried,* and one of them, the most glorious one, was called *Xanten.* For me, the Netherlands were the scenery of the Siegfried saga; and the boats went into saga-land. The *Xanten* was a blue-gold mysterium; the word started with a rare X, and the sound of the name excited me deeply; often I repeated it to myself as the formula that conjured up the world of heroic adventure. The boat was the physical connection to my dreams of deeds of honor and glory and of death resulting from meanness and trickery.

The magic of *Xanten* has not evaporated. The word still evokes the blue-grey and gold ships descending the Rhine, into a dreamland that is neither temporal nor spatial.

12. THE DUTCHMEN

From Holland there came the men with blue suits. They wore blue caps and on their shoulders they carried blue sacks. They roamed through the town, in twos or threes, hawking their merchandise: *Hollandse hering—Hollandse Kees!*

Purchasing cheese was no small ceremony. The man showed his big red balls, rubbed with linseed oil and grease, pressed them with authority and praised their quality. My mother examined different sizes and also pressed the balls with authority. When one seemed to appeal, the man pulled out a long, narrow knife and cut a conical piece out of the ball in order to show that the cheese was properly ripe down to the center. Only then the deal was made.

We children liked cheese and red herring. Holland had to be a beautiful country. The conviction deepened at the yearly fair; the most attractive stall was the Dutch-waffle bakery with its wide-spreading sweet odor.

It is remarkable how the various areas of experience remained separated from each other. As far as I remember, it never occurred to me that the Netherlands of the boats and the Holland of the cheese, the herring, and the waffles were the same country. That the blue-cheese vendors might come from Xanten was wholly unthinkable.

13. THE COMET

I must have been seven or eight when Halley's Comet appeared. In the evening we stood on the river-lane, looking up: there it was, with a big tail.

It was a week of excitement. Everywhere the comet was being

discussed. I heard that it was especially close to the earth, that there was the possibility we might pass through its tail, that one was not sure what the tail consisted of—possibly gas. Fears were voiced that the world might come to an end.

I had mixed feelings. I could not quite accept the fears, for I saw that the comet and its tail were pretty far away. How could we suddenly pass through this distant tail? But I also was impressed by all this talk and inquired how it would be if the world came to an end. It seemed that in this event the houses collapsed and people afterwards were dead. Now that was a fearful prospect; I did feel relieved when the comet had disappeared and the world was still there.

Of this fear of the world's end, there remained a shudder in the face of matter. "The starry heaven above me" fills my heart with admiration only as long as I see it as a firmament with glittering points; when I think of what these points are I am seized by a horror of the solitude in which globs of matter float around without meaning.

14. THE LOAF OF BREAD

Bread in the Rhineland has the form of French rolls— longish, somewhat pointed at the end. When a loaf was cut, from the end topward the middle, the slices were not cylindrical but conical; the crust ran on a slant; one surface was larger than the other. I always preferred to have my butter on the larger surface.

I cannot pinpoint the date when I became concerned with the problem how to get from the smaller to the larger surface. When slices are cut in a certain thickness, the surfaces are obviously of different size. How would it be, however, if one cuts very close to the previous cut so that the surfaces are still of the same size? When does the difference of size of the surfaces begin to increase so that in the end one still arrives at the larger surface?

My awkward questioning was rejected as nonsense. But I still remember my feeling that I had been wronged.

Today I believe to have intellectual mastery of Zeno's

paradoxes and their solution; but physically they are to me still a marvel, as they were then.

15. THE BOOK OF REALITIES

The Book of Realities was my favorite schoolbook. Between its covers it contained, with the exception of reading, arithmetic and religion, the entire material of the first four grades, i.e., the earth, plants and animals, physics, chemistry, physiology, and history. The realities of nature that were to be found in this book I do not remember; but history is still firmly retained. It was a most beautiful history—of course the history of the state of Prussia. The state seemed to consist mostly of kings, and besides them there was also Bismarck.

The most remarkable feature of this Prussian history was that it moved backwards. It began with William II, then went back to Frederick III, William I, and so forth. This arrangement occupied me quite a bit, and I remember having considered the possibility of reversing history. On the whole, however, I was satisfied, especially since a reversal would have encountered certain inner inhibitions. For history did not simply run backwards, but in retracing its steps its proportions changed in a way that seemed hardly reversible. The present had a normal human character; further back the kings grew and became even larger. In the nineteenth century it was not too bad: Frederick William IV was still quite human, like William II. Frederick William III grew noticeably in the halo of the wars of liberation. Frederick the Great already was a pretty large king. The Great Elector was a gigantic man on a white horse. And way back there loomed the gigantic shadow of a prince who because of his excellent qualities was named "The Bear." That seemed to be the right perspective: to look from the humanly comprehensible present into the depth of time and see the horizon closing with ever-larger figures that provided security.

Whatever capacity I have today to understand mythical images of history, like that of the Greeks, must have developed on occasion of this reversed Prussian history. I have always taken it for granted that the present was to be measured, with Thucydides, in human terms, that with increasing distance men grew to the size of a Solon and Lycurgus, that behind them there cavorted the heroes, and that the horizon was securely and dependably closed by the gods.

16. THE KAISER

To the Kaiser I had no clear relationship. He belonged to my life like a piece of furniture in daily use. At home he hung on the wall, together with wife, seven children, and a dog. In the reader at school he occupied a whole page, in white uniform. During music lesson we sang, with ardor, the pleasant melody of:

> The Kaiser is a goodly man
> He liveth in Berlin,
> And were it not so far away,
> I would go there today!

Many years later, when hearing *The Magic Flute,* I found the pleasant melody again—it was Papageno's song.

Maybe it was the everyday familiarity of the object that allowed not deeper feelings to form; the Kaiser remained no more than a spectacle. At any rate, no sentiments of special awe were generated in me. This psychically indifferent attitude to representatives of power has remained unchanged in my later life.

Once the Kaiser came into the Rhineland. He was expected in Bonn; and my mother wanted to go there with us children. On the day of the great event I capped a series of mischiefs by the willful busting of a window. That was serious, for it cost money. By way of punishment I was excluded from the expedition; my mother and sister set out alone. In the meantime the Kaiser's plans had changed; he did not go through Bonn but on our side of the Rhine, passing through Oberkassel. By chance I stood in front of the house and saw the Kaiser pass by in an automobile. He was very beautiful, with a golden helmet, on top of which there was a silver eagle. In the evening I celebrated a triumph.

During the following two days the triumph lost its splendor. The event of the Kaiser's passing through was much discussed. As I listened to the talks of the grown-ups, I became more and more certain that the beautiful man with the eagle-crowned helmet, whom I had taken for the Kaiser, was the equerry of the guards, next to the chauffeur. So I had not seen the Kaiser, after all. But I never let on.

17. THE SONG OF THE FLAG

Both at school and at home we children roared the Flag Song with wild enthusiasm; it stirred us deeply. It began:

> High from the ship's mast
> proudly waves
> its black-white-red
> the Flag

and it ended with a refrain in which one dedicates one's life to the Flag and promises to be faithful to it until death.

The song was so exciting because of its history. It must have been about 1900 when the gunboat *Iltis* was shipwrecked in a storm in East Asia, in sight of land but beyond any possible help. With the exception of a few survivors the entire crew went down with the ship, and in going down they sang this song.

The song and the story of the sinking affected me deeply. There seemed to be nothing greater and more glorious than to go down with a ship, its flag waving, while singing the Flag Song.

The flag is still waving, but time has done its work on it. Flags never had my whole sympathy; and quite early the flag that rather cracks in the wind than waves must have become a less noisy banner. Its colors then faded and turned to a glimmer of silver. It really was no longer a flag but just a silvery waving. And then the waving, too, disappeared and there remained only a sound of calling stillness—sometimes softly, from a distance, sometimes strong and close, so strong and close that it can hardly be distinguished from the call of the waves in which we go down.

18. THE EMPEROR'S NIGHTINGALE

Andersen's fairy tales were always my favorites. At first, my mother read them to us; then, when I learned to read, I could enjoy them as often as I wished. The stories themselves are almost forgotten; I remember only the tale of the Emperor's New Clothes. It is quite possible, however, that I do not really remember even this tale but that the story is so familiar to me because it is so frequently quoted. At any rate, the content did not especially impress me as a child. Apparently I was not told the moral of the story, and I did not find it myself. I only remember a certain embarrassment caused by the idea of the emperor in underwear.

Of the other stories I remember no contents at all. Only this or that image remains and the mood it aroused. I have re-read the fairy tales later; they are beautiful, but they are not the fairy tales that I heard and read as a child; the power of their magic is gone.

But the magic that the fairy tales had in my childhood is as strong as ever. One of the most exciting stories was that of the emperor—but not of the one with the New Clothes. It was the story of the emperor who lies stretched out on his bed; Death sits on his chest and takes away from him, one by one, the insignia of his power. Then comes the Nightingale and sings so gloriously that Death is moved and forced to return the crown and the golden sword and to let the emperor live.

The Nightingale still sings its heart-soring, throat-choking song against Death. The significance a musical composition has for me is determined by the degree to which it brings back again this sweet oppression between death and life.

19. THE CANNONS OF KRONBURG

The cannons of Kronburg speak in the story of Holger Danske. Again, nothing has remained of the story but the cannons. When the ships pass by, the cannons say "boom."

That is somewhere far away, in the north, where the world has gone farthest, with nothing beyond. Ships will pass there, and nobody asks whence they are coming and where they are going. Where they pass, without a sound, there is nothing; no human beings, only the cannons; and they say "boom" with solemn sadness, at the end of the world.

20. FIRST EMIGRATION

In 1910 my father accepted a position in Vienna. I was then nine years old. A move of this kind must have been in preparation for some time. I do not recall, however, that there was any kind of disturbance before the departure.

I still remember clearly the day when I went to school for the last time. The teacher, Mr. Corbach, whom I revered, said goodbye to me. He said something about my going into foreign parts but that it might not be so bad, since German was also spoken there. I was a little afraid, but I also was excited by the adventure and proud that something so important was happening to me.

What had happened only dawned on me several weeks later, when I first went to school in Vienna.

(October 25–November 7, 1943)

PART II

Experience and History

CHAPTER FOUR

What Is Right by Nature?

In classical philosophy "right by nature" was a symbol, with the help of which the philosopher interpreted his noetic experience of right human action. Through dogmatization of philosophy, which began with the Stoa and has not been wholly overcome until today, the symbol of noetic exegesis was gradually separated from its underlying experience and, under the title "natural law," turned into a topic of the philosophic schools. This topic, the idea of a body of norms with the claim of eternal and immutable validity, has had considerable effects since the seventeenth century, even though its noetic premises did not become very clear. Today the revived debate about natural law unfortunately still suffers from the topical character of its object, separated as it is from the experience containing its meaning. We shall try to get behind the topos of dogmatic philosophizing and to reconstitute the symbol of noetic exegesis.

To this end we shall examine the occasion on which the expressions "right" and "nature" first were related within a larger theoretical context, namely the Aristotelian *physei dikaion*. This case obviously merits our attention, not only because it is the first of its kind so that we may hope to discover in it the experiential bases of the symbol, but also and especially because the *physei dikaion* of Aristotle is supposed to be valid everywhere and for all time but all the same is a *kineton*, everywhere changeable. Thus the content of the original concept varies considerably from that of the later topos. The question of the transition of the one to the other is certainly worth a detailed investigation and is still to be accomplished, but it lies beyond the frame of the present undertaking. It suffices for us here to clarify the meaning of the *physei dakaion* and to unravel some of its philosophical implications.

I. *PHYSEI DIKAION*

The text in which the term *physei dikaion* occurs is so little clear that many have assumed that particular page of the *Nicomachean Ethics* (*NE* 1134b18 ss) to have come from a pen other than Aristotle's. That may be, but I would not go as far as that. Rather it seems to be a first version, possibly a dictation. Anybody who has himself struggled with the task of penetrating a large context of thoughts will recognize a mutual contamination of different series of thoughts. The page should have been worked over once more in order to put the associative sequence in discursive order. The text is not clear because (1) the concepts burst out of the logical scheme of general and special and because (2) the term *physis* occurs in those few sentences in several meanings so that only the expert reader can say with some certainty which meaning belongs to which passage. The first reason has to do with the total complex of the *philosophia peri ta anthropina* ("philosophy of human affairs", *NE* 1181b15 s), as Aristotle names the work that comprises the *Ethics* as well as the *Politics,* so we must deal with this reason first. Once the greater deficiency of clarity that affects the formation of concepts is removed, the smaller equivocations of the term *physis* offer no more difficulty.

The want of clarity in the concepts concerning the right by nature root in the dominant interest of the whole work in the theory of the polis and can be removed only through an interpretation of the text in the light of the larger theoretical context. To this end the definition in the *Politics* (1253a38 ss) as well as the overall structure of the *Nicomachean Ethics* must be examined.

In the just-mentioned passage of the *Politics,* Aristotle formulates three fundamental definitions: (a) justice (*dikaiosyne*) is a *politikon;* (b) Right (*dikaion*) is the order (*taxis*) of the *koinonia politike* (the political community); (c) the judicial decision (*dike*) is the determination of what is right (*dikaion*). We infer from the definitions that Aristotle wanted to put the questions of justice and judicial decision into an essential connection with the polis. For justice is a *politikon;* the *dikaion,* in turn, relates only to the polis but not to any other kind of association and its order; the judicial decision, whether it is to be understood as a legislative norm of a judge's decision, regards what is right within the framework of the community of the polis. Statements containing these concepts thus must not be generalized into an Aristotelian "philosophy of law," nor may one conclude from the relationship to the polis that this or that statement may not be valid for other types of association. The statements must be understood as "primarily related to the polis."

This rule of interpretation is confirmed by the curious structure of Book V of the *Nicomachean Ethics*. Aristotle begins with a distinction of justice in a general and a narrower sense; he then subdivides the latter in distributive and corrective justice. After the quite voluminous investigation has come to this point, he suddenly recalls that its object is the relation of what is generally right to what is politically right (*politikon dikaion*). Everything that was said after the section on justice in general appears as a single digression from which we now return—"we must not forget"—to the proper subject, the *politikon dikaion*. Together with this new beginning there are new subdivisions: The *politikon dikaion* consists of the *physikon* and the *nomikon;* the *nomikon* is eliminated since by definition it is concerned with the *adiaphora*, the essentially indifferent matters like traffic rules, measures, and weights; finally the investigation concentrates on the *physikon dikaion* as the right that is concerned with essentials. Within each of the two parts the formation of concepts thus clearly proceeds according to the scheme of general and special; the obscurity enters at the point of the break: there where justice in the general sense suddenly is related to the polis and the concept of the *dikaion politikon* is introduced.

What, then, is right in a political sense? Aristotle defines: "The just in political matters is found among men who share a common life in order that their association bring them self-sufficiency and who are free and equal, either proportionally or arithmetically. Hence, in a society where this is not the case, there is nothing just in the political sense in the relations of the various members to one another, but there is only something that bears a resemblance to what is just." Explaining this definition, he continues: "For the just exists only among men whose mutual relationship is regulated by law, and law exists where injustice may occur." This is possible only among men who are free and equal, for only among them there is public decision about justice (*dike*) that distinguishes between what is right (*dikaion*) and what is unjust (*adikon*). These sentences do not present

an argument but produce a curiously floating circle of meanings in which justice is closely linked with the polis and its relations between free and equal citizens, while the relations between men belonging to other associations drop down into a
just as curious shadowy condition of unreality.

The floating meanings receive a little more determination
from the term *nomos,* which these sentences introduced. *Nomos,*
the law, is to rule, not man. The ruler is to be no more than the
guardian of the *dikaion,* of that justice that distributively and
correctively obtains between men who are free and equal; if the
ruler violates the *dikaion* by acting in his own interest, assigning
to himself more than his equal share, he becomes a tyrant. For
Aristotle, the rule of *nomos* thus does not cover any content
whatsoever of statues or ordinances; rather one can speak of a
rule of law only when the law has a definite and essential content.

Now we are in a position to dissolve the obscurities that were
caused by Aristotle's dominant interest in the polis.

Above all, one must pay attention to the several layers of
meanings. Primarily the concepts refer to the polis as the
manifestation of right order, so on this level it appears as if
justice, law, right could be mentioned only with regard to the
polis. Since Aristotle, however, is aware that the problems
touched by these terms also concern men who live in other
associations than the polis, a second level of meaning is opened,
in which he touches the corresponding problems beyond the
polis. For Aristotle, there is not merely a *politikon,* but also a
despotikon, patrikon, and *domestikon dikaion,* only it must be distinguished from the more essential justice of the polis as a *homoion,*
a "resemblance." Nor does he deny to the "justice" of other
associations a *physikon,* even if it, too, is to be understood only in
the *modus deficiens* as a "resemblance," like the *dikaion.* Moreover, Aristotle has not much to say about these other types of
what is right by nature, since they do not interest him in the
course of an investigation of the *politikon.* Essential justice, then,
merges with what is right in the historical-concrete polis, while
the questions of right order for other types of association appear only sketchily on the edges of the investigation.

Given the dominance of the *politikon,* there can be no natural
law conceived as an eternal, immutable, universally valid nor-
mativity confronting the changeable positive law. This is so be-

cause the justice of the polis, its *nomos,* insofar it constitutes the rule of law among men free and equal, is itself right by nature. The justice of the polis is not positive law in the modern sense but rather essential law within which alone there arises the tension between *physei dikaion* and a possible derailment into the making of laws by arbitrary human will. Of course, the law of the polis is also legislated and obligatory in this capacity, but this attribute takes second rank behind the question whether the content of the statue is *physei* or rather the product of human *hybris.* This Aristotelian conception of *nomos* does not seem to differ in principle from the older one of Heraclitus or Sophocles. In Heraclitus we find the sentence (B 114) that all human laws (*anthropeoi nomoi*) are nourished by one that is divine (*theios nomos*), which governs as far as it will and is sufficient for all and more than enough. And Sophocles' Antigone speaks of the unwritten and irremovable commands (*nomima*) of the gods, of which nobody has seen how they arise; and she does not want to become guilty before the gods by conforming to ordinances that have sprung from the self-willed thought (*phronema*) of a man (*Ant.* 450–70). In Aristotle the place of the *theios nomos* has been taken by the *physei dikaion,* so *nomos* is subject no longer to the divine but to nature. Whether or what has changed through this mutation of the criterion can be ascertained only through a close examination of the concept of nature.

The second reason for lack of clarity is the changing meanings of the term *physis.* Now, after the first reason has been removed, we can go through the text with a view to the different meanings of *physis.*

Political justice is either *physikon* or *nomikon.* While *physikon* everywhere has the same validity (*dynamis*) and is independent of what men are thinking, *nomikon* concerns things that could be ordered one way or another, since from the point of view of essence they obviously are indifferent. After these definitions, Aristotle interrupts his train of thoughts and introduces a wide spread opinion: Many people think that all law is *nomikon;* for while that which by nature is the same always and everywhere—as, for example, fire burns both here and in Persia—the law seems indeed to be subject to changes. Against this view, he argues that the sentence, that law is changeable, does not seem to apply to gods, while among men, even though there is obviously something that is right by nature, it is indeed changeable. He adds that it is easy to recognize which *dikaia* are according to nature and which are not.

The difficulties of this text resolve themselves if one understands that the word *physis* has the three meanings of physical, divine, and human, without Aristotle indicating which of the three meanings he uses in each case. Furthermore, the hasty language of this passage does not distinguish carefully enough between the arbitrary making of laws characterizing the *nomika* and the not arbitrary but rather strictly limited legislation concerning the *physica*. Thus misunderstandings easily arise, when Aristotle talks of the *physikon dikaion* now as that which is valid everywhere (meaning in its divine essence), now as that which is changeable (meaning its realization of men in a concrete situation). When he now even begins to talk of *ta me physika all' anthropina dikaia* ("what is just not by nature but by human enactment"), one can indeed not make up one's mind whether by *physika* he means nature in the physical sense or the divine essence. The only thing that is certain is that the *anthropina* are not *nomika* as opposed to *physika* but rather the *physika* in the third sense of the human realization of what is by nature.

The *physei dikaion*, we may say by way of summary, is what is right by nature in its tension between divine immutable essence and human existentially conditioned mutability.

At the passage in which the *physika* are opposed to the *anthropina* (*NE* 1135a3), there begins a sentence which has got little attention because of the confusing context, even though it is of fundamental importance for Aristotalian ethics and politics. Aristotle has made a comparison (*NE* 1134b35 ss). The *nomika* are based on convenience and utility, as, e.g., one creates various standard measures for wholesale and retail commerce. Similar to the measures that are adapted to the market situation are also the *dikaia*, which are not *physika* but *anthropina*, for even the constitutions (*politeia*) are not everywhere the same, even though only one *politeia* is according to nature (*kata physin*), namely, the best one. In this passage, as we already mentioned, the *anthropina* must be understood as the natural in its human realization and, thus, are not equated with *nomika* but only compared with them, the *tertium comparationis* being the adaptation to the situation.

This passage is important, first of all, because it winds up the text about *politikon dikaion* by referring the reader, for his information, to the best constitution, the model of which Aristotle has worked out in *Politics* VII–VIII. Quite unlike the later ideas about natural law as the quintessence of eternal, immutable rules, the right by nature here is identical with the paradigm of the *ariste politeia.* The investigation about the *physei dikaion,* therefore, must not be understood as an autonomous set of teachings that could be further developed into a "doctrine of natural law", rather, it leads directly to the core problem of political science, the question of the right order of society. Inasmuch as this passage points in this direction, it is therefore, secondly, important for the overall structure of Aristotle's *episteme politike:* While the construction of the model only tries to get hold of the right by nature in its immutable aspect, the description of the different constitutions in the *Politics* survey the entire width of variations in the human attempts to realize the model. Both investigations together, in their relation toward each other, only make up the whole of political science.

The tensions between the immutable right of nature and the changing modes of its realization occur within the polis, the problems of which we have recognized as the dominant motive of the conceptualization. Since the polis is the community best by nature, justice as a whole has a fourfold determination as natural. First, it is right by nature insofar as the historical type of community of the polis is best by nature; second, it is natural insofar as it concerns the human essence, as contrasted with the *adiaphora;* third, within the tension it is the preeminently natural that is valid everywhere, akin to Heraclitus' *theios nomos;* fourth, it is the mutable natural, the *anthropinon,* in the concrete constitutions of the polis, in this sense akin to Heraclitus' *anthropeioi nomoi.*

This much for the commentary on the text about the *physei dikaion.*

II. *PHRONESIS*

What is right by nature is not given as an object about which one could state correct propositions once and for all. Rather, it has its being in man's concrete experience of a justice which is everywhere the same and yet, in its realization, changeable and everywhere different. There is, thus, an existential tension that cannot be resolved theoretically but only in the practice of the man who experiences it. Mediation between its poles is not an easy task. We know Solon's complaint on the occasion of his reform: "It is very hard to recognize the invisible measures of right judgment; and yet this measure alone contains the right limits [*peirata*] of all things" (Solon 4, 17). It is very easy to lose this invisible, divine measure, and then its place will be taken by a legislator's arbitrariness pursuing his special interest. In order to deal somewhat adequately with this task, man needs an existential power, a special quality, if his action is to mediate between the poles of the tension. This power Aristotle calls *phronesis*.

The problems of *phronesis* as the power of mediation run parallel to those of the tension between right and effective order in the polis. In dealing with what is right by nature, Aristotle permitted the politikon to dominate his conceptualization; similarly, when dealing not only with *phronesis* but with virtue in general, he puts his conceptualization under the idea of adjustment of the existential tension. This overall notion has not received much attention, as far as I know, and yet it is this that gives weight to any undertaking of ethics, not only Aristotle's. For purposes of characterizing its philosophical *locus*, it is advisable to speak on an *ontology of ethics*.

Aristotle's ontological interest manifests itself when he attributes to concrete action a higher degree of truth than to general principles of ethics. In (*NE* 1107a28 ss), he follows up a definition of virtue as the mean between extremes with an observation about the value of general concepts in ethics. We must not dwell on the generalities, says Aristotle, but we must look at the *hekasta*, the concrete facts or cases. In the science of human action, the general principles may have a wider application (or: are more widely accepted; the *koinoteroi* is not unambiguous), but the specifics are *alethinoteroi*, i.e., have more truth, for in action we are dealing with concrete things (*hekasta*) and must adjust to them. While other sciences endeavor to attain general principles with the widest possible area of application, in ethics the generalities are relatively uninteresting (possibly because they are already universally known). It is only on a lower level of abstraction, in the doctrine of particular virtues and in casuistics, that we get to the important things, and to these lower levels Aristotle attributes the greater amount of truth.

Now it does not go without saying that the lower levels deserve the attribute of more truth. Even if concrete action is more important, why should general principles and definitions be "less true" than decisions in particular cases? In this identification of truth with the concrete, there emerges the almost forgotten knowledge of the philosopher, that ethics is not a matter of moral principles, nor a retreat from the complexities of the world, nor a contraction of existence into eschatological expectation or readiness, but a matter of the truth of existence in the reality of action in concrete situations. What matters is not correct principles about what is right by nature in an immutable generality, nor the acute consciousness of the tension between the immutable truth and its mutable application (possibly even with tragic overtones), but the changeability, the *kineton* itself, and the methods to lift it to the reality of truth. The truth of existence is attained where it becomes concrete, i.e., in action.

The *kineton* of action is the *locus* where man attains his truth. That does not mean that ethics on the higher levels of abstraction would be superfluous for the truth of action, for correct action in concrete situations requires the deliberation of pro and contra in the tension of what is immutably right, and the premise for rational deliberation is ethical knowledge. Precisely in this question, however, Aristotle is willing, on the basis of his experiences to allow for other possibilities, inasmuch as he recognizes right action, which attains truth without the mediation of ethical knowledge. In the *Eudemian Ethics,* he speaks of *tyche,* the luck of right action. There would be no end of deliberation, he thinks, if reasons after reasons were to be considered and the deliberating reason (*nous*) did not have an absolute origin and beginning (*arche*) of its reasoning—the beginning of God. The reasoning about concrete action is part of a movement in being, which issues from God and ends in human action. Just as God moves (*kinei*) everything in the universe, the divine also moves all things in us (*EE* 1248a27). To be sure, the divine in us moves usually through knowledge (*episteme*), mind (*nous*), and virtue (*arete*), but it also can do without these instruments and move us without them, directly through *enthousiasmos.* Side by side with the capacity for correct action of the wise men there is, therefore, the capacity of the unwise (*alogoi*) to hit on a correct decision by divination (*mantike*). Such accuracy of true action without the instrumentary (*organon*) of knowledge and experience shows its possessor to be a fortune-favored one, a *eutyches*.

These reflections about the fortune-favored man reveal the connection between ethics and ontology, an ontology that still has a decidedly cosmological character. From the unmoved mover, as the first cause, the movement of being goes on through the cosmos down to the last thing that is moved, in the realm of humanity to human action. If what is right by nature is characterized as *kineton,* the translation of this term as "change-able" is correct but must be supplemented by the meaning of "being moved cosmically by the cause of all movement." The cosmological overtones should also keep us from understanding the content of particular cases as historical singularities in the modern sense. The constitution of the polis, which Aristotle uses as examples of the changeable right by nature, do indeed belong to the area that today we call history, but to the Hellenic thinker they appeared as belonging to an ahistorical realm of being. Let us not forget Aristotle's comparison with the market situation, to which one or another measure might be adequate. More about this question cannot be said at this time, for we are touching on a theoretical problem of the limits of history, which has hardly even been raised today.

Whatever these limits may be, for Aristotle the historical and ahistorical changeables merge into the one movement issuing from the Divine. The movement may take a short cut from the divine *arche* in man to his action, or it can use the instrumentalities of reason, knowledge, and habits of virtue. The normal case is not that of the fortune-favored unwise, but rather that of the wise man. The wise man, however, deliberates on the basis of his knowledge; and this knowledge may be ordered and expressed in the lasting form of propositions of various degrees of generality, which are called ethics. Insofar as this constant knowledge is the instrument used by the divine to attain truth in the reality of action, ethics itself is a phase in the movement of being that ends in the *kineton,* and its creation is a labor of serving the unmoved mover. The philosophical achievement of ethics has its dignity as a part of the divine movement that leads to the truth of action.

The ground for an ontology of ethics is the insight that ethical knowledge and deliberation are parts of the movement of being. Between the mover and the moved, however, there is man who either is, or is not, permeable for the movement of being. By no means all men are either wise or fortunate; rather most of them allow their action to be determined by their lusts (*hedone*) (*NE* 113a35). The next step, therefore, is the conception of the man in whom knowledge and deliberation occur.

The degree of permeability for the movement of being determines the rank of human beings, the highest of whom is the *spoudaios*. The *spoudaios* is the mature man who desires what is in truth desirable, and who judges everything right. All men desire what is good, but their judgment of what is good in truth is obscured by lust. If we tried to find out what is truly good by taking a poll in any given collectivity of men, we would get as many answers as the characters of those we have asked (1113a32), for each character considers that good what he desires. Hence, we must ask the *spoudaios*, who differs from other men in that he sees "truth in concrete things" (*hekastois*), for he is, as it were, their measure (*kanon kai metron*) (1113a34)—a principle of the method to which our "empirical" social scientists should pay attention.

The passages concerning the *spoudaios* show very clearly that, for Aristotle, what is right by nature cannot become a set of eternal, immutable propositions, for the truth of a concrete action cannot be determined by its subsumption under a general principle but only by asking the *spoudaios*. Appeal is made, therefore, not from the action to an immutably correct principle but to the existentially right order of man. The criterion of rightly ordered human existence, however, is the permeability for the movement of being, i.e., the openness of man for the divine; the openness in its turn is not a proposition about something given but an event, and ethics is, therefore, not a body of propositions but an event of being that provides the word for a statement about itself.

The ontology of ethics is completed by the theory of *phronesis*, that virtue that for Aristotle is the locus at which the movement of being in man becomes reality and simultaneous becomes articulate. *Phronesis* is the virtue of correct action and, at the same time, the virtue of right speech about action. More about the general characterization cannot be said on the basis of the text. Some Platonic premises, however, are implied but cannot be made explicit because of the dominance of cosmological thinking. Before we turn to details, a word is required about the doctrine of virtue in the *Politeia* and the relation to it of Aristotle's doctrine of virtue.

Plato distinguishes the three virtues of *sophia, andreia,* and *sophrosyne,* which by their respective dominance in the soul determine three types of characters, while the fourth virtue, *dikaiosyne,* guards the right relation of subordination and superordination of the others—in other words, the over-all order of the soul. By virtue of this role, Plato's *dikaiosyne* is first cousin to, although not identical with, Aristotle's justice "in the general sense." Outside of the closed system of the four cardinal virtues in the *Politeia,* there is *phronesis* as that virtue that is activated in man when he attains the *opsis,* the vision of the good. Resulting from the opening of the soul, it is a virtue thoroughly forming all of existence, within which formation only the system of the cardinal virtues operates. In order to distinguish it from the virtues with special functions, we call it an existential virtue. Aristotle's *phronesis,* too, is an existential virtue, but this character does not become sufficiently clear in the climate of cosmological thinking, for its activation through an experience of transcendence does not come up for discussion. Furthermore, its character is somewhat obscured by classifying *phronesis* among the intellectual virtues in Aristotle's bipartition of virtues into ethical and dianoetic virtues. The bipartition itself stems from Aristotle's difference from Plato, for whom the relation of action to the polis was still relatively beyond question and who, therefore, had no interest in such a bipartition. Aristotle, by contrast, places the *bios theoreticos* at the highest point of human existence, a form of existence that ambiguously oscillates between the primary experience of the cosmos, transcendental orientation, and immanent purposes. The equation of virtues in their bipartition between ethical and dianoetic virtues, however, does not work, as is demonstrated by the treatise on *philia* (*NE* VIII–IX), a treatise about a broadly conceived and many-layered phenomenon, the core of which is the love to the divine *nous.* The Platonic legacy of the experience of transcendence asserts itself and compels Aristotle to recognize the virtue he calls *philia,* which as noetic love comprises the love to God as well as the love to what is divine in us and in one's fellow man. This part of the encompassing investigation must be seen as the specifically philosophical version of the *imago Dei* problem. Further, one notes the reemergence in the *philia* treatise of Plato's direct relation between the experience of transcendence and the order of community. For the noetic *philia,* as love of the divine *nous,* which lives in all men and is common to them (here is an echo of Heraclitus' *nous* as the *xynon*), becomes the *philia politike*, the central virtue of the political community. Aristotle even makes the attempt to derive types of community, and particularly types of constitution, from types of *philia* (the relevant chapters, VIII, 9–11, are a little "Politics", the relation of which to the great *Politics* has unfortunately been hardly noted). Thus Aristotle, too, knows existential virtues but does not clearly characterize them as such or differentiate them from the other virtues. Of the three that can with certainty be recognized as existential virtues, he deals with "justice in the general sense" among the ethical virtues in *NE* V, with *phronesis* among the dianoetical virtues in *NE* VI, and with *philia*, without further characterization, in *NE* VIII–IX.

Let us now examine the main points of Aristotle's investigation of *phronesis*. They are the following:

(1) *Phronesis* is a virtue of deliberation about that which is good and useful for man. Not every deliberation of ends and means, however, comes under *phronesis*, but only the deliberation concerning the good life (*eu zen*) (1140a26 ss). Through the limitation to the "*eu zen* as a whole," the possessor of the virtue is identified with the *spoudaios*, the mature man; as the possessor of *phronesis*, however, he is called *phronimos*.

(2) Deliberation with a view to possible action can neither concern things that are not capable of being changed nor goals that cannot be realized (1140a32 s). *Phronesis* is not knowledge about the unchangeable order of the world; it concerns only human affairs (*anthropina*) and, among them, only those which can be objects of meaningful deliberation (1141b3 ss). The "changeability" in these passages must not be confused with the *kineton*. What is right by nature is changeable in the sense that in each case its realization is different. In the passages concerning *phronesis*, however, Aristotle does not speak of a *kineton* but rather of the possibility of action, i.e., of something capable of being different from what it is, so action can, or can not, have a changing effect.

(3) *Phronesis* thus must be distinguished from the dianoetic virtues of science (*episteme*), which enables us to draw conclusions from principles; the intellect (*nous*), which enables us to recognize first principles; and wisdom (*sophia*), which in a combination of science and intellect refers to things divine (VI, 6–7). Finally, *phronesis* must be distinguished from art (*techne*),

which does refer to things that can be changed but which produces artifacts and is not action that carries its end in itself (VI, 4).

(4) *Phronesis* possesses the same character (*hexis*) as political science. The two are identical as virtues, even though in general language there is differentiation between action in private affairs (*phronesis* in a narrow sense) and political questions (VI, 8). The identification is important for the understanding of the following point, in which *phronesis* is to be understood as always including political science.

(5) *Phronesis* is not identical with wisdom (*sophia*), for wisdom is a knowledge about the most eminent things (*timiotata*). It would be absurd to assert that political science, or *phronesis*, is the highest type of knowledge, for man is not the best thing (*ariston*) in the cosmos (*kosmos*). *Phronesis*, rather, is knowledge about what is salutory and good for each kind of living being respectively, and salutory and good for men is other than what it is for different kind of animals. There is no more *one* kind of *phronesis* for different living things than there is *one* medical art. Nor could one claim the term *sophia* for human *phronesis*, possibly by pointing to man's higher rank than the animals, for there are things that by nature are much more divine than man, e.g., the Highest Visibles (*phanerotata*), of which the cosmos is composed (VI, 7).

Combining the positive and negative determinations of these points, one may say: Aristotle's thinking is dominated by the experience of the cosmos, in which there are different kinds of things, among them also men. Man is not the highest being in a world become immanent, in which he might be thought to rank above all cosmic things and subject only to the transcendent God; rather, he is a "thing" above which there are higher things in the cosmos, namely, the star divinities (*phanerotata*). *Phronesis* thus becomes a knowledge with the help of which man realizes his *eu zen*, the specifically human mode of permeability for the order of the cosmos. Insofar as man optimally realizes the permeability in his existence, he is a *phronimos*; he is a *spoudaios* only insofar as he in that respect hold the highest rank in his kind of thing. A higher rank of being, among the *zoa*, is held by the star gods of whom we know through the virtue of wisdom, and for that reason *phronesis* is not the highest (*spoudaiotate*) kind of knowledge. Furthermore it is not knowledge at all, in the strict sense of a knowledge of principles and derived propositions, but only *episteme* in the sense of a kind of knowledge. These limitations, stemming from the pressure of the cosmos-experience, give rise within the *Nicomachean Ethics,* with its Platonic legacy, to certain difficulties. *Phronesis,* identical with political science, is supposed for that reason to be the *episteme kyriotate* and *architectonike,* the highest and master science of man, which alone assigns all other sciences their due places in the polis (1094a27 ss). This science, scarcely elevated to highest rank, is immediately afterwards characterized as a science of inferior precision (*akribia*), in which we cannot achieve more than a rough sketch of truth (1094b12 ss). There is thus a conflict the denigrating aspect of which is determined by Aristotle's insistence on preserving, at all costs, *phronesis* as a knowledge that has its truth not in general principles but in concrete action. His investigation therefore returns to this question again and again. In *NE* 1141b14 ss *phronesis* is knowledge not only of general principles but of concrete things, of *hekasta,* and for this reason it is possible that men who are ignorant of general principles are sometimes more effective in practice (*praktikoteroi*) than others who do have such knowledge. Still more pointedly Aristotle insists, 1142a24 s, that *phronesis* regards the last concrete thing, for the *praktikon,* the truly effective thing, is the *eschaton,* the last one. (To be noted here is the meaning of *praktikon:* it is not a matter of the ethical but rather of the effective aspects of action, right down to effective magic.)

Aristotle's insistence on this point elicits the final question whether *phronesis* can be adequately characterized at all as knowledge of right action, for this mode of expression puts between knowledge and action the subject-object of which Aristotle precisely wanted to eliminate. For him this knowledge merges into concrete action, and action is the truth of the knowledge; what separates the two is not the distance of subject and object but a noetic tension in the movement of being. That this is indeed the philosophical intention of Aristotle is confirmed by his distinction of *phronesis* from *synesis* and *eusynesia,* the virtue of right understanding and judgments (*NE* VI, 10). *Synesis* has the same scope as *phronesis* but is not identical with it, for *phronesis* issues into command (*epitaktike*) about what is to be done and what not, while *synesis* is the virtue of right judgment and understanding (*kritike*). The *synetos,* the man of good judgment, knows how to assess action correctly, but he does not thereby become a *phronimos,* who acts correctly with effectiveness. Since *synesis* indeed puts the subject-object distance between knowledge and action and precisely in this is distinct from *phronesis,* this distance must be understood ontologically. The virtue that Aristotle calls *phronesis,* or political science, is an existential virtue; it is the movement of being, in which the divine order of the cosmos attains its truth in the human realm.

CHAPTER FIVE

What Is Nature?

Any assertion that this or that is, or is not, "right by nature" must remain void of meaning unless we know what is nature. In this matter we are not too well off. From the text that we have so far consulted, we conclude that Aristotle lived in a tradition going back beyond Plato to the tragedies and the older philosophers and that he counted on being understood when speaking of nature. The contexts in which this term is used indicate that nature refers to constant structures in the movement of being, comprising gods and men, organic and inorganic—in other words, to something like a constitution of being. That, however, is all that can be inferred. Where can we learn more precisely what is meant by nature?

Whoever is looking for an answer to this question will probably first think of the philosophical dictionary in *Metaphysics* delta, which offers precise definitions of nature and related concepts. This source, however, is a disappointment. It develops the concept of nature in its three meanings of (1) matter, (2) form or gestalt (*eidos kai morphe*), and (3) the unity of form and matter in a thing, through the experiential models of organism and artifact. Now if, after reading the dictionary, anyone should feel pride in possessing exact metaphysical knowledge that animals and statues consist of form and matter, we do not want to spoil his fun, but we still must ask ourselves: What can one do with this knowledge in the area of man and society, where the question is one of right order? When we recall the texts about what is "right by nature," we recognize immediately that the meanings of the term nature in *that* context do not fit the definitions of *Metaphysics* delta. And when Aristotle himself attempts to apply his pattern of form and matter to society, he gets into insoluble difficulties: In *Politics* III he posits, faithful to his definitions, the constitution as form and the citizens as matter of the polis; he then concludes with logical precision that every revolutionary change of the constitution must bring about a new polis not identical with the previous one; this brings him up against the problem that every time when in Athens the Democrats overthrow a tyrant or the Oligarchs push the Democrats out of power, a new Athens arises that has nothing in common with the old one except the name; he even finds that, alas, metaphysically talented politicians follow his idea or even anticipate it, as they refuse to acknowledge the public debts of the previous regime; finally, since he, as much as we, is interested in the Athens that in the change of constitutions has maintained its identity, he can only leave the impasse in midair.

Similar difficulties result from the attempt to apply the *Metaphysics* pattern to man by having the soul, as *anima rationalis* or *intellectiva,* function as form and the body as matter. At first glance it may appear as if this attempt would have better chances of succeeding, for unlike society, which frequently changes its constitution, man has only one forming soul for the time of his life. (My assumption that man has only one and not several souls follows the philosophers and the saints, bracketing out both ancient Egyptians who have several souls and modern psychologists who with great inner strength assert that they have none at all.) But even if man has only one soul, and therefore does not present the difficulty that, in the case of society arises from the change of its forms in time, there are still other but similar difficulties. They arise in the mysterious life-of-its-own of which a soul is capable by virtue of its special relation to divine eternity. We human beings in time cannot completely gauge it, but what we learn of it does make one wonder whether the term "form" adequately characterizes the metaphysical status of the soul. Let us take a look at the experiences of the philosophers and the saints.

The Hellenic philosophers from Pythagoras to Plato have shared the saddening experience that the body is the prison, nay even the grave of the soul, and that we owe a sacrifice to the god of healing when death liberates the soul from the sickness of temporal life. Whatever may be the processes culminating in such experiences, it is obvious that the soul may convey to man the desire that it would rather not be linked to the body. This kind of aloofness one would really not expect of a form that is firmly imposed on its matter and penetrates it solidly. The kind of relationship that such occasions reveal points not so much to the soul as form but rather to the body as having the solidity of form with which it holds and surrounds the soul, contrary to the latter's will. As they interpret this curious relationship, the philosophers use not at all the form-matter pattern but rather myths of a prehistorical fall that has doomed souls to prison for the time of temporal existence, or myths of an Ultimate Judgment, or metempsychosis, of the reincarnation of the soul and its final release to true existence in eternity. When it is a matter of the soul's relation to eternity, myths are the symbols that adequately express the soul's fate.

The image produced by the sad experiences of the philosophers resembles that emerging in the joyful experiences of the saints. The saint's soul also lives with a view to eternity, but if it, like the philosopher's, also places disparaging accents on time, body, and world, still in the realm of the Gospel there is certainty that all things work together for good to them who love God. Again, the transformation effected in human nature by God's grace through Christ elicits a corresponding language akin to the myth. We hear of changes, conversions, renewal, and rebirth, of a new creatureliness, and of the great transformation that puts a new man in the place of the old one who has died. The gestalt, the *morphe*, is subject to *metamorphosis*, and the *forma* to the *re-formatio*. The rhetorical exuberance of Augustine can never find enough new expressions for the experience of a being that changes its form from time to eternity: *de forma in formam mutantur . . . de forma obscura in formam lucidam . . . a deformi formam in formam formosam* and finally *de forma fidei in formam speciei* (*De Trin.* XV, 8, 14). The problem of symbolic expression is especially clear in Thomas. He subjects the relation of soul and body strictly to the form-matter pattern (*ST*, I, 76, 1) and thus finds himself impelled to a radically antimythical formulation when he wants to speak of the changes effected in the soul by grace (*ST* I-II, 110, 2 and 3): The habitus of grace is not a mutation of the soul but a new creation; men are newly created out of nothingness—*in novo esse constituuntur ex nihilo*. In the myth things can change, they can acquire a new form without losing their identity. In the strict language of Thomas, in which the truths of revelation are rethought in metaphysical rationality, a thing cannot mutate but a new thing must take the place of the old one, the new one having its origin, just as the old one, in the *creatio ex nihilo;* nor can the form mutate, as in Augustine, but the *forma supernaturalis* must rather be added to the *forma naturalis*.

Let us formulate the result of these preliminary reflections on the question of what is nature:

If we mean by nature the constants of the order of being, man's and society's nature obviously comprises much more than the complex of the form-matter pattern. If, however, we orient our concept of metaphysics in accordance with a still valid tradition created by Aristotle, only the form, but not the constants of movement, can metaphysically be seen as the nature of being. A wider philosophical concept of nature thus opposes a narrower metaphysical concept, or, more precisely speaking, a comprehensive understanding of what is nature has been narrowed by the development of metaphysics. This problem was both clear and acute for Aristotle, for he was a philosopher and not a systematizer, and he did not allow his own definitions to obstruct his view of reality. In the section on *physei dikaion* he speaks of a nature that is not form in the sense of *Metaphysics;* in the same way, in *Politics* I, he deals with the nature of a polis that has nothing to do with the form-problems of Book III; and when in the latter he indeed employs his metaphysical definitions, he allows the conflict between definition and reality to come to the surface and there remain unresolved, and he is not concerned with possible charges of inconsistency. This situation of the problem has not essentially changed to this day. If one wishes to penetrate and, if possible, solve it, one must answer the question that imposed itself in the course of the reflections: In the history of Hellenic thinking, why was the comprehensive, philosophical conception of nature narrowed to the metaphysical concept of form?

The Hellenic thinkers knew that their philosophizing about the nature of things (*peri tes physeos*) was one configuration among several others in which the question of the ground of being could be pursued. In his historical survey in *Metaphysics* alpha, Aristotle reports about the Ionic philosophers that Thales of Miletus, having been the first to raise the question of *physis*, thought the origin (*arche*) of all things to be water; he reports further that even before this time the poets had given the same answer in the figure of the myth of Okeanos and Tethys as the ancestors of all becoming (*tes geneseos pateres*); finally, using the term created by Plato, he calls the older figure "theologizing" in order to distinguish it from the younger, "philosophizing." There are thus at least two figurations of the question of the ground of being which we today would distinguish as mythical and philosophical. Following Aristotle's hint, we shall first characterize the Ionic form of the question by means of a comparison with the related cosmogonic myths of Egypt.

In the numerous cultural centers of Egypt, different gods were worshipped as the creators of the cosmos: In Heliopolis, it was Re or Atum, the energy of the sun; in Elephantine, Khnum, a god who creates all things on a potter's wheel; in Thebes, Amon, the hidden god of the wind; in Memphis, Ptah, the earth's energy. If one places next to the list of Egyptian gods the list of the elements water, air, fire, and earth, which the Ionians saw as the *arche,* both lists point up the similarity of the attempts to find the origin of the cosmos in elementary forces. The same type of speculation about the origin or beginning of being may realize itself in either one or the other of the symbolic media that Aristotle called "theologizing" and "philosophizing." The first of his variants, the cosmogonic speculation, employs the language of the myth that arose from the primary experience of the cosmos, including the gods whose activity permeates it. The second variant uses philosophical language emerging as the expression of an experience of which we shall say at this point only that, in accordance with a remark by Aristotle, the gods of polytheism are excluded from it. At the beginning of philosophy there is thus the dissociation of a cosmos-full-of-gods into a dedivinized order of things and a divinity whose relations to the newly discovered character of the universe is still unclear. The Hellenic thinkers named that which revealed itself to their differentiating experience *being;* and ever since then being has been for philosophers the subject of all propositions about order and nature.

The tremendous problems of the constitution of being that were raised by the act of differentiation could not be mastered on the first try. The Ionic attempt to identify the nature of being by a material *arche* was no more than the beginning of a process of thought, which is as yet incomplete. We shall briefly characterize its hellenic development in terms of the three main complexes of problems. They have to do with (1) the dependence of philosophy on the myth and its separation from the myth, (2) the relation of the divine to being, and (3) the relation of man and his cognition to being.

About the first of these: The Ionic attempt leans on the figure of cosmogonic speculation and borrowed from it the form of the myth in the sense of a story or narration about events in the cosmos. The *arche* of the Ionians is not any longer a member of the society of gods, but it stands at the beginning like a god from whose initiative a chain of events passes right down to the being that is experienced here and now. The form of the mythic story imposes on the being of the Ionians the character of becoming, the mythical *genesis*. Since, however, being is experienced not only as a stream but also reveals constant and recurring forms that abide in the midst of flux, the nature of being as a becoming must necessarily be supplemented by its characterization as abiding and recurrent form. Experiences of this kind motivate the speculation about being as eternally immutable. When they are reinforced by the experience of transcendence, they can elevate the character of permanence of being to the point of the truth of being before which "coming-into-being is quenched" (*Parm.* B 8, 21). This truth, if not logically compelling but still a compelling vision, indeed results in an inclination of philosophy toward form as the true being. Since the original insight into the nature of being as a coming-to-be goes back to the primary experience of the cosmos and its expression in the myth, one can define metaphysics, inasmuch as it narrows the insight to the form-matter pattern, as the extreme anti-mythical form of philosophizing.

Second, when the order of being no longer comprises the polytheistic gods, the relation of the divine to being remains in that suspension which can still be sensed in the fragments of Anaximenes. On the one hand, the Ionian thinker says: "As our soul, being air, holds us together, so do breath and air (*pneuma*) surround the whole universe," (B 2) seeming to posit an element as that nature which governs being and possibly even produces the gods (A 10); on the other hand, although the tradition is vacillating, he seems to have said that the air is God (A 10). In retrospect, the hyletic speculation of Anaximenes is still very close to the cosmological speculation of the Egyptian type; looking forward, however, one perceives the possibility of recognizing the unmythical god (for air is not one of the gods, but precisely God) as the origin of being, which would relieve the elements of the responsibility for acting the role of *arche*. If we also consider the equation God-Air-Governor of Souls, we sense something of the experience of transcendence in which the soul stands before God and, with the experience of itself as the place of God-openness in being, also obtains a new, philosophical relationship to the myth, as we find it in Plato. The state of suspension is broken only through the experiences of transcendence, especially that of Parmenides; in it there is a recognition of the divine as the Beyond in relation to a world which in turn, through this insight, becomes immanent, i.e., this-side-of-God. Only after this separation there is no more need for the divine mythically and genetically to send off being into its becoming, and the divine can be related to the appearance of the world as the transcendent-creative, the demiurgic reality. Experience of being and experience of transcendence thus are closely linked with each other, inasmuch as the implications of the still compact experience of being of the Ionians fully unfold through the experience of transcendence. Only in the light of the experience of transcendence, God, as well as the things of the world, obtains that relative autonomy that makes it possible to relate them to the common denominator of being.

When the gods, having become homeless through the dissociation of the cosmos, are again found in the truth of God, and thereby the relation of the divine to the world has become clear, this clarity still leads to new problems, as soon as the relationship is interpreted in the language of being. The difficulties are caused by a slowly vanishing obscurity on a number of points. In order to avoid extended historical investigations, we prefer to formulate them as theses:

(1) The being of philosophical experience is not a newly discovered entity to be added to the things that are already given in the primary experience of the cosmos.

(2) The experience of being differentiates the order of things (*a*) in its autonomy, (*b*) in the relation of things with each other, and (*c*) in its relation to the beginning. It discovers the order of the cosmos.

(3) The divine ground of being is not an existent thing of the type of things existing in the world.

(4) Things existing in this world, in addition to the order of

their autonomous existence and that of their relations to each other, also have a dimension of order in relation to the divine ground of being. There are no things that are merely immanent.

(5) The world cannot be adequately understood as the sum total of relations of autonomously existing things. That is not possible even when the directly experienced relations are extrapolated into infinity, for the indefinite progression is itself a world-immanent event. The mystery of a world permeated by divine activity is not eliminated by dissociating the transcendental experience of the cosmos into God and world. The impossibility of construing the world as a purely immanent complex of experiences is even today a central problem of theoretical physics.

The historical-concrete problems will become more understandable in the light of these theses.

The cosmos is dissociated by the experience of being, but all that it formerly comprised in a compact way, which includes the gods, must now be interpreted in the language of being. In other words, the now world-transcendent God must philosophically be included in the order of being. This is a philosophical necessity—for where and what would be the world's order of being if it issued not from the divine presence as its creative source?—which runs into the difficulty that divine being and worldly being are not things on either side of a spatial dividing line. Rather, they are indices that are placed on being when the cosmos is definitively dissociated by the experience of transcendence. Now being is nothing but a network of relations of order under the primary experience of things given in the cosmos (*not* in the world), in the right understanding of which we are interested. Hence as we are thinking about being, which itself is no thing (thesis 1), the prephilosophical, cosmic things have a tendency to suggest themselves as models of being. When, as in Parmenides, God is the model of being, then the being of the world is demoted to *doxa*, in comparison with the eminently-being being of truth; when the nondivine things provide the model for being, the predicates are derived from immanent existence, and even the predicate being itself can apply to God only by way of analogy. The aporia of this type are not soluble on the basis of objectivizing thought about being. In order to solve them, the philosopher must acknowledge that the figures of cosmic primary experience are still present in his thinking about being, and he must include the truth of the primary experience of a divine-worldly cosmos in his philosophy. For the cosmos may indeed be dissociated into divine and worldly being, by the experience of being, but that dissociating knowledge does not dissolve the bond of being between God and World, which we call cosmos.

When consciousness of the cosmic bond of being as the background of all philosophy declines, there arise the well-known dangers of the dedivinized world and the unworldly God, the unwordly world as nothing but a nexus of relations between immanent things, and the dedivinized God reduced to mere existence. Modern suffering from such effective reductions and the resulting tensions between the full God and the God of being are evidenced in Pascal's *Mémorial:* "Dieu d'Abraham, Dieu d'Isaac, Dieu de Jacob, non des philosophes et des savants." Plato was aware of this cosmic background of philosophy and therefore carefully separated thought about being and myth: The problems of the transcendent idea belong to the dialectic of thought about being; the problems of the destiny and judgment of the soul (*Gorgias, Politeia*), the cycles of order and disorder (*Politikos*), and the creation by the demiurge (*Timaeus*) are formulated through myths.

Third, and finally, the experience of being confronts us with the problem of the relation between the order of being and the knowing human being. Contrary to the possibility that the order of being might be unknowable for man or that man with his capacity for mental order might confront a being without order, reality demonstrates a remarkable agreement between order of the mind and order of being. Today that agreement may appear as a marvel, insofar as one thinks about it at all, as in Einstein's dictum: "The only thing unintelligible about the universe is its intelligibility." Alternatively, it may be laboriously regained, as a basic problem of philosophy, by means of an argument with modern objectivist thought that is obviously considered necessary—as Heidegger did in his *Satz vom Grund.* For the Hellenic thinker, though, it was an assured experience that he needed to interpret. Heraclitus (B 1) plays back and forth between the two meanings of the term *logos* as the order according to which things come into being and the didactic discourse that explains things (*hekasta*) according to their nature (*kata physin*); and Parmenides (B 3) says bluntly: "For it is the same thing to think (*noein*) and to be (*einai*)." The experience of being activates man to the reality of order in himself and in the cosmos; only he who lives in this movement is a man awake, who has the one and unique world (*cosmos*) in common with others who are awake, contrary to the sleepers every one of whom lives in his own world (Heraclitus B 89). The background of the experience of being is the primary experience of the cosmos in which man is consubstantial with the things of his environment, a partnership that in philosophy is heightened to the wake consciousness of the community of order uniting thought and being. The awareness of these relations remained alive in Greek thinking down to Plato and Aristotle. For Plato, as for Heraclitus, the philosopher is man awake, who communicates to his society the knowledge of its right order, while the tyrant is the sleeper who gratifies his lusts in public and commits crimes belonging to the phantasies of dreams. For Aristotle the *spoudaios* is the fully developed man who is in the highest degree permeable for the cosmic-divine movement of being and who, by virtue of this quality, becomes the creator of ethics and the source of knowledge about what is right by nature. This classical conception of the fully developed man, once the cosmic background of philosophy has been lost, is subject to the same dangers as the conception of the full God: Man, reduced to being, becomes a thing-in-being in a world construed as wholly immanent, and his relation to the order of being is no longer one of partnership but rather reduced to the subject of cognition.

To return to the question why, in the history of Hellenic thinking, the philosophical concept of nature is narrowed to the metaphysical conception of form: our survey has shown the cause; the problems of the new thinking about being could obviously be mastered only step by step. The philosophic conception still preserves the nature of being as a coming-to-be that was already given in the primary experience of the cosmos; while the metaphysical concept accentuates the nature of things as a being ordered by form. The two tendencies are in tension with each other. It can be observed in a noteworthy passage of Aristotle's *Metaphysics* delta, which deals with the interpretation of a statement by Empedocles. In Aristotle's version (the text B 8 in Diels-Kranz has a different one), Empedocles says: "Nothing that is has nature (*physis*), there is only a mixing and separating, and 'nature' is but a name men give to the mixture." He seems to say that the reality of the being of things is found in their elemental coming-to-be or coming-to-unbe, rather than in the figures of their ephemeral existence. Aristotle adds the astonishing and antimythical commentary that, even when the elemental reality of the being-reality of things is found, we attribute it to a nature only if it has form or figure (*eidos kai morphe*). The problem of coming-to-be, still dominant in Empedocles' mind, is shoved aside in favor of the form. In view of the rivalry of these dominances, we have to ask ourselves why the two concepts of nature got into mutual tension. Why could not one supplement the other without conflict?

The tension has been caused not so much by the technical difficulties of thinking through the problems and finding adequate terminology (even though the difficulties are big enough not to have been mastered until even now), as rather by the emotional block created by the fact that the experience of being is at the same time an experience of God.

The survey has shown that the dissociation of the cosmos began with the Ionic experience of being but was completed only through the experience of transcendence on the part of later thinkers. The partners in the cosmos separate into an immanent world of relatively autonomous things and a transcendent divine ground of being. Between them is man as that being in whom the dissociation occurs, in whom, however, God and world again are united in the manifold of experiences that elicits the rich vocabulary of *philia, pistis, elpis, eros, periagoge, epistrophe,* etc., as the corresponding manifold of expressions. Where the question is about the autonomous nature of existing things in the world, there is also the question of the nature of God, without whom, understood as transcending the world, there could not be any this-worldly immanence of things with autonomous natures; and wherever God and world are separated by the experience of being, there is also the question of man, who experiences the order of being and himself as an experiencing being. Man enters into the known truth of his own order, i.e., of his nature, through the experience of himself as one who is experiencing order. This ontological complex makes sense only as a whole. Philosophy becomes senseless if it isolates one of its parts without regard to the others.

When the experience of being differentiates itself from the primary experience of the cosmos, it elicits the new image of the demiurge. One can gauge the fascination of this newly grasped forming power by considering that Aeschylus in Prometheus could give expression to the human derailment corresponding to the demiurgic God even before Plato had created the myth of the demiurge. The new experience of God is the source of disturbances in which the form of being attains dominance over its coming-to-be. Some examples may illustrate the power of illumination radiating from the experience of a demiurgic god.

In the myth of the *Timaeus,* the demiurge is the craftsman who creates the cosmos by imposing form on matter. In the *Politikos,* the statesman is seen as the cosmocrator who puts into form the human psychic matter of society. In *Sophistes* (265 E), Plato places human works parallel to the divine: "I will only lay it down that the products of nature, as they are called, are works of divine art. Accordingly, there will be two kinds of production (*poietike*), one human, the other divine." In *Metaphysics* alpha, Aristotle further pursues this idea. In connection with his report on the Ionic speculation, he asks himself how matter could be the cause of change, since the wood does not make the bed nor the bronze the statue. How could fire, earth, or any other element cause things to be good and beautiful? Since these qualities of things cannot be attributed to automatism or chance, one must look to other causes (*aitia*) besides matter, above all for an *arche* of the movement. After the confused ideas of his predecessors a relief of sobriety had come when a thinker (*Anaxagoras*) said that the *nous* is present (*eneinai*) not only in animated beings but also in nature, and that it is the cause (*aition*) or order (*cosmos*) and all coherence (*taxis*). It now becomes clear why Aristotle developed his concept of nature by the model of an artifact, even though he was aware of the philosophical inadequacy of his procedure. The otherwise shocking fact now becomes understandable through the illumination radiating from the experience of a demiurgic god. Its dominance resulted in the mutual coordination of the images of God and man. I emphasize the mutuality, since the correspondences would be grossly misunderstood if one were to use the cliché of anthropomorphism and thus to assert that the forming God had been inferred from the image of a forming man. This assumption would presuppose that there is an autonomous and exclusively immanent experience of man according to which one could derivatively shape an image of God. That would violate the previously established principle of the indivisibility of the ontological complex. The differentiating achievement of the experience of being consists precisely in having attained clarity about the correlation of the reality of being and the truth of knowledge, of *einai* and *noein,* of divine creation of the order of being, and of human participation in it through knowledge of the order of human being. Ordering man and society through right action is a part of the ordering that governs the cosmos. As we recall, for Aristotle the *spoudaios* is the man who in the highest degree is permeable for the movement of being that proceeds from the unmoved mover; and ethics has its dignity in the human creation in which the ordering movement of being is articulated for the human realm. Thus the agreement of the image of God and the image of man must be seen as the symbol expressing the experience of human attunement to the divine ground of being.

Even though the demiurgic experience of God induces the conceptualization of nature as form and figure, the wide philosophical horizon encompassing being and becoming still remains open for Aristotle. Of special interest in this context are the remarks regarding aetiology, the question of origin and coming-to-be, in *Metaphysics* alpha, since they start out from the Ionic experience of being and analyze its meaning. The text begins (994a1) with the statement that there must be a definite beginning (*arche*), for the reasons (*aitia*) for things are not infinite in number. The material coming-to-be of things, traced to its causes, cannot be regressed infinitely so that flesh would come from earth, earth from air, air from fire, and so *ad infinitum.* Reversely, one cannot follow the chain of causes in descending order infinitely so that, beginning with the higher term (e.g., from fire, water; from water, earth; and so on, forever), some other kind of being is generated, without coming to an end product. In particular, however, an infinite regress is impossible in the area of human action and its purpose (994b9): "The wherefor is an end (*telos*), and an end of the sort that is not for the sake of something else but for the sake of which other things are. Hence, if there is a last term of this sort (*eschaton*), the process will not be infinite (*apeiron*); and if there is not, there will be no wherefor. But those who assume an infinite regress fail to notice that they remove the nature of the good (*ten tou agathou physin*). For nobody would try to do anything if he were not going to arrive at a limit. Rationality (*nous*), at least, is incompatible with such an infinite series; for the reasonable man (*noun echon*) always acts for the sake of something, and this end (*telos*) serves as a limit (*peras*)."

The passage stands in need of a discursive loosening-up to comprehend it fully. The question is about the concept of *aition* and of the finiteness or infinity of the series of causes ascending to the origin, *arche*. The difficulties of understanding the text are caused by the three different meanings of the compact term *aition*. First, it contains the meaning of cause in the sense of "cause and effect," i.e., the causality as an immanent, temporal process regarding phenomena. This meaning of *aition* turns the discussion to the nature of beings in the world this-side-of-God. The question comprises the nature of things in their autonomy as well as in their relations to each other, to which belongs the possibility of indefinite progression from the present state of a phenomenon, in the dimensions of space and time and in the causal chain. In *Physics*, Aristotle explicitly maintains the infinity of the temporal dimension of the cosmos. Thomas follows him in this respect, for since there can be no philosophical argument against the infinity of the world in time, the conviction that the world is created depending on revelation.

The second meaning of *aitia* overlies the first. It signifies the four *causae* (*causa materialis*, *efficiens*, *formalis*, and *finalis*) by which one comprehends not so much being things in general but rather those things that primarily belong to the class of organisms. In Aristotelian metaphysics, the experience of organism is an independent factor entering the definition of "Nature" but also running over into the conception of human nature, insofar as the *forma* of organism is suited to support the definition of nature as form. The idea of man as an immanently formed thing that has its fulfillment in a this-worldly happiness, is something definitely influenced by the model of organism. It is only in the third meaning of *aition*, when the discussion turns to the *causa finalis* of human action, that we come to the question of the order of human existence through the *nous*. In this area only, Aristotle rejects the infinite regress in the chain of causes as inadmissible. With respect to action, he insists on a limit (*peras*) of the series, since otherwise the *nous*, the highest good, and the meaning of the term *aition* must not be dismissed as equivocations; they must be acknowledged as a phase in the unfolding of the thought about being, a phase in which the problems of the order of being already appear in their differentiation but have not yet severed their connection to the background of cosmological thought. In the light of our analysis of the ontological complex one could say about the first meaning of *aition* that it refers to that being that, as a consequence of the experience of transcendence, has received the index "immanent." This being of immanence, which we call "world", contains no problem of *arche* (except possibly in the sense of what transcends the world) but only one of indefinite progression. If we ask whether "the world" has a beginning in time or not, we have loaded the question by hypostatizing the order of being into a being thing, inasmuch as we have forgotten that "being" and "world" do not exist but are rather relations of order with respect to the cosmos in which we still are living. The question of the *arche*, the origin or beginning, does not arise from the experience of being but rather belongs to the prephilosophic primary experience of the cosmos. It may appear in a variety of symbols, according to the respective degree of symbolic differentiation, down to the philosophical differentiation of being in which it is also expressed: In the myth it appears as cosmogonic speculation; in the symbolism of revelation it figures as the divine creation out of nothing; in philosophy as the question of the ground of being of the world. The differentiation that is new in philosophy is the experience of man as a being who experiences the order of being and his own order as something in accord with it. This is the experience whose problems come to the fore in the third meaning of *aition*, on occasion of the question of the meaning of human action, and that compels Aristotle to reformulate the question of the *arche*, the origin.

The question of the *arche* is reformulated insofar as it no longer regards the origin of the world but rather the disposition of human order in the order of being through the accord of the human *nous* with the divine *nous*. In order to grasp it properly, certain misunderstandings must be avoided: The *nous* must neither be confused with the Hebrew *ruach* of God, nor with the Hellenistic, Christian, or gnostic *pneuma*, nor with

the *ratio* of the Enlightenment, nor with Hegel's *Geist*. Rather it
is to be understood strictly in the sense of the Hellenic thinkers
as the place where the human ground of order is in accord with
the ground of being. As Aristotle, linking the limit of human
action with the *nous*, raises the question of this place, he transcends the demiurgic image of God and man and goes back to
the ground itself, which alone can legitimize the images. As he
leaves behind the images, his question of the *peras* of action
bursts out of the definition of human nature as form, for when
the question is raised of action's limit in the *nous*, one "sees" no
form; rather, the form is realized only in and through action.
At its core human nature, therefore, is the openness of the
questioning knowledge and the knowing question about the
ground. Through this openness, beyond all contents, images,
and models, order flows from the ground of being into man's
being.

I have spoken of questioning knowledge and knowing question in order to characterize the experience that I have called
noetic, for it is not the experience of some thing, but the experience of questioning rising from the knowledge that man's
being has not its ground in itself. The knowledge that being is
not grounded in itself implies the question of the origin, and in
this question being is revealed as coming-to-be, albeit not as a
coming-to-be in the world of existing things but a coming-to-be
from the ground of being. The experience of constant and
recurring figures in being as temporal becoming leads us to
being as form; the noetic experience that transcends being as
form and the demiurgic images leads us to coming-to-be out of
the ground of being—that coming-to-be that prephilosophi-
cally is symbolized by mythical narratives of the genesis of
things. Through its time of the narrative, which is not the time
of becoming in the world, the myth expresses the coming-to-be
from the ground of being. The ensuing great problems of a
philosophy of the myth cannot be treated here. The problem
has been mentioned only because it is related to the aetiology of
Aristotle.

The cited passages from *Metaphysics* alpha were peculiar because the links in the causal chain, for which a limit was postulated, were the elements that in the Ionic speculation of being
function as *arche*. Thus the postulate of a limit of causalities
really has nothing to do with chains of causation composed of

pheonomena in the world, but it has to do with the coming-to-be out of the ground of being, which does have its limit in that ground. Aristotle's postulated limit, therefore, is already contained in the premise in which the elements figure as archaic entities. As the coming-to-be from the ground of being, which was to be expressed in terms of cosmogonic and Ionic speculation about being, was subsumed under the concept of *aition,* which concept at the same time also designated the causalities in the world; and as this coming-to-be even was represented by a chain of causes, we have the possibility of those derailments that one calls proofs of the existence of God. For statements like "The great Mighty one is Ptah who gave life to all gods," or "The *Apeiron* is the origin of existing things," or "In the beginning God created heaven and earth" are not propositions about events in the world's time but myths that tell of the archaic coming-to-be in the time of the narrative; and the "existence" of the divine beings who appear in them as actors cannot be "proved" by world-immanent syllogisms. That existence does not stand in need of any such proof, for the truth of the myth consists in its adequacy as a symbol of the directly given experience of being as not grounded in itself. This experience always implies the question of the origin of being; the question of the origin implies knowledge about the ground of being at which the question aims; the knowledge about the ground of being implies knowledge of its character as being that is grounded in itself. The proofs of the existence of God cannot add anything to this complex of experiences. These proofs, going back to certain hints in Aristotle, are a still unexplained phenomenon, for Kant's demonstration that they are based on fallacies does not explain why they were conceived. One may approach a solution of the problem if one recognizes them as a *sui generis* form of myth that arises only when the *nous* is demoted to world-immanent *ratio* and that *ratio* is at the same time hypostatized as an autonomous source of truth.

We have come to the end of our exploration of the question: What is nature? Let us recapitulate the main phases. In the first part we had to examine the definition of nature as the form of things, and we concluded that it was inadequate. The second part concerned the question of why, in the history of hellenic thought, the wider philosophical concept of nature, which marks the beginning of the experience of being, is narrowed down to the metaphysical concept of nature as form. The third part contained the answer, in that the narrowing turned out to be motivated by the demiurgic experience of God. The fourth and last part dealt with the noetic experience of Aristotle, which transcends the demiurgic experience of God. It showed that the core of man's nature is the openness of his being in questioning and knowledge about the ground of being.

CHAPTER SIX

Reason: The Classic Experience

Though reason is the constituent of humanity at all times, its differentiation and articulation through language symbols is a historical event. The genius of the Hellenic philosophers discovered reason as the source of order in the *psyche* of man. This chapter will be concerned with reason in the sense of the Platonic-Aristotelian *nous*, with the circumstances and consequences of its differentiation as an event in the history of existential order.

I shall not deal with the "idea" or a nominalist "definition" of reason but with the process in reality in which concrete human beings, the "lovers of wisdom," the philosophers as they styled themselves, were engaged in an act of resistance against the personal and social disorder of their age. From this act there emerged the *nous* as the cognitively luminous force that inspired the philosophers to resist and, at the same time, enabled them to recognize the phenomena of disorder in the light of a humanity ordered by the *nous*. Thus, reason in the noetic sense was discovered as both the force and the criterion of order.

Moreover, the rise of reason to articulate self-consciousness was accompanied by the philosophers' consciousness of the event as an epoch that constituted meaning in history. Once man's humanity had become luminous for its order, one could not return from this meaningful advance of insight to less differentiated modes of experience and symbolization. The discovery of reason divided history into a before and after. This consciousness of epoch expressed itself in the creation of symbols which intended to characterize the new structure in the field of history. The central symbol was the "philosopher" in whose psyche humanity had become luminous for its noetic order; parallel symbols were Plato's "spiritual man" (*daimonios aner*) and Aristotle's "mature man" (*spoudaios*). The man who was left behind in a less differentiated state of consciousness remained the "mortal" (*thnetos*) of Homeric language; the man who insensitively resisted the advance of insight became the "unwise" or "dull-witted" man, the *amathes*. In Aristotle's *Metaphysics,* "myth" and "philosophy" denoted the two symbolisms by which, in historical succession, compact cosmological and differentiated noetic consciousness expressed the respective experiences of reality. And regarding the same epochal advance, Plato developed in the *Laws* a triadic symbolism of history in which the ages of Kronos and Zeus were now to be followed by the age of the Third God—the *nous.*

The epochal consciousness of the classic philosophers, however, did not derail into apocalyptic expectations of a final realm to come. Both Plato and Aristotle preserved their balance of consciousness. They recognized the noetic outburst for the irreversible event in history that it was, but they also knew that reason had been the constituent of humanity before the philosophers differentiated the structure of the *psyche,* and that its presence in human nature had not prevented the order of society from falling into the disorder which they resisted. To assume that the differentiation of reason would stop the rise and fall of societies would have been absurd; Hellas was not expected to develop into the federation of paradigmatic poleis that Plato desired. On the contrary, Plato rather foresaw, and Aristotle witnessed, the fall of the polis to the new type of imperial-ecumenic society. The classic philosophers thus kept the field of history open for social processes in a future that could not be anticipated, as well as for the possibility of further differentiations of consciousness. Plato especially was very much aware that man, in his tension toward the ground of existence, was open toward a depth of divine reality beyond the stratum that had revealed itself as the *nous;* as a philosopher he left consciousness open to the future of theophany, to the pneumatic revelations of the Judaeo-Christian type as well as to the later differentiations of mysticism and of tolerance in doctrinal matters.

Reason in the noetic sense, it should be understood, does not put an apocalyptic end to history either now or in a progressivist future. It rather pervades the history which it constitutes with a new luminosity of existential order in resistance to disordering passion. Its *modus operandi* is not revolution, violent action, or compulsion, but persuasion, the *peitho* that is central to Plato's existence as a philosopher. It does not abolish the passions but makes reason articulate, so that noetic consciousness becomes a persuasive force of order through the stark light it lets fall on the phenomena of personal and social disorder. To have raised the tension of order and disorder in existence to the luminosity of noetic dialogue and discourse is the epochal feat of the classic philosophers. This epoch has established the life of reason in Western culture in continuity to our own time; it does not belong to the past, but is the epoch in which we still live.

The discovery of reason as the epochal event in the history of existential order cannot be exhausted by an essay. I have to be selective. As our own situation as philosophers in the twentieth century A.D. resembles closely the Platonic-Aristotelian situation in the fourth century B.C., and as we are today engaged in the same type of resistance against the disorder of the age, it will be suitable to concentrate on the discovery of reason as the ordering force in existence.

I. THE TENSION OF EXISTENCE

In their acts of resistance to the disorder of the age, Socrates, Plato, and Aristotle experienced and explored the movements of a force that structured the *psyche* of man and enabled it to resist disorder. To this force, its movements, and the resulting structure, they gave the name *nous*. As far as the ordering structure of his humanity is concerned, Aristotle characterized man as the *zoon noun echon*, as the living being that possesses *nous*. The phrase caught on. Through the Latin translation of the *zoon noetikon* as the *animal rationale*, man has become the rational animal and reason the nature of man. On the topical level of discourse, the characterization developed into something like a word definition.

The philosopher, however, was not interested in word definitions but in the analysis of reality. The characterization of man as the *zoon noun echon*, or *zoon noetikon*, was no more than the abbreviating summary of an analysis concerning the reality of order in man's *psyche*. If the analysis was concerned not with man's personal order, but with the order of his existence in society, it arrived at the abbreviating characterization of man as the *zoon politikon*. And if the analysis of man's existence in historical reality, of man's "historicity" as the moderns call it, had been carried by the classic philosophers further than it actually was, they might have arrived at the summarizing characterization of man as the *zoon historikon*. All three of the characterizations are true inasmuch as they summarize a valid analysis of reality experienced, but every single one of them would become false if it excluded the two others and claimed to be the one and only valid definition of the nature of man. Moreover, man is not a disembodied psyche ordered by reason. Through his body he participates in organic reality, both animal and vegetative, as well as in the realm of matter; and in his psyche he experiences not only the noetic movement toward order but also the pull of the passions. Besides his specific nature of reason in its dimensions of personal, social, and historical existence, man has what Aristotle called his "synthetic" nature. Of specific and synthetic nature together we can speak as man's "integral" nature. This integral nature, comprising both the noetic psyche with its three dimensions of order and man's participation in the hierarchy of being from the *nous* down to matter, Aristotle understands to be the subject matter of the philosopher's study *peri ta anthropina*, the study of things pertaining to man's humanity.

For the present, we only have to be aware of this comprehensive field of human reality as the field in which reason has its place and functions as the cognitively luminous center of order in existence. I shall now discuss the classic experience and symbolization of this ordering force in man's *psyche*.

The reality experienced by the philosophers as specifically human is man's existence in a state of unrest. Man is not a self-created, autonomous being carrying the origin and meaning of his existence within himself. He is not a divine *causa sui;* from the experience of his life in precarious existence within the limits of birth and death there rather rises the wondering question about the ultimate ground, the *aitia* or *prote arche*, of all reality and specifically his own. The question is inherent in the experience from which it rises; the *zoon noun echon* that experiences itself as a living being is at the same time conscious of the questionable character attaching to this status. Man, when he experiences himself as existent, discovers his specific humanity as that of the questioner for the where-from and the where-to, for the ground and the sense of his existence.

Though this questioning is inherent in man's experience of himself at all times, the adequate articulation and symbolization of the questioning consciousness as the constituent of humanity is, as I have stated, the epochal feat of the philosophers. In fact, one still can discern in the Platonic-Aristotelian formulations the shock of the transition from the compact to the differentiated modes of consciousness. With Plato we are closer to the discovery. The Socrates of the *Theaetetus* recognizes in the experience (*pathos*) of wondering (*thaumazein*) the mark of the philosopher. "Philosophy has indeed no other beginning" (155d). A generation later, when the initial impact had worn off, Aristotle could open his *Metaphysics* with the programmatic statement: "All men by nature desire (*oregontai*) to know (*eidenai*)." All men, not the philosophers only; the philosopher's enterprise has become humanly representative. Everyone's existence is potentially disturbed by the *thaumazein*, but some express their wondering in the more compact medium of the myth, others through philosophy. By the side of the *philosophos*, therefore, stands the figure of the *philomythos* and "the *philomythos* is in a sense *philosophos*" (Met. 982b18 ss). When Homer and Hesiod trace the origin of the gods and all things back to Ouranos, Gaia, and Okeanos, they express themselves in the medium of theogonic speculation, but they are engaged in the same search of the ground as Aristotle himself (*Met.* 983b28 ss). The place on the scale of compactness and differentiation does not affect the fundamental identity of structure in man's humanity.

Nevertheless, the epochal event of differentiation has occurred and the philosophers have created the coherent body of language symbols by which they signify the stations of their analysis. There is, first, the group of symbols which express the experience of restless wondering: wondering—*thaumazein;* seeking, searching—*zetein;* search—*zetesis;* questioning—*aporein, diaporein*. The questioning, then, is experienced with an index of urgency. It is not a game to be played or not. The philosopher feels himself moved (kinein) by some unknown force to ask the questions, he feels himself drawn (helkein) into the search. Sometimes the phrase used indicates the urgent desire in the questioning, as in the Aristotelian *tou eidenai oregontai;* and sometimes the compulsion to raise the question that rises from the experience is grandly elaborated as in Plato's Parable of the Cave where the prisoner is moved by the unknown force to turn around (*periagoge*) and to begin his ascent to the light. Not always, however, will the unknown force have to break the fetters of apathy. The unrest in a man's *psyche* may be luminous enough to understand itself as caused by ignorance concerning the ground and meaning of existence, so that the man will feel an active desire to escape from this state of ignorance (*pheugein ten agnoian, Met.* 982b21) and to arrive at knowledge. Aristotle formulates succinctly: "A man in confusion (*aporon*) or wonder (*thaumazon*) is conscious (*cietai*) of being ignorant (*agnoein*)" (*Met.* 982b18). The analysis thus requires further language symbols: ignorance—*agnoia, agnoein, amathis;* flight from ignorance—*pheugein ten agnoian;* turning around—*periagoge;* knowledge—*episteme, eidenai.*

The part of the experience articulated up to this point provides the infrastructure for the noetic insights proper. I have presented it with some care because it is less well known than it ought to be. Plato and Aristotle were so successful in elaborating the exegesis of their experiences that the postclassic development of philosophy could attach itself to the upper stratum of noetic "results," while the differentiated experience of existence which had engendered the symbolism of "philosophy was relegated to a limbo of semi-oblivion. Against such neglect I must stress that the infrastructure was the catalyst that brought the pre-Socratic occupation with noetic problems into focus as a concern with the ordering of the psyche through its tension toward the divine ground, the *aition,* of all reality; by virtue of its catalytic function it is the key to the understanding of the *nous* in the classic sense.

The *nous* had attracted the attention of pre-Socratic thinkers, especially of Parmenides and Anaxagoras, in connection with their experiences of intelligible structure in reality. Parmenides had given the name *nous* to man's faculty of ascending to the vision of being, and the name logos to the faculty of analyzing the content of the vision. He concentrated the preanalytical content of his vision in the nonpropositional exclamation *Is!* The experience was so intense that it tended toward the identification of *nous* and being, of *noein* and *einai* (B 3); in the rapture of the vision the knower and the known would fuse into the one true reality (*aletheia*), only to be separated again when the logos became active in exploring the experience and in finding the suitable language symbols for its expression. From the Parmenidean outburst, the classic experience has inherited the noetic endowment of man (the Aristotelian *zoon noun echon*) that makes his psyche a sensorium of the divine *aition,* as well as the sensitiveness for the consubstantiality of the human *nous* with the *aition* it apperceives. While Parmenides differentiated the noetic faculty to apperceive the ground of existence, Anaxagoras was concerned with the experience of an intelligible structure in reality. Could the divine *aition* indeed be one of the elements as earlier thinkers who were still closer to the gods of the myth had assumed, or would it not, rather than an element, have to be a formative force that could impose structure on matter? Anaxagoras decided for the *nous* as the source of intelligible order in the cosmos and was praised highly for his insight by Aristotle. Thus, from the side both of the knower and the known, the experiences of intellectual apperception and of an intelligible structure to be apperceived, having gone their separate ways, were ready now to merge in the discovery of the human *psyche* as the sensorium of the divine *aition* and at the same time as the site of its formative manifestation.

The differentiation of the psyche expands the quest of the ground by the dimension of critical consciousness. The more compact symbols of the myth or of the pre-Socratics cannot remain unchallenged once the empirical source from which the symbols derive their validity is recognized to be the experiential processes of the *psyche.* The man who asks questions, and the divine ground about which the questions are asked, will merge in the experience of questioning as a divine-human encounter and reemerge as the participants in the encounter that has the luminosity and structure of consciousness. In the Platonic-Aristotelian experience, the questioning unrest carries the assuaging answer within itself inasmuch as man is moved to his search of the ground by the divine ground of which he is in search. The ground is not a spatially distant thing but a divine presence that becomes manifest in the experience of unrest and the desire to know. The wondering and questioning is sensed as the beginning of a theophanic event that can become fully luminous to itself if it finds the proper response in the psyche of concrete human beings—as it does in the classic philosophers. Hence, philosophy in the classic sense is not a body of "ideas" or "opinions" about the divine ground dispensed by a person who calls himself a "philosopher," but a man's responsive pursuit of his questioning unrest to the divine source that has aroused it. This pursuit, however, if it is to be responsive indeed to the divine mover, requires the effort of articulating the experience through appropriate language symbols; and this effort leads to the insights into the noetic structure of the *psyche*.

The consciousness of questioning unrest in a state of ignorance becomes luminous to itself as a movement in the *psyche* toward the ground that is present in the psyche as its mover. The precognitive unrest becomes a cognitive consciousness, a *noesis,* intending the ground as its *noema,* or *noeton;* at the same time, the desire (*oregesthai*) to know becomes the consciousness of the ground as the object of desire, as the *orekton* (*Met.* 1072a26 ss). The ground can be reached in this process of thought and be recognized as the object desired by the meditative ascent through the *via negativa:* the ground is not to be found among the things of the external world, nor among the purposes of hedonistic and political action, but lies beyond this world. Plato has introduced the symbol of the beyond, the *epekeina,* into philosophical language as the criterion of the creative, divine ground (*Rep.* 508-9); and Aristotle speaks of the ground as "eternal, immovable, and separate from the things of sense perception" (*Met.* 1073a3-5). Positively Plato identifies the One (*to hen*) that is present as the ground in all things as *sophia kai nous* (*Phileb.* 30c-e); and Aristotle identifies the actuality of thought (*nou energeia*) as the divine life eternal "for that is what God is" (*Met.* 1072b27-31). The complex of the *nous* symbols thus covers all steps in the philosophers' exegesis of man's tension toward the ground of his existence. There is both a human and a divine *nous,* signifying the human and divine poles of the tension; there is a *noesis* and a *noeton* to signify the poles of the cognitive act intending the ground; and there is generally the verb *noein* to signify the phases of the movement that leads from the questioning unrest to the knowledge of the ground as the *nous.* While the usage has certain disadvantages, it brings forcefully home the philosophers' understanding of the process in the soul as a distinct area of reality with a structure of its own. This structure can be unfolded either by ascending from the existential unrest at the bottom of the cave to the vision of the light at its top, or by descending from the consciousness that has become luminous down: without the *kinesis* of being attracted from above there would be no desire to know about the ground; without the desire, no questioning in confusion; without questioning in confusion, no consciousness of ignorance. There would be no existential unrest moving toward the quest of the ground unless the unrest was already man's knowledge of his existence from a ground that he is not himself. The movements of the divine-human encounter are understood to form an intelligible unit of meaning, noetic in both substance and structure.

This is the unit of meaning to which I have succinctly referred as man's tension toward the divine ground of existence. The abstract "tension" (it would have to be the Greek *tasis*), however, is not part of the classic vocabulary; when Plato and Aristotle speak of the divine-human movement, they prefer the symbols, inherited from their predecessors in the exploration of the psyche, which denote various concrete modes of the tension, such as *philia, eros, pistis,* and *elpis.* I must now touch upon the problems in man's existence as a *zoon noun echon* which necessitate the various levels of abstraction in the analysis.

II. PSYCHOPATHOLOGY

The Platonic-Aristotelian concentration on the concrete modes of the tension is of decisive importance for the understanding of the symbol *nous,* because it puts the experiential context in which the differentiation of reason occurs beyond a doubt: reason is differentiated as a structure in reality from the experiences of faith and trust (*pistis*) in the divinely ordered cosmos, and of the love (*philia, eros*) for the divine source of order; it is differentiated from the *amor Dei* in the Augustinian sense, not from the *amor sui.* Thus, the reality expressed by the *nous* symbols is the structure in the *psyche* of a man who is attuned to the divine order in the cosmos, not of a man who exists in revolt against it; reason has the definite existential content of openness toward reality in the sense in which Bergson speaks of *l'âme ouverte*. If this context of the classic analysis is ignored and the symbols *nous* or reason are treated as if they referred to some human faculty independent from the tension toward the ground, the empirical basis from which the symbols derive their validity is lost; they become abstracts from nothing, and the vacuum of the pseudo-abstracts is ready to be filled with various nonrational contents. The concept of the "tension toward the ground," denoting both the preanalytic and noetic modes of the tension, is meant to ward off certain misunderstandings of reason by stressing unequivocally the existential *philia* as the reality that becomes noetically luminous in the *philosophia* and the *bios theoretikos* of the classic philosophers. In face of the breakdown of philosophy in modern Western society, the bond between reason and existential *philia,* between reason and openness toward the ground, must be made thematically explicit.

The concept of the tension, as it leaves no doubt about the bond between reason and existence in openness toward the ground, is essential for understanding the fundamental issue of psychopathology: if reason is existential *philia,* if it is the openness of existence raised to consciousness, then the closure of existence, or any obstruction to openness, will affect the rational structure of the *psyche* adversely.

The phenomena of existential disorder through closure toward the ground of reality had been observed and articulated at least a century before the classic philosophers. Heraclitus had distinguished between the men who live in the one and common world (*koinos kosmos*) of the logos which is the common bond of humanity (*homologia*) and the men who live in the several private worlds (*idios kosmos*) of their passion and imagination, between the men who lead a waking life and the sleep-walkers who take their dreams for reality (B 89); and Aeschylus had diagnosed the Promethean revolt against the divine ground as a disease or madness (*nosos, nosema*). In the *Republic* then, Plato used both the Heraclitian and Aeschylean symbols to characterize the states of attunement and closure to the ground as states of existential order and disorder. Still, it took the shattering experiences of ecumenic imperialism and, in its wake, existential disorientation as a mass phenomenon, to let the bond between reason and existential order arrive at conceptual fixation. Only the Stoics created the terms *oikeiosis* and *allotriosis*, translated by the Latins as conciliation and alienation, to distinguish between the two states of existence which respectively make the life of reason possible or condition disorders of the *psyche*.

In the *Tusculan Disputations*, Cicero relates the principal Stoic formulations:

> As there are diseases of the body, so there are diseases of the mind (*morbi animorum*); the diseases are generally caused through a confusion of the mind by twisted opinions (*pravarum opinionum conturbatio*), resulting in a state of corruption (*corruptio opinionum*); the diseases of this type can arise only through a rejection of reason (*ex aspernatione rationis*); hence, as distinguished from diseases of the body, mental diseases can never occur without guilt (*sine culpa*); and since this guilt is possible only for man who has reason, the diseases do not occur in animals.[1]

The analysis behind such formulae can be gathered from a passage of Chrysippus: "This change (of the mind) and withdrawal from oneself happens in no other way than through a deliberate turning-away (*apostrophe*) from the logos."[2] The *apostrophe* is the movement opposite in direction to the Platonic *periagoge* or *epistrophe*. In turning away from the ground man turns away from his own self; thus, alienation is a withdrawal from the humanity that is constituted by the tension toward the ground.

Moreover, in this context there appear the first attempts at expressing the experience of "anxiety." Cicero's *anxietas* in the *Tusculan Disputations* is too uncertain in its meaning to be unreservedly identified with modern "anxiety"; it may denote no more than a state of mind given to unreasoned fears.[3] But statements attributed to Chrysippus make it clear that anxiety is understood to be a variety of ignorance (*agnoia*). A man is altogether raving, says the passage in question, when he is ignorant (*agnoian echon*) about his self and what concerns it; this

---

1. *Tusculan Disputations* IV, 23–32. Arnim, *Stoicorum Veterum Fragmenta* III, pp. 103–105.

2. *SVF* III, p. 125, 20–21.

3. *Tusculan Disputations* IV, 27. SVF III, p. 103, 10–17.

ignorance is the vice opposite to the virtue of true insight (*phronesis*); it is to be characterized as an existential state in which the desires become uncontrolled or undirected, a state of fluttering uncertainty and overexcitement of passions, a state of being scared or terrified because existence has lost its direction. The description is summarized in the term *agnoia ptoiodes* as the Stoic "definition" of madness (*mania*).[4] To the *zoon noun echon* there corresponds, as its pathological opposite, the *zoon agnoian echon*.

The Stoic exploration of the pathological countertype gives further precision to the meaning of noetic existence. The critical point to be noted is the appearance of *agnoia*, of ignorance, as a characteristic in the states of both health (*sanitas*) and unhealth (*insania*). The questioning unrest, as I have neutrally called the initial phase of the noetic experience, can either follow the attraction of the ground and unfold into noetic consciousness, or it can be diverted from the ground and follow other attractions. The pathological derailment thus occurs in the phase of questioning unrest, in man's attitude toward the tensional structure of his existence, not at the upper levels where the derailment becomes manifest in discrepancies between a well-ordered life and a disoriented existence, or between rational articulation of reality and equally articulate "twisted opinions," the *pravae opiniones*. The manifest symptoms of disorientation will, of course, attract primary attention. From the *Tusculan Disputations* one can collect a list of syndromes that sounds quite modern: restless money-making, status-seeking, womanizing, overeating, addiction to delicacies and snacks, wine-tippling, irascibility, anxiety, desire for fame, stubbornness, rigidity of attitude, and such fears of contact with other human beings as misogyny and misanthropy. But a symptomatology of this kind, though valuable as an approach on the common sense level, is analytically not precise enough. For there is nothing wrong with passions as such, nor with the enjoyment of external and somatic goods, nor with occasional indulgences or excesses. Unless the lines are drawn more clearly, one would arrive at the situation ridiculed by Horace in *Satirae* II, 3. Cicero is careful, therefore, to distinguish between acute manifestations of passion and the habits that have become

4. *SVF* III, no. 663.

chronic, as for instance, between *angor* and *anxietas, ira* and *iracundia;* and the habituation must be of such gravity as to imbalance the rational order of existence, it must amount to a rejection of reason, to an *aspernatio rationis.* This last criterion connects with the earlier concern of Chrysippus about the man who is impermeable to argument because he considers his indulgence to be the rational thing to do. The phenomenon of rational argument in defense of the escape from noetically ordered existence impressed Chrysippus so strongly that he assumed the logos itself to be capable of corruption; Poseidonius had to reject the fallacy and to return to the force in man's existence that can use the passions as the means of escape from the noetic tension and, at the same time, reason as the means of justifying the escape from reason.[5]

The Stoics thus recognize mental disease as a disturbance of noetically ordered existence. The disease affects both the passions and reason, but it caused neither by the one nor the other; it originates in the questioning unrest, the *agnoia,* and in man's freedom to actualize the meaning of humanity potentially contained in the unrest or to botch the meaning.

The health or disease of existence makes itself felt in the very tonality of the unrest. The classic, especially the Aristotelian, unrest is distinctly joyful because the questioning has direction; the unrest is experienced as the beginning of the theophanic event in which the *nous* reveals itself as the divine ordering force in the *psyche* of the questioner and the cosmos at large; it is an invitation to pursue its meaning into the actualization of noetic consciousness. There is no term for "anxiety"; the tonality of being scared or frightened by a question to which no answer can be found is characteristically absent from the classic experience; the "scare" had to be introduced by the Stoics, as a pathological phenomenon, through the adjective *ptoiodes.* In the modern Western history of unrest, on the contrary, from the Hobbesian "fear of death" to Heidegger's *Angst,* the tonality has shifted from joyful participation in a theophany to the *agnoia ptoiodes,* to the hostile alienation from a reality that rather hides than reveals itself. A Hobbes replaces the *summum bonum* by the *summum malum* as the ordering force of man's existence;

5. For this technically complicated controversy cf. Max Pohlenz, *Die Stoa* (1947), I, pp. 141–47.

a Hegel builds his state of alienation into a system and invites all men to become Hegelians; a Marx rejects the Aristotelian quest of the ground outright and invites you to join him, as a "socialist man," in his state of alienation; a Freud diagnoses the openness toward the ground as an "illusion," a "neurotic relict," and an "infantilism"; a Heidegger waits for a "parousia of being" which does not come, reminiscent of Samuel Beckett's *Waiting for Godot;* a Sartre feels "condemned to be free" and thrashes around in the creation of substitute meanings for the meaning he has missed; a Lévi-Strauss assures you that you cannot be a scientist unless you are an atheist; the symbol "structuralism" becomes the slogan of a fashionable movement of escape from the noetic structure of reality; and so forth.[6]

However, as this list of cases shows, there is more to the matter than a mere difference of tonality between classic and modern unrest, for the representatives of the modern *agnoia ptoiodes* aggressively claim for their mental disease the status of mental health. In the modern climate of opinion, the *zoon agnoian echon* has replaced the *zoon noun echon.* The perversion of reason through its appropriation by the mental cases that had already worried Chrysippus has grown, in the modern period of deculturation, into the murderous grotesque of our time.

Still, man cannot live by perversion alone. Parallel with the culmination of the grotesque in Hitler, Stalin, and the orgy of the "liberation rabble" after the Second World War, there has also grown the awareness of its pathological character. In the nineteenth century, it is true, Schelling had already coined the term "pneumopathology" when he had to deal with the progressivism of his time, but until quite recently it would have been impractical to treat the "opinions" which dominate the public scene as psychopathological phenomena. By now the "reductionist fallacy," the creation of imaginary "second realities," and the function of philosophies of history in creating an illusion of "immortality" have become widely known as pathological symptoms: an author like Doderer has, in his *Daemonen,* recognized the *Apperzeptionsverweigerung,* the refusal

6. The enumeration refers to well-known sources: Hobbes, *Leviathan;* Hegel, *Phaenomenologie;* Marx, *Nationaloekonomie und Philosophie* (Paris MS 1844); Freud, *Die Zukunft einer Illusion;* Heidegger, *Einfuehrung in die Metaphysik;* Sartre, *L'Etre et le Néant;* Lévi-Strauss, *La Pensée Sauvage.*

to apperceive, as the syndrome of the *zoon agnoian echon;* and in existential psychology, as for instance in the work of Victor E. Frankl, the "noological dimension" of man, as well as the treatment of its diseases by "logotherapy," have been rediscovered. It would not be surprising if sooner or later psychologists and social scientists were to find out about the classic analysis of noetic existence as the proper theoretical basis for the psychopathology of the "age."

III. LIFE AND DEATH

The life of reason in the classic sense is existence in tension between life and death. The concept of the tension will sharpen the awareness for this "in-between" character of existence. By "in-between" I translate the concept of the *metaxy* developed by Plato in the *Symposium* and the *Philebus.*

Man experiences himself as tending beyond his human imperfection toward the perfection of the divine ground that moves him. The spiritual man, the *daimonios aner,* as he is moved in his quest of the ground, moves somewhere between knowledge and ignorance (*metaxy sophias kai amathias*). "The whole realm of the spiritual (*daimonion*) is halfway indeed between (*metaxy*) god and man" (*Symp.* 202a). Thus, the in-between—the *metaxy*—is not an empty space between the poles of the tension but the "realm of the spiritual"; it is the reality of "man's converse with the gods" (202-203), the mutual participation (*methexis, metalepsis*) of human in divine, and divine in human, reality. The *metaxy* symbolizes the experience of the noetic quest as a transition of the psyche from mortality to immortality. In the language of Socrates in the *Phaedo,* right philosophizing is the practice of death (*melete thanatou*) that will let the psyche, in death, arrive at its divine, immortal, and wise status in truth (*alethos,* 81a); in Aristotle's language, noetic philosophizing is the practice of immortalizing (*athanatizein, NE* 1177b33). "Such a life, however, is more than merely human; it cannot be lived by man qua man but only by virtue of the divine (*theion*) that is in him . . . If then the *nous* is divine compared with man, so is the noetic life divine compared with human life" (*NE* 1177b27 ss). Because of the divine presence that gives the unrest its direction, the unfolding of noetic consciousness is experienced as a process of immortalizing. With their discovery of man as the *zoon noun echon,* the classic philosophers have discovered man to be more than a *thnetos,* a mortal: he is an unfinished being, moving from the imperfection of death in this life to the perfection of life in death.

Historically, the experience of immortalizing in the unfolding of rational consciousness has been, and still is, the storm center of misunderstanding, fallacious misconstruction, and furious attacks.

If man exists in the *metaxy,* in the tension "between god and man," any construction of man as a world-immanent entity will destroy the meaning of existence, because it deprives man of his specific humanity. The poles of the tension must not be hypostatized into objects independent of the tension in which they are experienced as its poles. The misconstructions can assume the form of elementary logical mistakes such as the previously rejected transformation of the summarizing symbol *zoon noun echon* into a word definition. Or they can, more elaborately, misuse man's bodily existence for the purpose of reducing the metaleptic tension, through causal explanation, to the organic and inorganic strata of being in which it is founded. Or, since the discovery of the *nous* and the symbolization of the *metaxy* are facts in the history of humanity, they can psychologize the symbols engendered by the tension into projections of an immanent psyche. Moreover, the authors of the misconstructions can make their purpose explicit through one of the direct attacks on the noetic structure of existence of which I have given representative examples. Whatever the degree of elaboration or consciousness of purpose, the deformations of the human pole of the tension into a world-immanent entity are attacks on the life of reason, an *aspernatio rationis* in the Stoic sense. They are psychopathological phenomena. Since this cruder class of misconstructions which dominate the modern period of ideologizing has by now become notorious, no more need be said about it.

The classic analysis of noetic order in existence has been more subtly distorted through a restrictive concentration on the conflict between reason and the passions. The distortion is of millennial standing. Even the Stoics were bewildered when, in their attempt at a psychopathology, an excess of passion did not satisfactorily explain the syndrome of mental disease. Harping on the passions as the only source of disorder could lead to the ludicrous impasse satirized by Horace; and besides, no indulgence of the passions could explain the rejection of reason in the name of reason that had Chrysippus worried. There was a mysterious force at work, back of the passions, that would disturb the noetic order of existence and become manifest in the *agnoia ptoiodes*. The mystery was caused, and still is, by the isolation of both reason and the passions from their context in the tension between life and death. In the *Laws*, Plato has developed the myth of the puppetplayer who pulls the human puppets by the various metal cords, by the golden cord of reason and by the lesser cords of the passions. One could, and still can, refer to this myth for understanding the interplay of the pulls in man's existence, but one must not forget the cosmic drama in which it has its place. The pull (*helkein*) of reason and the counterpulls (*anthelkein*) of the passions are real enough but they are movements experienced by the *psyche* in its state of entombment in a mortal body. The reason why man should follow one pull rather than another is not to be found in the "psychodynamics" of the puppetplay, nor in some standards of "morality," but in the potential immortality offered by the divine presence in the *metaxy*. In the classic experience of noetic existence man is free either to engage in the action of "immortalizing" by following the pull of the divine *nous*, or to choose death by following the counterpull of the passions. The psyche of man is the battleground between the forces of life and death. Life is not given; the God of the *Laws* can only offer it through the revelation of his presence; life to be gained requires the cooperation of man.

The differentiation of life and death as the moving forces behind reason and the passions requires further refinements in the analysis of the *metaxy*. Plato has given them in the *Philebus* by symbolizing the mystery of being as existence between (*metaxy*) the poles of the one (*hen*) and the unlimited (*apeiron*) (16d–e). The one is the divine ground (*aitia*) that is present as the formative force in all things, to be identified with wisdom and mind (*sophia kai nous*) (30b–c). The unlimited is Anaximander's *apeiron*, the cosmic ground (*arche*) from which things are brought forth into being (*genesis*) and into which they perish again (*phthora*), "for they pay one another penalty for their injustice (*adikia*) according to the ordinance of Time" (B 1).

Behind the passions there is at work the lust of existence from the depth (i.e., the injustice on which the law of the cosmos has set the penalty of death in Time). In Christian psychology, this apeirontic lust of existence has become the *superbia vitae,* or *libido dominandi,* which serves the theologians as the definition of original sin. The conflict between reason and the passions thus receives its specific character from the participation of the psyche in the *metaxy* whose poles are *apeiron* and *nous.* In the *psyche* of man, the tension in reality achieves the status of consciousness. The consequences for the meaning of man's existence have been stated by Plato in the *Timaeus:*

> Now, when a man abandons himself to his desires (*epithymia*) and ambitions (*philonikia*), indulging them incontinently, all his thoughts (*dogmata*) of necessity become mortal, and as a consequence he must become mortal every bit, as far as that is possible, because he has nourished his mortal part. When on the contrary he has earnestly cultivated his love of knowledge and true wisdom, when he has primarily exercised his faculty to think immortal and divine things, he will—since in that manner he is touching the truth—become immortal of necessity, as far as it is possible for human nature to participate in immortality. (90a–b)

Nevertheless, even if a man "mortalizes," he cannot escape from his existence as a *zoon noun echon;* even if he rejects reason, the rejection must assume the form of reason or he will fall into the moods of dejection, *taedium vitae,* acedia, and so forth; the more intensely he indulges his mortalizing *libido dominandi,* the more is the death he works in need of being cast in the image of life. Hence, a radical, fully conscious *aspernatio rationis,* as it is to be found in modern ideologies, requires an equally radical symbolization as a rational system, if possible as a *System der Wissenschaft* in the Hegelian sense. In fact, the radical modern systems, especially of history, have considerably helped in the clarification of the issue because as early as the eighteenth century their purpose has been explicitly stated and criticized. In his lecture on *Universal History* (1789), Schiller declared the purpose of a progressivist philosophy of history to be the achievement of imaginary immortality through participation in the imaginary meaning of history; the meaning of a universal history progressing toward the realm of reason would replace the meaning of existence that had been lost with the loss of faith in personal immortality. But five years earlier Kant had observed that participation in the meaning of history was no substitute for the meaning of personal existence because it offered no answer to the problem of a man's personal death in time.[7] Today, almost two hundred years later, the Kantian observation has become shocking news to Eastern European Marxists who have discovered that belief in the Communist dogma is not much of a consolation in the face of death.

In the *Philebus* passage just quoted Plato has articulated the theoretical implications of the issue through the creation of analytical concepts which are still in use, or rather misuse, today. Man exists in the tension between mortality and immortality, between the apeirontic depth and the noetic height. The *apeiron* and the *nous* reach into his *psyche* and he participates in them, but he is not identical with, or in control of, either the one or the other. This area of metaleptic reality is the proper domain of human thought—its inquiries, learning, and teaching (*skopein, manthanein, didaskein*). To move within the *metaxy*, exploring it in all directions and orienting himself in the perspective granted to man by his position in reality, is the proper task of the philosopher. To denote this movement of thought or discussion (*logos*) within the *metaxy*. Plato uses the term "dialectics" (17a). Since, however, man's consciousness is also conscious of participating in the poles of the metaleptic tension (i.e., in the *apeiron* and *nous*), and the desire to know is apt to reach beyond the limits of participatory knowledge, there will be thinkers—"those who are considered wise among men these days"—who are inclined to let the In-Between reality (*ta mesa*) escape (*ekpheugein*) them in their libidinous rush toward cognitive mastery over the *hen* or the *apeiron*. To denote this type of speculative thought Plato uses the term "eristics" (17a). Again the modern radical deformations of consciousness have contributed substantially to the understanding of Plato's

---

7. Schiller, *Was heisst und zu welchem Ende studiert man Universalgeschichte* (1789), last paragraph. Kant, *Idee zu einer allgemeinen Geschichte in weltbuergerlicher Absicht* (1784).

problem by providing object lessons of "eristics." Phenomena in the *metaxy*, of an economic or psychological nature, are rashly fused in an act of libidinous transgression with the apeirontic depth in such symbols as the Marxian being which determines consciousness, or in the Freudian symbol of the libido, with the declared purpose of mobilizing the authority of the acheronta against the authority of reason.[8] As the symbol of this revolt, furthermore, the unconscious appears in such variegated contexts as Freud's psychoanalysis, Breton's surrealism, or in Jung's psychology of a collective unconscious which transforms the symbols found by man for expressing his experiences in the *metaxy* into apeirontic archetypes. Most instructive, however, is Hegel because as a knowledgeable and conscientious thinker he feels obliged to support his deformation of the classic philosophers' noetic experience with specific references. There is a passage in Aristotle's *Metaphysics* which can be misunderstood if one wants to misunderstand it at all costs, because it is pervaded by the exuberant joy of touching immortality for a moment when touching (or apprehending, *thigganein*) the divine *nous* in cognitive participation. Hegel attaches this passage (*Met.* 1072b18–31) as an appendix to his *Encyclopaedie*, indicating by this strategic placement its central importance for him. The critical sentence in the passage is the following: "Thought (*nous*) thinks itself through participation (*metalepsis*) in the object of thought (*noeton*); for it becomes the object of thought through being touched (*thigganon*) and thought (*noon*), so that thought (*nous*) and that what is thought (*noeton*) are the same" (*Met.* 1072b20 ss.) Whe read in the Aristotelian context, the sentence articulates the dynamics of sameness and difference of the knower and the known in the act of noetic participation, the joy of momentary sameness with the divine notwithstanding. When read in the context of the *Encyclopaedie*, the sentence expresses the beginnings of a philosophical enterprise that has been brought to its successful conclusion by Hegel. For in the Hegelian conception, philosophy begins as the "love of wisdom" in the classic sense and moves from this imperfect state toward its consummation as "real knowledge" (*wirkliches Wissen*) in the System. From the classic participation in the divine *nous* it

8. *"Flectere si nequeo superos, Acheronta movebo"* is the motto of Freud's *Traumdeutung.*

advances through the dialectical progress of the *Geist* in history, to identification with the *nous* in self-reflective consciousness. The tension toward the ground of existence, considered by Hegel to be a state of diremption (*Zerrissenheit*) or alienation (*Entfremdung*), is meant to be superseded by a state of conciliation (*Versoehnung*), when the ground has become incarnate in existence through the construction of the System. The *metaxy* has been transmuted into immanence. This speculative magic (*Zauberworte, Zauberkraft*) by which the thinker brings the divine ground into his possession is what Plato has called "eristics"; Hegel, on the contrary, calls it "dialectics." Thus, the meaning of the terms has been inverted.

Moreover, being a first-rate thinker, Hegel plays on the Pauline symbols of the divine pneuma and the "depth of God" (I Cor. 2:6–13) the same tricks as on Aristotle's *nous*. Again placing his inversion in a strategic position, on the last page of the *Phaenomenologie* he draws the divine pneuma into the *metaxy* by presenting his System as the exhaustive revelation of the depth that had been intended, but only partially achieved, by Christ and Paul.

In a clean sweep he transfers the authority of both reason and revelation to his System and to himself as its creator. The libidinous drive in this egophanic revolt against theophanic reality becomes manifest in his conviction that his construction of the System is the noncombatant's equivalent to the combatant's death on the battlefield of the revolution; and from his comments on Napoleon he even emerges as the world-historic great man who has made of the French Revolution the sense that has been miscarried by the emperor.

The imperial style, developed to perfection by Hegel, is in general characteristic for the modern egophanic revolt against reason in its ideological varieties and subvarieties. Beyond the individual cases of existential disorder, the style becomes a public grotesque when, with the lapse of time, the social scene fills up with little emperors who each claim to be the possessor of the one and only truth; and it becomes lethal when some of them take themselves seriously enough to engage in mass murder of everyone who dares to disagree. As an instructive case in which the transition from intellectual imperialism to the support of mass murder can be studied in its well-reasoned detail, I recommend Maurice Merleau-Ponty's *Humanisme et Terreur* (1947). Granted that the general social situation favors the expansion of the style at all rather than its oblivion, this evolution toward a mass phenomenon both grotesque and murderous is determined by its origin in the destruction of the life of reason in the *metaxy*. In Hegel's case—and one should never forget that only a technically competent thinker of Hegel's stature could perform such a feat—one can observe how man's consciousness of his tension toward the divine ground is transmogrified, through the *Zauberworte* of the System, into a "dialectical" process, internal to an imaginary "Consciousness" that can be brought under control by the speculative thinker. Since "dialectical Consciousness," however, is not the consciousness of concrete human beings but a symbolism that has its status in reality as the eristic fantasy of a libidinously disturbed psyche, the System does not have the authority of reason which it has tried to usurp. Once the divine *nous* has been submitted to human construction, God is dead indeed. What has come to life instead is the imperial appeal of the System to the *libido dominandi*. This appeal does not attach to any particular System (as for instance the Hegelian or the Comtean) but to the form of the System as such and to its eminent flexibility. For reason can be eristically fused with any world-content, be it class, race, or nation; a middle class, working class, technocratic class, or summarily the Third World; the passions of acquisitiveness, power, or sex; or the sciences of physics, biology, sociology, or psychology. The list is not meant to be exhaustive. One may even say that the appeal of a particular System lies less in the tenets of its creator than in the possibility of tampering with them under the title of "revision" while retaining the imperial style of absolute truth.

And yet, there is some order to be observed in this libidinous grotesque. It becomes visible when the eristic fantasy is exposed to the pressure of reality. Since the meaning of existence in noetic tension is the process of immortalizing, the mortalizing pressure of the apeirontic depth makes itself increasingly felt when the *nous* has been successfully deformed by the eristic fusion. Hence, in the so-called modern interpretation of existence, there is to be noted the shift of accent from the exuberant *aspernatio rationis* in the name of reason which has given the eighteenth century its name, to the contemporary preoccupation with existence in the name of depth, death, and anxiety. Moreover, since eristic fantasy blends reason with a world-content, the truth of the System becomes questionable when the knowledge of the world-content advances beyond the state at which the eristic thinker incorporated it into his construction. Hence, the epigonic adherents of a System will develop the well-known variety of devices which are meant to protect the respective Systems against the inevitable friction with reality. There is the just-mentioned device of "revision," frequently used to preserve the plausibility of the System, though it may lead to dissent among the adherents and to angry redefinitions of orthodoxy and dissent. There is the fundamental taboo on questions concerning the premises of the eristic fusion, explicitly demanded by Marx and conscientiously observed by the followers of the Marxian variety of eristics. There is the dignified tactic of not taking cognizance of fatal criticism, and the less dignified procedure of personally defaming the critic. And finally, where the adherents of a System have gained governmental power, they can resist the pressure of reality by jailing or killing dissenters or by summarily building a physical wall around the territory under their jurisdiction.

All this may sound obvious, and it is as far as the facts are concerned. What is perhaps less obvious is that I have just described the social process in history of a mental disease, a *kinesis* in the Thucydidean sense, in terms of the classic insights into the tension of existence. Regarding both its nature and its course, the modern *kinesis* can be made intelligible if the categories developed by the classic philosophers in their analysis of the *metaxy* are used; and inversely, the phenomena which can be empirically observed as the phenomena of friction between an eristic fantasy and the noetic structure of reality confirm the validity of the classic analysis.

IV. APPENDIX

The unfolding of noetic consciousness in the psyche of the classic philosophers is not an "idea," or a "tradition," but an event in the history of mankind. The symbols developed in its course are "true" in the sense that they intelligibly articulate the experience of existential unrest in the process of becoming cognitively luminous. Though the classic analysis is neither the first nor the last symbolization of man's humanity in quest of its relation to the divine ground, it is first in articulating the structure of the quest itself: of the unrest that offers the answer to its questioning, of the divine *nous* as the mover of the quest, of the joy of luminous participation when man responds to the theophany, and of existence becoming cognitively luminous for its meaning as a movement in the *metaxy* from mortality to immortality. The articulation of the structure has been so successful indeed that even the modern egophanic revolt against the theophanic constitution of man's humanity has to use the language of the noetic analysis if it wants to be intelligible, thereby confirming the validity of the philosophers' articulation.

True insights concerning reason as the ordering force in existence were certainly gained, but they had to be gained as the exegesis of the philosophers' resistance to the personal and social disorder of the age that threatened to engulf them. To separate the "truth" of insight from the effort of resistance would make nonsense of the insight into the in-between structure of existence. The life of reason is not a treasure of information to be stored away, it is the struggle in the *metaxy* for the immortalizing order of the psyche in resistance to the mortalizing forces of the apeirontic lust of being in time. Existence in the in-between of divine and human, of perfection and imperfection, of reason and passions, of knowledge and ignorance, of immortality and mortality is not abolished when it becomes luminous to itself. What did change through the differentiation of reason was the level of critical consciousness concerning the order of existence. The classic philosophers were conscious of this change as an epochal event; they were fully aware of the educational, diagnostic, and therapeutic functions of their discoveries; and they laid the foundations of a critical psychopathology that was further elaborated by the Stoics. They could not foresee, however, the vicissitudes to which their achievement would be exposed once it had entered history and become an integral factor in the cultures of Hellenistic, Christian, Islamic, and modern Western societies. They could not foresee the incorporation of philosophy into various revelatory theologies, nor the transformation of philosophy into propositional metaphysics. And above all, they could not foresee the radical separation of the noetic symbolism they had created from its experiential context, so that the philosophical vocabulary would be set free to endow the attack on reason with the appearance of reason. The dynamics of their resistance moved from the decay of the cosmological myth and from the Sophistic revolt toward the "love of wisdom"; they did not anticipate a distant future in which the egophanic revolt would have perverted the meaning of the noetic symbols, the extensive *dégradation des symboles* as Mircea Eliade has called this modern phenomenon, so that the dynamics of resistance would have to move from the System of thinkers in a state of alienation again toward noetic consciousness.

To present the classic insights as doxographic relics not only would be pointless, it would destroy their very meaning as the expression of man's resistance to the mortalizing disorder of the age. Not the insights are to be remembered, but the resistance against the "climate of opinion" (Whitehead) is to be continued, if the life of reason is to be kept truly alive. The present essay obviously is an act of resistance in continuity with the classic effort. The tactics used will have become clear. In the first place, the practically forgotten experiential context on which the meaning of reason depends had to be restored. Moreover, as far as that was possible in the brief space, I have tried to establish the inner coherence of pieces of analysis which in the sources are scattered over a vast body of literature. From the basis of the restored experience, then, it was possible to branch out into the psychopathology of alienation and the *aspernatio rationis.* And from this basis broadened by the Stoic analysis, finally, it was possible to characterize the modern revolt against reason as well as the phenomenon of the System. In this critical characterization, however, I had to concentrate selectively on flagrant cases; the general importance of the classic analysis as an instrument of critique did not become fully visible. It will be apposite, therefore, to present a diagram of the points to be considered in any study of human affairs, of the *peri ta anthropina* in the Aristotelian sense:

	PERSON	SOCIETY	HISTORY
Divine Nous			
Psyche—Noetic			
Psyche—Passions			
Animal Nature			
Vegetative Nature			
Inorganic Nature			
Apeiron—Depth			

The left vertical column lists the levels in the hierarchy of being from the *nous* to the *apeiron*. Man participates in all of them; his nature is an epitome of the hierarchy of being. The arrow pointing down indicates the order of formation from the top down. The arrow pointing up indicates the order of foundation from the bottom up.

The top horizontal column lists the dimensions of man's existence as a person in society and history. The arrow pointing to the right indicates the order of foundation.

Principle of completeness: A philosophy *peri ta anthropina* must cover the grid determined by the two coordinates. No part of the grid must be hypostatized into an autonomous entity, neglecting the context.

Principle of formation and foundation: The order of formation and foundation must not be inverted or otherwise distorted, as for instance by its transformation into a causality working from the top or the bottom. Specifically, all constructions of phenomena on a higher level as epiphenomena of processes on a lower one, the so-called reductionist fallacies, are excluded as false. This rule, however, does not affect the conditioning causality which is the very essence of foundation. Neither are inversions of the order of foundation in the horizontal column permitted. Specifically, all "philosophies of history" which hypostatize society or history as an absolute, eclipsing personal existence and its meaning, are excluded as false.

Principle of metaxy *reality:* The reality determined by the coordinates is the in-between reality, intelligible as such by the consciousness of *nous* and *apeiron* as its limiting poles. All "eristic phantasies" which try to convert the limits of the *metaxy*, be it the noetic height or the apeirontic depth, into a phenomenon within the *metaxy* are to be excluded as false. This rule does not affect genuine eschatological or apocalyptic symbolisms which imaginatively express the experience of a movement within reality toward a beyond of the *metaxy*, such as the experiences of mortality and immortality.

The diagram has proved of particular value for students because it gives them a minimum body of objective criteria for "true" and "false" in their struggle with the flood of contemporary opinion literature. With the help of the diagram it is possible to classify false theoretical propositions by assigning them their place in the grid. On occasion it has become an exciting game for the students to place ideas which enjoy the popularity of the moment in one of the twenty-one squares. Beyond its function as a technical aid in mastering contemporary phenomena of intellectual disorder, the diagram had the important psychological effect of overcoming the students' sense of disorientation and lostness in the unmanageable flood of false opinions that presses in on them every day.

CHAPTER SEVEN

Eternal Being in Time

Eternal being realizes itself in time.

If one understands this sentence as an attempt to say something essential about history in the language of philosophical concepts, then it elicits the question whether there is such a thing as essence of history that could be grasped by philosophical analysis. For the drama of history is not yet completed and thus not given as a thing about the essence of which one could state propositions; and the philosopher does not look at this nonthing as an observer but, in philosophizing, turns into an actor in the drama about which he wants to make statements. The model of a subject of knowledge confronting his object is not applicable to a knowledge in which the act of knowing is part of the process that is to be known. This reflection compels us to recognize, beyond the concepts of thing and essence, a reality of being that comprises both philosophy and history.

This reality may be divided into four relations which we shall attempt to characterize:

(1) Eternal being did not wait for philosophy in order to realize itself in time. Thousands of years of history passed before philosophers appeared in it. The first relation thus characterizes philosophy as a phenomenon in the field of history.

(2) Philosophy, however, is not an indifferent happening that at some time emerges in the stream of time only to submerge again. Rather, it is an event of specific significance for history insofar as through it history is lifted into consciousness, as the realization of eternal being in time. Knowledge, hitherto confined to the compact experience of the cosmos and its expression through the myth, then affected by the experience of transcendence, is thereby differentiated and fully articulated through the formation of philosophical concepts. Philosophy thus engenders a consciousness of epoch in the philosophers. The men in whom philosophy becomes an event are aware that it constitutes an epoch in history, a mark from which one dis-

tinguishes between a before and an after. In this second relation therefore, philosophy, is a constituent of history.

(3) A consciousness, even when it does not intend the knowledge of a thing, is still consciousness of something. In order to grasp the nonobjective something of philosophical consciousness, we must consider that philosophy becomes a constituent of history and a factor of its structure because, first, history is the process in which eternal being realizes itself in time and, secondly, philosophy makes conscious the differentiated knowledge of this process. Eternal being is not an external object that could be discovered and studied or not studied *ad libitum,* but rather it is a compelling experience whenever it irrupts into time, thereby realizing itself in it. The place of this realization, as it occurs, is the soul of the philosopher, the lover of wisdom, who desires eternal being and, in love, opens his soul to its irruption. There is no philosophy without philosophers, namely without men whose soul responds to eternal being. If the history is the process in which eternal being being unusually complex, cannot be fully covered but can only realizes itself in time, philosophy is a historical event in the precise sense that eternal being becomes real in time as the response of the philosopher. Philosophy becomes a constituent of history because, in the third relation, history is the constituent of philosophy.

(4) There are other souls than the philosophers' where eternal being irrupts into time, and more than one mode of irruption. Among other experiences of transcendence the philosophical experience is distinct in that in it the logos of realization becomes transparent; and the symbolism of this experience is the language of philosophical conceptions. Insofar as philosophy develops the concepts symbolizing the realization, it also makes possible the recognition of the logos of realization in nonphilosophical symbolisms. Thus the logos of history can be explored through the logos of philosophy and can be translated into its language. In the fourth relation, therefore, history becomes a field of phenomena for philosophical investigation.

The four relations will determine the order of the following discussion. It is useful to list again their titles:

(1) Philosophy as a phenomenon in history

(2) Philosophy as a constituent of history
(3) History as a constituent of philosophy
(4) History as a field of phenomena for philosophical investigation

Before entering into the study, two points may be noted for a better understanding:

First: Reality may be divided into relations but does not cease being the one, undivided reality. The relations are not autonomous things. As we investigate the four relations, one after the other, we do not mean to exclude the remaining three. In the succession of the following four sections a series of thematic overlays and repetitions are therefore inevitable.

Second: The historical-phenomenal aspect of this reality, being unusually complex, cannot be fully covered but can only be touched upon in this chapter. All propositions about the meaning of historical phenomena must thus be understood in the strictest sense of the context. They should not be rashly generalized into a material philosophy of history.

I. PHILOSOPHY AS A PHENOMENON
IN THE FIELD OF HISTORY

Philosophy is not an indifferent happening which emerges in time, only to submerge again, but a phenomenon in the field of history. This sentence combines statements into a higher unity which, in the introductory characterization of the relations, appear in the first and second one. For philosophy, while figuring (in the second relation) as a specific constituent of history, is by no means the sole phenomenon that determines history's structure. When philosophy appears in history (in the first relation), it therefore becomes a part of a field that is structured also by other phenomena than philosophy. The combining statement takes its meaning from the concept of "the field" into which philosophy enters as it also contributes to its constitution. By field we mean the fact that historical phenomena do not appear without context but as part of meaningful configurations. To consider philosophy in the field of history means to circumscribe the configuration to which philosophy belongs, according to its meaning.

Since the configurations in their turn do not occur without

context but are parts of wider structures, ultimately of all known history, the question to which configuration philosophy belongs does not admit of an unambiguous answer as long as we do not have a limiting criterion. We posit as criterion the minimum of configurations below which we would lose the meaning of philosophy as it was understood by its originators. This minimum is circumscribed by the configuration of the three phenomena: Spiritual outburst—Ecumenic empire—Historiography.

According to various degrees of retrospective insight, the three phenomena, as they appeared, were understood as factors that independently determined the configuration of history.

Romanticism already understood that philosophy is one of the spiritual outbursts to which also belong the prophets, Zoroaster, the Buddha, Confucius, and Lao-tzu and that these outbursts belong together and configuratively determine the history of mankind. The earliest use of these phenomena for a construction of a material philosophy of history that is known to me is that of Fabre d'Olivet, *De l'État de l'homme, ou vues philosophiques sur l'histoire du genre humain* (1822). Even today this factor in its independence is a continuing motive, as, e.g., in Jasper's construction of the period from 800–200 B.C. as the "axis time" of mankind, a time in which these outbursts remarkably accumulated. Precisely this construction, however, shows that, and why this factor, taken independently of the configurative context, is not adequate to determine the meaning of a period. The thesis of the critical meaning of the axis time can be maintained only if one ignores and downplays other spiritual outbursts of equal or even greater historical significance, which, however, like the appearance of Moses or Christ, occurred before 800 or after 200. Thus if one determines the structure using the spiritual outbursts as an independent factor, one loses the specific meaning of that accumulation to which philosophy also belongs. That meaning, which the construction of an axis time rather adumbrates than captures, can be clarified only by seeing it as part of a configuration which also comprises the ecumenic empires and historiography.

The second phenomenon, the ecumenic empires, has also been seen first as an independent configurative factor. Attempts to use it for the determination of the structure of history go back to the time of the ecumenic empires themselves, i.e., to the Daniel Apocalypse and the speculations about the *translatio imperii*. The most important modern attempt is Hegel's philosophy of history. That may sound strange as one remembers that Hegel defined "the states" as the "object of history in a more definite shape," but it appears less strange when one examines Hegel's world history of states materially. For then it turns out that for old and middle history "the states" are empires, and particularly ecumenic empires.

The principle of construction, and at the same time its defect, can be discerned in Hegel's *Lectures on the Philosophy of History*, at the section on the Persian empire, i.e., precisely at the point where Hegel's concept of world history as an apocalypse of empire cuts across the material of the Daniel Apocalypse. The Persian empire, for more than one reason, seems to Hegel to have a key position in the structure of history. Above all, it is the first "empire in the *modern* sense—like that which existed in Germany, and the great imperial realm under the sway of Napoleon; for we find it consisting of a number of states, which are indeed dependent but which have retained their own individuality, their manners, and laws." This institutional designation of the Persian empire as a supranational structure—following Polybius, we would call it an ecumenic empire—is then supplemented by its processual characterization as the first empire that, unlike China and India, has "passed away," by succumbing in the collision with the Greek power of Alexander. The Persian empire and its fate manifest the "historical transition," the *translatio imperii*, the "transmission of sovereignty—an occurrence which from this time forward is ever and anon repeated." Finally the Persian empire constitutes a transition in a still different sense, from the Eastern "worlds immersed in nature," which endure, to the "principle of Free Spirit," which advances while its natural existence perishes. With the transition from the oriental to the Greek world "Spirit bids adieu to Nature."

This is not the place to pursue a thorough analysis of Hegel's material philosophy of history, which to this day remains a desideratum. We confine ourselves to the statement that the equation does not work with the "states," but requires in principle the "empires" and "worlds." For us the essential meaning is that which Hegel, in the tradition of the apocalypse, has attributed to the empires as determinants of the structure of world history. On the one hand, this recognition stems from an awareness of the empires' significance, which is as correct as that of the author of the Daniel Apocalypse. On the other hand, considerable difficulties result from the use of the factor without considering the configurative context, the historical field. One notes with astonishment, above all, that the history of the oriental world unfolds dialectically from China by way of India to Persia. As a result of this construction the entire Middle East (Egypt, Babylonia, Assyria, the Davidic Empire, Israel, and Judah), which is more ancient than China, can be embodied in world history only as the variety of the "states" conquered by Persia. In the place of the Mesopotamian empires, which in the Daniel Apocalypse precede the Persian and Seleucid empires, Hegel has posited China and India. The Asiatic civilizations had not been within the ken of the author of the Daniel Apocalypse, while the level of knowledge of Hegel's time required that they be included in the picture of world history, but that did not necessitate a tampering with the entire construction of history. The reason for Hegel's misconstruction might well be that for him Voltaire's tableau of the East-West parallel histories appeared more binding than the alternative picture stemming from the tradition of the *historia sacra,* which was valid until Bossuet and which placed the beginning in the Middle East. Thus in the case of Hegel's construction, we arrive at a similar result as in the case of Jasper's "axis time." On the one hand, the accumulation of ecumenic empires from China to Rome, occurring in about the same period of time as the spiritual outbursts that induced Jaspers to conceive of his axis time, can no longer be neglected as a configurative factor. On the other hand, one gets into manifest misconstructions if one sees this factor as an autonomous determinant of history. Just as Jaspers cannot cope with the spiritual outbursts that do not occur in his time span, so Hegel is embarrassed by the imperial history of the Middle East, which he can escape only by incorporating it into the Persian empire that comes at its end. The affinity of these misconstructions calls attention to the affinity of the motives that stem from the opposition of the Enlightenment to the overall picture of the *historia sacra.* The material philosophy of history of modern times is held together by a line of Enlightenment from Voltaire to Hegel to Jaspers. We can now state more completely that the problems of material philosophy of history raised by the imperial apocalypses of the *historia sacra* and the Enlightenment cannot be solved as long as the meaning of the particular factors is not determined in the context of the entire configuration.

Historiography does not appear as an independent factor in the construction of images of history, as do the spiritual outbursts and the ecumenic empires, unless one wants to see a case of this kind of the epochal consciousness of Ssu-ma T'an and Ssu-ma Ch'ien, the creators of Chinese historiography. It seems that the historiographer is so absorbed in the act of his craft, which just as much as the other two phenomena determines the structure of the historical field, that he does not become objectively conscious of his constituent function. It is not that such a consciousness is utterly lacking. In Hellenic times the oriental and western, the Greek and Roman historians compete with each other in the endeavor to legitimize their respective civilizations and peoples as the most ancient and thus highest-ranking ones. But the Hellenistic historiomachy already belongs to a second generation of historiography, in which the first, that of the real meaning of history, is presupposed. The earlier layer is that which interests us because in it the problem of the configurative meaning can be clearly discerned.

Historiography has arisen in mankind's history at three places: In Hellas, Israel, and China. The three cases are independent of each other. In all three, however, the events that seem deserving of special attention were linked with a struggle involving society and ecumenic empire. In the case of Israel, where the historiographic beginnings occur earlier, there also figures the conflict with the older cosmological empires. Herodotus' object is the collision of Hellas with the ecumenic empire of the Persians. Ssu-ma Ch'ien's historiography encompasses classical China and its absorption into the empires of the Ch'in and Han Dynasties. In Israel the royal history of the Deuteronomists ends with the destruction of Jerusalem by Babylon, while the work of the Chronicler is induced by the restoration of the Temple after the Persian conquest of Babylon, and the Books of the Maccabeans by the conflict with the Seleucid Empire. What seems to be a general relation between the appearance of historiography and the conflict with an empire, however, is not reversible. In all cases known to us, historiography occurs only when the order of a society collides with an imperial order, but there are numerous conflicts of this kind that have not led to the creation of historiography. The configuration of two factors, even though it has produced an interesting result, is too loose; it still remains below the minimum that empirically would permit the assertion of an unambiguous context of meaning.

If we now include the third factor, one can establish empirically that in those societies in which historiography has arisen, spiritual outbursts preceded both historiography and the ecumenic empires: in Hellas, the Ionic philosophers, Parmenides, Heraclitus, and Xenophanes; in Israel, the Prophets; in China, Confucius and Lao-tzu. In the case of Israel one also needs to recall that its conflicts with cosmological empires were preceded by spiritual outbursts, and that especially in the internal argument with the Davidic-Solomonic empire—on the occasion of which the David memoirs appeared as the probably earliest work of historiography—the prophets played a decisive role. Even when the three factors are combined, one still does not attain a fully satisfactory relation of mutual coordination. Still, the indefinitely large field of exceptions with regard to the combination of historiography and ecumenic empire has been reduced to the two cases of Persia and India. In Persia we find the spiritual outburst of Zoroaster and an ecumenic empire, but no historiography; in India the spiritual outbursts of the Buddha and Mahavira, numerous conflicts with ecumenic empires of the Persians and Alexander, as well as the internal even though imitative, development of the Maurya Empire, but again no historiography. A complete empirical investigation thus would have to include still other factors in order to make clear the configurative complex. This we have to renounce for the present, when we must limit ourselves to indicate the method by which, in principle, the investigation would have to be completed.

The meaning of the empirically established configuration can be expressed only in the conceptual language created on occasion of that spiritual outburst that we call philosophy, in which is symbolized the logos of the realization of eternal being in time. We would have to use statements belonging to the fourth relation of reality, history as the phenomena of philosophical investigations. Such statements, however, are possible only when the preliminary questions of philosophy as a constituent of history and history as a constituent of philosophy have been clarified.

II. PHILOSOPHY AS A CONSTITUENT OF HISTORY

The event philosophy is one among many that constitute history, but it constitutes history in a special way insofar as in the philosophical experience eternal being not only realizes itself in time, but in the same movement also makes the logos of realization transparent. It causes the field of history to become visible as a field of tensions in being. This is why we can speak of the philosophical experience as an ontic event, inasmuch as on this occasion being is recognized as the field of historical tensions. We also can speak of it as a noetic experience, inasmuch as through the event the illuminative quality of the *nous* is brought to understand itself. As for the structures in being that thus become visible, we speak of them as the logos of realization.

In our context it is a question of primarily two tensions in being. The first is the tension of the soul between time and eternity; the second the tension of the soul between its order before and after the ontic event. Because of the illuminative character of the philosophical experience the description of the tensions is inevitably burdened by the difficulty that the grammatic subjects of the statements are not names of subjects referring to the world of things. Neither the poles of the tensions in being nor the experiences of the tensions or the states of order in being are things of the external world, but rather they are terms of the noetic exegesis in which the ontic event interprets itself. Plato, whose philosophizing will serve us as an example of the tensions, has sought to express them through the symbolism of the myth. We shall not follow his example by merely referring to the Platonic myths, but rather we shall try to describe them, even if only briefly. This is necessary because historically the terms of the exegesis have again and again been objectivized, made into objects of philosophically derailed propositions about which we have to say something in the following paragraphs.

Primarily, the philosophical experience discloses the soul as the place of the tensions between the temporal being of the experiencing man and eternal being, the realization of which is experienced. Let us try to determine more precisely the meaning of this statement.

The term "soul", or *psyche,* in this statement must not be understood as if it were an object about which one could make philosophical propositions concerning its immateriality or immortality, its pre- or post-existence. Rather it is strictly the name of a predicate of which "place of the tensions" is the subject. The classical philosophers felt the need to develop a term to designate the place of experiences of being and gave this meaning to the term *psyche.* This fact may be explained on the analogy of the physiological placing of sensual perceptions: Just as the eye, ear, and hand are the organs of optic, acoustic, and haptic perceptions, man also needs an organ to perceive the tensions of being (the philosophical meaning of the term *noein* is also preceded by its meaning of sensual perception, *percipere*). In this sense the soul must be understood as sensorium of the tensions in being, in particular as sensorium of the transcendence.

The subject of the experience also is a matter of difficulty. The sensorium of the tensions in being is just as little the subject of the experiences as eye and ear are the subjects of optic and acoustic perceptions. Rather, it is the man who sees and hears. We have spoken, therefore, of "man in his temporal being" as the subject of the philosophical experience, which is simultaneously an experience of being and of the *nous.* The concept, however, is unsatisfactory, for, were it to be taken in its strict meaning, the experience of eternal being by a man in temporality would remain unintelligible. Since neither the temporal being of man nor his experience of eternal being can be doubted, there must be in man something nontemporal through which he participates in eternal being. This requirement points back to the sensorium of transcendence, to the soul, by virtue of which man has a part in eternal being. (This sentence should not be understood as a simplistic plea for the "status of reality" of the soul, even though it contains a hint about the structure of the problem of the soul's reality). When man by virtue of his soul experiences his participation in eternal being, he is more than merely "man in temporal existence."

We suspect therefore that the qualifications of man's status as "temporal being"—even though we do not doubt its correctness—is not to be understood as the attribute of a thing but rather as an index stemming from the very noetic experience, i.e., from the illumination of being, in which temporal being is experienced as the counterpole to eternal being. We shall have to say more about this problem of indices. At this point we merely state that it would be more cautious to speak of man simply as the subject of experience, as long as this caution does not hide from us the paradox of a being in time which is more than a temporal being.

What, now, is the kind of experience of which we are speaking? We are dealing with the experience of a tension between the poles of temporal and eternal being, not with objective cognition either of the poles or of the tension itself. Whatever may be the case of man as the subject of experience, he does experience in his soul a tension between two poles of being of which one, called *temporal,* is within himself, while the other lies without, albeit not seen as an object in the temporal being of the world, but experienced as being beyond all temporal being of the world. From the temporal pole the tension is experienced as a loving and hopeful urge toward the divine eternity, from the pole of eternal being as a call and irruption of grace. In the course of the experience neither does eternal being become intelligible as an object in time nor is the experiencing soul transfigured from temporal into eternal being. Rather, the process should be characterized as an ordering of self or the soul permitting itself to be ordered by its loving opening to the irruption of eternal being. This process of the soul, however, does not again result in an order that would be a new object beyond the tension. Even when an enduring order results that governs the soul's life until death, it does not become a possession but endures only in the flow of the tension itself, which at any time can collapse through sloth or the self-closing of the soul.

The subject of the experience confronts us with problems no less than does the experience itself. For if the experience must be characterized as tension between nonobjective poles of being, if it does not deal with an object of experience because it is identical with the tension, then it may appear as if the experience is an event in being without a subject. Just as with regard to "man in temporal being" we suspected that the temporality is an index of being stemming from the noetic experience itself, so now we suspect that the "subject of noetic experience" is an index that man gains only from the experience itself. If the tension of being gives us the impression of an event without subject, we should leave it this way, in order not to obscure the insight into the problem of man as subject of the philosophical experience. But, on the other hand, one should not take this impression with literal seriousness, for then the subjectless event would project being, in which it occurs, as its subject. Being would replace the human subject of the experience, and the tensions of being would become propositions about being as a subject so that being, the terminus of the exegesis, would become the object of speculative thought. On the one hand, then, the impression of a subjectless event in being must not be rejected as a false appearance; that would open the way for psychologization: for sophistic theories concerning the gods as the invention of a "clever" man as well as for Feuerbach's psychology of the divine as a projection of the soul. On the other hand, one must not hypostatize the impression of being, when it is noetically illuminated, into being as an object; that would deliver being to the *libido dominandi* of the speculators and activists, and philosophy would derail into speculations of the theogonic or historical-dialectic type. Pending further analyses concerning the problem of indices, we thus leave alone the impression of a subjectless, nonobjective event in being; still, we recognize the psyche as the place of the event through which it becomes an experience. We thus recognize, with the psyche as the sensorium, man as the subject of the experience; and with man in his material existence, the spatio-temporal order of the ontic event.

The difficulties of expressing the philosophical experience adequately, and yet without derailing, roots in the fact that philosophizing about the nonobjective field of the tensions of being is tied to a language the grammar of which depicts objective images of the world of things. There is, however, the additional possibility of expressing the tensions through the symbolism of the myth, as Plato did. It is a matter of the two previously mentioned tensions that primarily constitute history: (1) the tension of the soul between time and eternity and (2) the tension between the order of the soul before and after the ontic event. We now shall turn to these two tensions in the special mythical form of expression which they received on the occasion of Plato's philosophizing.

The *locus classicus* for the first tension and its mythical expression is the speech of Socrates in the *Symposium*. The poles of temporal and eternal being are represented by the mortals and the gods. Between them there are relations: "worship and prayers" on the part of men, "commands and graces" on the part of gods. Rather, the relations should run back and forth but cannot, for "god and man do not mingle"—we have pointed out that it remains inscrutable how man, in temporal being (Plato's *thnetos*), could experience eternal being. There is, then, need of a mediator who reports and interprets to the gods that which happens with men and to men that which happens with gods. The role of the mediator is attributed by Plato to "a very powerful spirit," for the realm of the spiritual (*pan to daimonion*) lies between (*metaxy*) God and man. This spirit (*daimon*), by virtue of his position in between, is to mingle what does not mingle as long as it stands objectively opposite and to "merge both sides together into one great whole." The symbolism discreetly points up what is the core of the matter, man who is not simply *thnetos* but experiences in himself the tension to divine being and thus stands between the human and the divine. Whoever has this experience grows above the status of a mortal and becomes a "spiritual man," *daimonios aner*. We have mentioned the index of the "subject of philosophical experience" that emerges only from this human experience; Plato expresses the same problem when he, in talking about man, supplements the *thnetos* of the epical language by the *daimonios aner* of the philosophical one.

The "great spirit," the mediator, is Eros, the symbol of the experienced tension between the poles of temporal and eternal being. Now the tension itself becomes explicit through the myth of Eros' descent. His mother is Penia (poverty, need), his father is Poros (fullness, wealth), the son of Metis (wisdom, counsel). Penia seduces Poros, who is intoxicated by the feast that the gods celebrated on the birth of Aphrodite, and from the liaison springs Eros. The sad-loving quest of penury for fullness, and the inebriated penetration of richness into poverty certainly bespeak personal aspects of Plato's experience. Beyond that, however, they introduce a material element into the analysis that we have not touched so far and that attains its full weight through its further development by Boëthius. For the poles of tension are materially no longer determined by time and eternity, or by mortals and gods, but by penury and fullness, incomplete and complete being. This is all the more remarkable since Boëthius's determination of eternity as perfect being refers not to the *Symposium* but to the *Timaeus*, where the tension is symbolized through the demiurge, between eternity and time, as the *eikon* of eternity. The relations between time-eternity and penury-fullness, which are here manifested, require still further investigation. In our context the shifting of the material determination is important chiefly because it serves Plato as an instrument to describe the philosophical experience as the tension between wisdom (fullness) and ignorance (penury). "The gods are not seekers after truth and do not long to become wise, for they already are wise," to which Plato adds ironically, "why should the wise be seeking the wisdom that is already theirs?" But if "the wise" will not concern themselves with philosophy, neither will the ignorant (*amatheis*), for the depressing fact of ignorance is that it is satisfied with what it is. The man who does not feel his condition of need does not desire what he is lacking. The philosopher, too, is *amathes*, but his *amathia* is the one pole of the tension in which he experiences the other pole, *sophia* (wisdom). That *amathia* that is not a pole of philosophical experience characterizes the man without tension, who is spiritually dull.

Plato's description of the complacent ignoramus introduces a third type of man. The first type was the mortal, *thnetos*, who in the language of the epic is the opposite of the *athanatoi;* the second type was the spiritual man, *daimonios aner,* who lives in the tension between needy and full being; the third one is the *amathes*, the man of spiritual dullness. As we reflect about the sequence of the three types, there emerges the field of history which is constituted by the event of philosophy. For the man who through philosophical experience enters into the tension of differentiated knowledge about the order of being recognizes, not only himself as the new type of the *daimonios aner,* but also the man who still lives compactly in the cosmic primary experience, as the historically older type. Further, once the humanly representative level of differentiating experience has been attained, no way leads back to the more compact levels.

Whoever closes himself to the new order sinks down to the dullness of the *amathes*. The order of the soul moved by Eros thus is not a completed event. Beyond its characteristic tension of being, it constitutes, by virtue of its essence, a field of tensions to types of order that historically have not attained the differentiation of philosophy, as well as to types of resistance or of self-closing to the new order. The logos of realization, once having become visible, furnishes, together with the noetic understanding of itself, also the criteria for judging orders of lower rank or of different kind. The insights that are at stake do not constitute an indifferent body of knowledge, since they regard the right relation of man to the divine ground of being; the philosophical tension between time and eternity is recognized as the right order of the soul, which implies the claim of fulfillment for all. From this claim to be the right order of human existence, there stems the inexorability characteristic of the constitution of the historical field. For the man in whom the experience has happened feels judged, not as a private person, but in his capacity as man. The experience has occurred in him as a representative for every man, and for that reason every man is judged by it, even and precisely when he refuses himself to its claim. The myth of judgment therefore serves Plato as an expression of the historical tensions. In the *Gorgias,* Socrates and Callicles confront each other as the representatives of the new order and the resistance to it. The decision about the right order, which in time is made by the verdict of the Athenians about Socrates, is in eternity accomplished by the judgment of the dead. The poles of the psychic tension in the historical field become visible as those men who are beholden to "time" and the others who live with a view to "eternity"; or the "living ones" who through the splendor of time go toward death, and the "dead ones" who through their life in the tension of judgment go to eternity. Through the historical character of the philosophical experience other types of men become visible, in whose life and death contest the field of history is constituted.

By way of conclusion, this section requires a reflection about the field of history.

In the first part, concerning phenomena, we understood "field" as the structure of being by which phenomena occur, not without context but as part of meaningful configurations. In the present section, concerning the constitution of the field, it was understood as a field of tensions in being. When talking of meaningful configurations of the phenomena, we presupposed a meaning which was more concretely determined by the subsequent analysis of the meaning of the tensions. The second determination is still not sufficient for the characterization of the field, for being threatens to assert itself as the place of the tensions, while in reality it is not an object but a terminus of the noetic exegesis. In order to characterize the field adequately we must go back to the experience of being and its peculiar problems, for the nonobjective character of the experience of being extends it beyond into the field of history, which that experience constitutes.

Let us first eliminate the misunderstanding that motivates the objectivizing constructions of the field of history. The question of the field is a question of the place of tensions in the same way in which the question of the place of experiences of being arises. We accepted *psyche*, in the sense of the word created by the philosophers, as the designation of the place of the tensions; further we spoke of the *psyche* as the sensorium of transcendence; finally we posited man as the possessor of the sensorium and the subject of the experiences he had by virtue of it. The layers of the problem correspond essentially to Plato's layers of *nous*—in *psyche*—in *soma*. These tiers, which apply to concrete man, must not be projected beyond man into history. In particular it is not admissible to construe the place of history as an expanded *psyche* (collective, of mankind, cosmic, divine), however often this may have been attempted ever since Plato, in the *Timaeus*, spoke of a *psyche* of the *cosmos*. For the *Timaeus* is a myth, and Plato knew what he was doing when he gave to the *anima mundi* a place in the myth. We gain nothing by pretending that the mythical symbol stands for an object of knowledge. Rather, we should ask about the experience that has elicited the mythical symbol, in the light of which that symbol appears meaningful. In philosophy, therefore, the *psyche* is for us the place of the experience of being, the subject of which is the concrete human person; the assumption of a *psyche* without spatio-temporal location in a concrete man as the subject of its experiences is philosophically inadmissible. If, however, we exclude the expanded *psyche* as the place of the tensions and thus exclude one subject of experience, then the field of historical tensions, which we doubtless experience, refers us back to the personal soul as the field of the experiences of being where we would find the general characteristicum.

Let us then go back to the experience of being itself, the experience of a tension between the poles of time and eternity, the experience of mutual encounter and mutual penetration of temporal and eternal being. In the course of the analysis of this experience we raised the question how man, in his temporality, could possibly have any experience of eternal being; and by way of an answer we stated the presumption that temporality is an index that we impute to man and to the world only in the light of the experienced tension. The immanence of the world of things and the time of the immanent world are not primarily experienced. They are indices for a complex of reality which becomes visible in its own structure when through the occurrence of philosophy one recognizes its position at the time-pole of the tension between time and eternity. It is only when these indices are objectivized that there arises the aporia of having to put together the objects called temporal and eternal being, which not only were never separated but which as objects do not exist at all. If we accept the theory of indices the difficulty disappears, for then the experience of being does not occur in the "temporal" time—from the point of view of which an experience of eternity is hard to understand—but rather occurs where it is experienced, in the "in between," Plato's *metaxy*, which is neither time nor eternity. The tension of being itself, its genesis, exegesis, and interpretation, its effects of order, its decline, and so on, are indeed experienced as a process. But this process occurs in the *metaxy*. It may appear to occur in wordly time inasmuch as one can relate mundane events to the process in the *metaxy*, for the subject of the experience is a human person, who, belonging to a number of structures of order, also belongs to the world. This possibility of dating the process is certainly a fundamental problem of ontology, but it does not give us the right to place the *metaxy*—in which the experience unfolds—into the world and its time. In order to keep the layers apart it is advisable to introduce some terminological distinctions. In order not to depart unduly from conventional language, we shall speak of the series of immanent worldly dates, of the embedding of the *metaxy* in the world, as the temporal process of the experience. Similarly we shall speak of a temporal process of history that designates the series of immanent-worldly dates that can be related to the field of history. More difficult and more important, however, is the task of finding an adequate term for the process of the experience in the *metaxy*. To this end let us recall once more that, in the philosophical experience, neither does eternal being become an object in time nor is temporal being transposed into eternity. We remain in the "in between," in a temporal flow of experience in which eternity is present. This flow cannot be dissected into past, present, and future of the world's time, for at every point of the flow there is the tension toward the transcending, eternal being. This characteristic of the presence of eternal being in temporal flow may be best represented by the term *flowing presence*.

If we understand the event of philosophy as flowing presence, then the realization of eternal being in time is neither an event in the past or the future of worldly time, nor the assured condition of a being thing (whether it be a man, a society of humans, or the entire humanity); rather, it is the permanent presence of the tension toward eternal being, related to wordly time. Two aspects account for the permanent tension of the flowing presence becoming "history": First, the tension in being is not an object that could be known "intersubjectively" and thus would present about the same phenomenal image to everyone. Rather, it is indeed a tension that must be experienced personally and that therefore, presents itself in a manifold of experiential modes on the scales of compactness and differentiation, of transparency and obliqueness, of anxiety and faith, of *libido dominandi* and charity, of despair and hope, of acquiescence and rebellion, humility and defiance, opening and closing oneself, apostasy and return, promethean revolt and fear of God, joy of life and *contemptus mundi*. Secondly, the field of experiences is not a disorderly multiplicity but manifests intelligible traits of order, insofar as between the modally differing experiences flowing from the "truth" of ontic experience, there arise those relations that give to the field direction and that hardness of irreversibility, which Plato has caught in his myth of judgment. How can the flowing presence, with its modes of experiences, the tensions between them, its epochally representative events indicating direction and judgment, how can all this constitute a field in such a way that it becomes, in the world's time, an intelligible process of history, a kind of biography of the flowing presence? This structure of reality is as little intelligible as the intelligibility of the world through the natural sciences. It must be called the mystery of history.

III. HISTORY AS THE CONSTITUENT OF PHILOSOPHY

Philosophy and history constitute each other mutually. The two relations are difficult to keep apart in the description. Hence, what must be said under the title of history as a constituent of philosophy has to a large extent already been included in the preceding section. This section will therefore be limited to a formulation of the fundamentals of the problem.

If we understand history as the realization of eternal being in history, the historical constitution of philosophy presents the two aspects that have already been dealt with in the preceding section. First of all, the philosophical experience, in which eternal and temporal being encounter each other, is itself an historical event of realization, its type being represented by Socrates' speech in the *Symposium*. Secondly, the experience has a modal character, i.e., it is one mode of experience among others in the field of the flowing presence. The philosophical experience that renders the logos of realization transparent can be understood as historically constituted only when it is related to the primary experience of the cosmos and its expression in the myth. Reversely, only when we consider philosophy as an event in the field of history do we understand its specific accomplishment as differentiated knowledge of the order of being. It is this second aspect that concerns us here.

The philosophical experience does not discover objects that until then were unknown, but it discovers relations of order in a reality that was also known to the primary experience of the cosmos. Aristotle indicated the critical point of discovery when he observed that the poets placed at the beginning the gods Okeanos and Tethys, whereas the Ionian philosopher places water there, and when he then distinguished the poets as the theologizing thinkers from the Ionians as the philosophizing ones: The cosmos that also comprises the gods is dissociated, by the philosophical experience, into a world without gods and a world-transcendent God. The tension between nondivine tem-

poral being and divine-eternal being, experienced as an illumination, results in the new order of a world-this-side-of-God and
a world-transcending God, taking the place of the cosmic relations of order.

It is difficult to dwell on the character of this differentiation
of relations of order without succumbing to the possibilities of
an objectivization. For instance, one should not speak of a dedi-
vinization of the cosmos, for when dedivinized it is no longer
the cosmos; nor should one speak of a dedivinized world, for
the gods were never in the world. In order to prevent derailments of this and other kinds, which obscure the problem, we
need a theory of indices. The preceding section has already
identified its chief points. A few examples of its application will
help to clarify the matter.

Let us consider, above all, the term *being:* It designates, not
an object, but a context of order in which are placed all experienced complexes of reality after the dissociation of the cosmos,
and which, before the dissociation, were placed in the context
of the cosmic order. The new context of order called *being*
replaces the older one called *cosmos.* The term being, if it is to
function as the index of the new order, must decisively change
its meaning that it had in the context of the cosmic primary
experience. Particularly instructive for the genesis of the indices is the process, in the course of which the cosmo-logical
meaning of *ta onta* in Homer's language mutates into the ontological meaning of the philosophers' language.

Let us next consider the spatial metaphors, like *this world—the
other world [diesseits–jenseits]*, or *immanent–transcendent:* they do
not define attributes of beings, but rather are indices that, in
the light of the experienced tension of being, are associated
with the mundane and divine complexes of reality respectively.

Finally, there is the term *world:* Neither is the world an object
that exists, but rather the index for the complex of reality of
things and the relations between them, as soon as their nondivine, autonomous structure becomes visible through the experience of being. If one forgets the character of the term as an
index, i.e., its genesis in the experience of being, and if one
objectivizes the indexed autonomous structure, there appear
the antitheistic, ideological "worlds," e.g., the world of the
sense-perceptible things, with its claim to a monopoly of reality.
This type of derailment is of special interest for the political

theorist because under its influence a tragicomic situation arose in the period of the ecumenic empires, when "rulers of the world" discovered that a piece of real estate, even though its boundaries may be extended ever so far, does not become a world and that more than spatial extension is required for an empire. This insight led to the historical processes of experimentation with imperial theologies designed to supply the missing ingredients of a world. They entered into tentative associations with spiritual movements, they summoned ecumenical councils that served to bend the spiritual movement for imperial purposes, and they eventually created an imperial orthodoxy. Even today we suffer from empires that seek their "world" by means of expansion rather than advance into the *metaxy* of the flowing presence.

The examples are meant to emphasize once more that the core of philosophy is the experience of the tension of being, from the ordering truth of which the indices radiate toward the complexes of reality. Wherever the tension of being results in a concern with the autonomous world of things, there also is concern with God, without whom, understood as world-transcending, there could be no world of autonomous things. Wherever God and world are kept apart by the experience of being, in which they meet, there also is concern with man who, in the experience of himself as one who experiences order, enters into the knowing truth of his own order. This complex of problems seems to me to be the historically constituted core of all philosophy.

IV. HISTORY AS THE FIELD OF PHENOMENA OF PHILOSOPHICAL INVESTIGATION

Philosophy is the event of being on the occasion of which the logos of realization becomes transparent. Philosophy, therefore, is that phenomenon in the field of history, with the help of which not only are other phenomena recognized as phenomena of realization but also is the field of history recognized as the field of tension between the phenomena. One would be led to expect that, following the event of *being* and its self-interpretation as a historical event, there would immediately begin attempts to construct a material philosophy of history in the grand style. This, however, did not happen. The inklings of a material philosophy of history, which are in principle present in Plato's work, did not immediately lead to further attempts to explore and survey the field of history as a whole.

The absence of such attempts may be explained on a number of grounds: There were no critically validated comparative materials from the older Middle Eastern cultures or the contemporary Far Eastern ones; since such materials did not invite an overall construction, no philosophical concepts required for the theoretical mastery of such materials were evolved. These are good reasons that must not be carelessly shoved aside. A more important one, it seems to me, is the polemical situation created by the event of history, a situation which required the concentration of energy in the philosophical experience itself and its defense against the types of tradition and resistance. "Warfare and battle" are the words with which the *Gorgias* begins. The first sentence makes clear that it is a matter of that "warfare and battle" that Socrates had chosen, by appearing at this historical hour. Insofar as this event is historical action, insofar as the representative creation of a new order with its claim of recognition gets into conflict with the existing order of society, it seems to demand all available strength and thus to bar the unfolding of possibilities that are prepared in principle. At any rate, we find that not only the philosophical experience of transcendence but also the Israelite and the Christian experiences have at first a tendency to form types within a relatively narrow horizon—one could say, a horizon of contemporary history. The emerging types are adequate for this narrow purpose. One recalls the reduction of history's problems to the pairs of types dominating the field of history, as, e.g., Hellenes and barbarians, Israel and the nations, Plato and the Sophists, Christ and the Pharisees, and finally, the Christian concept of *pagani* for all non-Christians insofar as they are not Jews. Even when we go beyond this initial situation, we find that the improvement and increase of conceptualized types occurs in situations of conflict. A more precise definition, e.g., of what is Christian, results from the need for debate with contemporary types of opponents: Irenaeus and the Gnostics, Athanasius and the Arians, Augustine and the Manicheans, Thomas and the Muslims (who to him are still *pagani*). Even in our own time, the philosophical debate with the ideologies, the exploration of their long prehistory and their relations with the Gnostics of antiquity and the sects of the Middle Ages, did not get seriously underway until the ideologies appeared as world powers that threaten Western civilization from within and without. The wave of "philosophies of history" since Voltaire, which indeed did work with global masses of material, did not originate in a sudden eruption of contemplative interest. Rather, it followed upon the imperial era of the discoveries and conquests, through which the globe and its peoples became a domain of the West. We therefore dare to generalize empirically that the philosophical investigation of the realm of phenomena has received its dynamism always from contemporary situations of struggle. If the horizon of phenomena today is indeed global, the reason is that the entire globe has become a contemporary field of tension.

If this thesis turns out to be tenable, an important insight into the reciprocal constitution of philosophy and history would have been gained. The historical constitution of philosophy then would not be a one-time event but rather a historical process, in which philosophy attains a more profound understanding of itself by actualizing its noetic potentiality for investigation of the historical realm of phenomena. Today we are at the beginning of great philosophical developments, through the development of a philosophy of history, which for the first time must explore the realm of phenomena in its global breadth and temporal depth.

The confinement to a situation of struggle was not the sole obstacle for the unfolding of a philosophy of history in its full material breadth, an unfolding that would have been possible at any given time. The widening of the horizon in classical as well as Christian philosophy was impeded in that the working-out of philosophical concepts on the basis of the beginnings encountered certain barriers. These barriers began to fall in modern times, and today they have fallen to such an extent that the field of work has been cleared of them. It is a matter of partialities, the possibilities of which are contained in the tension of being.

In the experience of flowing presence, there is a meeting of time and eternity, man and God. An experience of this *metaxy*, therefore, cannot place its accents wholly on either the human seeking-and-receiving pole nor one the divine giving-and-commanding pole. When the accents of mode are placed on the human seeking-and-receiving pole in such a way that the knowledge of the *metaxy* and the order of being become dominant, we speak of philosophy. When the accents of modality are placed on the divine giving-and-commanding pole in such a way that human knowledge of the experience is reduced to a communication of the divine irruption, we speak of revelation. Either mode conditions typical attitudes toward the temporal sequence of experiences. In the Hellenistic development of the philosophical experience, during the classical period from Hesiod to Plato, each newly differentiated experiential position relegates the older, more compact experiences to the category of *pseudos*, a term the meaning of which extends all the way to the lie. Vis-à-vis the older *pseudos*, the younger experience represents *aletheia*, the truth. Not until the late works of Plato, and in Aristotle, does one find the beginnings of the formation of types and the formation of a conceptual language in which the symbolism of the older myth is understood, not as *pseudos* but as truth in a different mode of experience, as, e.g., in Aristotle who distinguishes between theologizing and philosophizing thinkers, both of whom express the same truth in different symbolisms. These beginnings, however, were not followed up in Hellenistic times. A wholly different relationship prevails between the Christian thinkers and their predecessors. Above all, a prophet cannot lie, for he speaks the word of God. Further, the statements of the experience of revelation, together with the historical reports of their circumstances, melt into a gigantic literary corpus that as a whole is put under the category of revelation. If, in reading these *sacrae litterae*, conflicts emerge between the reader's predecessors, or if the reading successor has beliefs different from his canonized predecessors, certain rules of interpretation must be applied in order to avoid collisions between truths. Augustine formulated this principle: "All *divina scripta* are compatible with each other in peace" (*Serm.* I, 1, 4), and when passages do appear incompatible, one must consider that "another prophet is speaking, not another spirit" (*In Ps.* 103, 1, 5). The method to overcome apparent conflicts is allegorical exegesis. Categorizing as a lie and allegoresis are the two attitudes toward the phenomenon of the predecessor that correspond to the modal accents on the temporal or the eternal pole of the experience of transcendence. Neither one nor the other attitude, however, is suitable to the exploration of the phenomena of the flowing presence. Not until the historical research of theologians and the science of comparative religion have those obstacles been definitively removed.

We must not claim for our time all that is to be done in this field, for it is precisely the great principle of material philosophy of history that we owe to an insight of Augustine. In his *Enarrationes in Psalmos* (64.2) this text is found:

> *Incipit exire qui incipit amare.*
> *Exeunt enim multi latenter,*
> *et exeuntium pedes sunt cordis affectus:*
> *exeunt autem de Babylonia.*

> He begins to leave who begins to love.
> Many the leaving who know it not,
> for the feet of those leaving are affections of the heart:
> and yet, they are leaving Babylon.

Augustine places the conflicts between the Chosen People and the empires under the symbol of the exodus and understands the historical processes of exodus, exile, and return as figurations of the tension of being between time and eternity. Whichever figure the exodus may adopt—that of a real emigration or that of a collision, within the society, between the representatives of higher- and lower-ranking orders—the dynamism and direction of the process stem from the love of eternal being. The exodus in the sense of *incipit exire qui incipit amare* is the classical formulation of the material principle of a philosophy of history.

PART III

What Is Political Reality?

Science and Reality

When the chairman of our association invited me to deliver a paper at this meeting, he stipulated a paper on fundamentals.* In order to meet the requirement I proposed as subject the question "What is Political Reality?"

The proposed subject is not as obvious a response to the requirement as its generality might cause one to assume. Principles of logic are the topmost, nonderived propositions that a science presupposes and that can be made explicit by analysis, if they are not already known. Fundamental principles are the axioms of a science—they are not axioms of the reality that the science investigates. Consider, e.g., the great achievement of axiom research in our century, the *Principia Mathematica* by Russell and Whitehead. In the *Principia* the mathematical knowledge was assumed as given. The authors sought to explore the axioms of the known state of the science, axioms they developed in sections 1–43 of their work. In the light of the axioms, they could, then, in the bulk of the work, work through and newly formulate a series of mathematical problems with a view to their axiomatic content. As we consider mathematics and physics as models of science, it does not seem to be a matter of course to raise the question of the reality of the object in the form of a paper on fundamental principles.

Let us assume that it makes sense to raise the question in this form. We have thereby at least implied something essential about the relation of political science to its object, as well as characterized the point at which that relation differs from the corresponding one in mathematics and physics.

In order to penetrate to this essence and character, we state, above all, that no corollary to the axiomatization of mathematics by Russell and Whitehead can be provided for political sci-

*What is Political Reality? Paper delivered at the Annual Meeting of the *Deutsche Vereinigung für Politische Wissenschaft* on June 9, 1965, in Tutzing; published in: *Politische Vierteljahresschrift*, vol. VII, no. 1 (1966).

ence because there is no body of propositions of political science that could be compared with mathematics. We further state: The absence of such a body of proposition follows essentially from the special relation between science and reality in the field of politics, so it is not a defect that could be remedied in the future. If we now continue to ask why such a body of propositions does not and cannot exist—what is the special character of the relation between science and reality that inhibits such a body of propositions—we could answer, in a first approximation: The core of political science is a noetic interpretation of man, society, and history that appears with the claim of critical knowledge of order vis-à-vis the order of that society in which, respectively, it emerges. Political science in the sense of noetic knowledge of order finds itself in the peculiar situation, other than the sciences examining the phenomena of the external world, in that the intended object, "political reality," is itself structured by a knowledge that aims at that object.

Let us try to characterize this peculiar relationship in its chief traits:

(1) Whoever seeks to interpret, noetico-critically, the order of man, society, and history finds that at the time of his attempt the field is already otherwise occupied. For every society is constituted by the self-understanding of its order. Hence every known society in history produces symbols—mythical, revelatory, apocalyptic, gnostic, theologic, ideological, and so on—through which it expresses its experience of order. I name these acts of self-interpretation, which are found in political reality, the non-noetic interpretations.

(2) A further characteristic of the relationship is its historical dimension. The non-noetic interpretations historically precede the noetic ones by thousands of years. The earliest known case of a noetic interpretation, the case to which all later ones are linked, occurs in the context of Hellenic philosophy. There the noetic interpretation received the name of political science, the *episteme politike*. The non-noetic interpretations not only precede the noetic ones in time, but, after the emergence of noetic interpretation, they also remain the form of society's self-interpretation, which the noetic attempt always finds confronting it. There are no societies whose constitutive self-interpretation is noetic. This peculiarity of the relationship suggests the supposition that the noetic interpretations, for rea-

sons later to be explained, can function as a corrective or additive to the non-noetic ones but cannot replace them.

(3) A noetic interpretation does not arise independently of the conception of order of a society but rather in critical contention with it. Wherever noesis emerges, it appears in a relation of tension to the self-consciousness of society. One recalls the world-historical tensions between philosophy on the one hand, and myth and sophism on the other; between philosophy and theology; and today between philosophy and ideology. The opposition is the origin of that differentiation, in the course of which the noetic interpretation becomes a "science," relating to political reality as its "object." The opposition, further, is mutual, so that the representatives of the non-noetic interpretation are not helpless vis-à-vis the objectivization on the part of their noetic critics. Not without resistance do they let themselves be maneuvered into the role of an "object of investigation," but they, in turn, objectivize their noetic opponent from the point of view of their own order: The philosopher, seen from the point of the cult of the polis, becomes an atheist; from the point of revelation he becomes a heretic; from the point of revolutionary ideology, he becomes a reactionary who represents a rival ideology.

I have put the terms "science" and "object" in quotation marks, for the listed characteristics of the relationship have made clear that it is a two- or three-layered phenomenon of interpretations, which layers, moreover, not only overlay each other but also interpret each other mutually. Were we to detach from this complex phenomenon one or the other layer as "science" or "object," we would at this point only get entangled in questions of the following kind: Does the noetic interpretation, by virtue of its generic kinship as a concept of order, belong to the reality to which it is opposed? Alternatively, should the same principle of generic kinship of self-interpretations elevate the self-interpretation of society to the rank of a science? At this moment nothing is sure except that the phenomenon cannot be dealt with according to the natural science model of science and object.

Although the phenomenon is complex, an analysis can make it transparent. If today it is so difficult to realize that the questions "what is political science?" and "what is political reality?" require clarification, the reason must be found in the conceptual confusion characteristic of the era of ideologies. In the ideological climate of our time, the term *science* has become a *topos* designed to lend prestige to a variety of non-noetic interpretations of social order. Whether we consider the older ideologies—the progressivism of Enlightenment, the Positivism and Marxism of the nineteenth century—or the more recent ones, German historism, American behaviorism, and the newest production, post-Stalinist "scientific Communism" of the Soviet empire, all have doubtlessly the character of non-noetic self-interpretation. Their representatives would indignantly reject the suspicion that they are engaged in a noetic interpretation in the sense of classical philosophy, but they still claim the character of a "science."

In this situation, determined on the one hand by the dominant model of science and object and on the other by the scientist claims of the ideologies, there seems to be no sense in trying to solve the question of "political science" through the frontal attack of a nominal definition. It makes no sense to define, through methods or topics, a political science that does not exist as a corpus of propositions and principles, for in that case we would only accept the useless model of science and object. Still less does it make sense to allow oneself to be drawn into an ideological debate about which of the claims to the title *science* might be justified. We must recognize that debate as the dilettantism of epigonic ideologists; we must put it behind us and turn to the matter itself.

In order to minimize the possibility of stirring up a sterile discussion of what is political science, I introduced the term "noetic interpretation," designating the matter with which we are dealing: It is the tension in political reality that presses beyond the self-understanding of society to the noetic interpretation and thereby pushes the social reality into the position of an object.

CHAPTER EIGHT

The Consciousness of the Ground

The tension in political reality, which historically produces the phenomenon of the noetic interpretation, is not a thing about which objective propositions could be formed. Rather, it must be traced back to its origin in the consciousness of men who desire true knowledge of order. The consciousness of concrete men is the place where order is experienced. From this center of experience radiate the interpretations of social order, both the noetic and the non-noetic. The experience of concrete-human order, too, is not knowledge of an object but itself a tension, insofar as man experiences himself as ordered through the tension to the divine ground of his existence. Nor does any of the terms that emerge in the exegesis of this experience relate to an object. Neither the tension is an object, nor are its poles. Nor is the relation of man to his ground an object for propositions that could turn into possessive truth; rather, it is precisely the tension itself and man's abiding in it. Far as we might push the game of objectivizing language, we must keep dissolving it negatively, in order to keep free our awareness of the experience of order as a nonobjective reality. The nonobjective character of the experience of order admits of no so-called knowledge of order; rather, the intangibility of the reality, which is no ineffability, allows room for a variety of experiences that motivate a corresponding number of symbolic expressions of the experience. In the dynamism of the effort to find the right expression of order we find the origin of the tensions in political reality.

Noetic as well as non-noetic interpretations expound the experience of order for society. Both types, and also their variants, claim that their interpretation is the only true one. As far as the content of the experience is concerned, all interpretations conceive order in terms of their ground. The various modes of the experience, with their corresponding multiplicity of symbolic expression, all revolve around the founding of right order through insight into the ground of order. The multiplicity of interpretations, even when known, can never be understood as referring to a multitude of grounds, but the interpretation is always joined to the consciousness that it expresses the experience of the *one* ground. In the mythical language, the origin of the imperial order is built into the cosmogony, the myth of the creation of the one cosmos; in the noetic language the *aition* coincides with the ground of being. Behind the historical variety of interpretations, then, we find the unity of the question about the ground.

Noetic interpretations arise when consciousness, on whatever occasion, seeks to become explicit to itself. The endeavor of consciousness to interpret its own logos shall be called noetic exegesis. Since the prototype of such an exegesis, the classical one, was essentially successful, the present attempt can relate to it. With regard to the symbols we can even follow the classical vocabulary, especially that of Aristotle.

In the experience and language of Aristotle man finds himself in a condition of ignorance (*agnoia, amathia*) with regard to the ground of order (*aition, arche*) of his existence. He could not recognize his own ignorance as such, were he not in the throes of a restless urge to escape from ignorance (*pheugein ten agnoian*) in order to seek knowledge (*episteme*). Since the term *anxiety*, which in modern languages signifies this restlessness, has no equivalent in Greek, Aristotle uses specific terms in order to characterize questioning in confusion or doubt (*diaporein, aporein*). "But whoever is perplexed (*aporon*) and wonders (*thaumazon*) is conscious (*oetai*) of being ignorant (*agnoein*)" (*Met.* 982b18). From questioning restlessness there arises man's desire to know (*tou eidenai oregontai*). The restless search (*zetesis*) for the ground of all being is divided into two components: the desire or grasping (*oregesthai*) for the goal and the knowledge (*noein*). Similarly, the goal (*telos*) itself is divided into the components of desire (*orekton*) and the known (*noeton*) (1072a26 ss). Since the search is not a blind desire but rather contains the component of insight, we may characterize it as knowing questioning and questioning knowledge. Although the quest implies a component of direction, it still may miss its goal (*telos*) or be satisfied with a false one. That which gives direction to the desire and thus imparts content to it is the ground itself, insofar as it moves man by attraction (*kinetai*). The tension toward the ground, of which man is conscious, thus must be understood as a unity that may be interpreted but not analyzed into parts. Tracing the exegesis backward, we therefore must say: Without the *kinesis* of being attracted by the ground, there would be no desire for it; without the desire, no questioning in confusion; without questioning in confusion, no awareness of ignorance. There could be no ignorant anxiety, from which rises the question about the ground, if the anxiety itself were not already man's knowledge of his existence from a ground of being that is not man himself. This directional factor of knowledge in the tension of consciousness toward the ground Aristotle calls *nous*. Since in his language the terms *nous* and *noein* carry a variety of meanings, while the directional factor of knowledge in the tension toward the ground is the material structure of consciousness and its order, it is advisable, for the purpose of our essay, to identify this factor and to fix it terminologically. I shall, therefore, call the directional factor *ratio*. With a view to the thus complete exegesis, we may speak of the *ratio* as the material structure of consciousness and its order. Further, we may characterize that which Bergson has called the open soul its rationality; and the closing of the soul with regard to the ground, or the missing of the goal, as its irrationality.

Aristotle adds to the exegesis of the noetic desire for the ground and the attraction by the ground the symbol of mutual participation (*metalepsis*) of two entities called *nous* (1072b20 ss). By *nous* he understands both the human capacity for knowing questioning about the ground and also the ground of being itself, which is experienced as the directing mover of questions. In Aristotle's thinking, which is in the process of detaching itself from the symbolism of myth, synonymity of expression means equality of genus by genesis. "We note that all primary things come into being out of something with the same name" (1070a4 ss). "To explain a thing (*ousia*) it is necessary to know which among a number of things that have a name in common gives that name to the others (*ek synonymou*), for it is it which explains what other things are (*malista aouto*)" (993b20 ss). To the synonymity of the two entities corresponds the genesis of the human from the divine nous. In the sense of the mythic symbolism of synonymity through genesis, Aristotle thus can understand the tension of consciousness as the mutual participation (*metalepsis*) of the two *nous* entities. On the part of the human *nous,* the knowing question and the questioning knowledge, i.e., the noetic act (*noesis*) is the apprehending participation in the ground of being; the noetic participation, however, is possible by virtue of the preceding genetic participation of the divine in the human *nous.*

Through the symbols of synonymity, genesis, and mutual participation of the two *nous* entities, myth enters into the exegesis. What is the meaning of this entry?

The noetic exegesis does not occur in a vacuum but historically renders conscious the tension toward the ground as the center of order of the differentiated consciousness, in contrast to a preknowledge of man and his order that stems from the compact primary experience of the cosmos, with its expression in the myth. It is a differentiating correction of the compact preknowledge, but it does not replace the latter. Our knowledge of order remains primarily mythical even after the noetic experience has differentiated the realm of consciousness and noetic exegesis has made its logos explicit. Our habits of thought, however, are so uncritical that this fact is hardly noticed. We casually work with the concept of human nature as if we considered it constant, as did the classics, or malleable, as do the ideologues. We forget that that concept was not developed inductively but as an expression of the love for the divine ground of being that a philosophizing human being experiences concretely as his essence. What applies to the philosophical experience of nature also applies to the presence under God, which a prophet experiences pneumatically as his essence. The statement that the known nature is not merely the nature of one person who concretely has the experience of his essence, but rather that of all men, implies the premise that all men are equal *qua* men, regardless of whether or not they experience their human essence in the clarity of differentiated consciousness. The knowledge of the premise, however, comes not from the concrete experience of essence on the part of the respective noetic or pneumatic person, but from the cosmic primary experience, in which things are already experienced as participating—men as men, and gods as gods—even when we do not know too well what precisely they are. Without that premise, the noetic experiences would remain a biographical curiosity; only with the premise as background do they attain their ordering function in society and history, inasmuch as the premise is the basis of the claim that they are representative and binding for all men. The community-creating content of the premise is so important that in the context of philosophy special symbols were developed for it. Heraclitus speaks of the logos as what is common (*xynon*) to men, in which all participate *qua* men, and thus it demands of them conscious *homologia*. For Aristotle, the common element is the *nous,* and the symbol of the common order through participation in the *nous* is thus *homonoia.* Alexander takes over the *homonoia* as the symbol for his imperial religion; and finally, St. Paul introduces it into the symbolism of the Christian community. The entering of the myth, therefore, is not a methodological derailment; rather it is the residue of prenoetic knowledge of order and the background without which the noetic knowledge of order would have no function.

In the light of this insight, let us consider the *metalepsis* of Aristotle. Socrates, in the *Phaedo,* quotes a dictum concerning the Orphic mysteries: "Many bear the emblems (i.e., take part in the cult), but the devotees (i.e., those akin to the god) are few." The devotees, he believes, are the true philosophers; and he has done everything in his life to become one of them (69c). The Platonic-Aristotelian philosophy is preceded not only by the myth of the primary experience but also by the symbolism of a probably quite differentiated pneumatic experience of the divine. When the classical noesis lifts the logos of consciousness to highest clarity, it interprets the logos of an area of reality that Plato identifies as initiation into the mysteries. The "Bacchus" who, in the quoted dictum, is both the god as well as the human akin to God becomes in Aristotle the *nous,* which is both divine and also the human *nous* participating in the divine. Nor is the identity of the area of reality dissolved if we trace the mythical symbolism still further, clarifying its logos, and substituting the ground (*aition*), for Bacchus or *nous.* Even when the noetic exegesis, coming from the more compact experiences of reality, differentiates its logos, it still abides in this same area of reality. The myth, then, ingresses into the noetic exegesis because the noesis egresses from the myth, as it interprets its logos.

Behind the metaphors of ingress and egress there lies the problem of objectivization by noesis. We must resolve and remove the aporias pertaining to this problem before we can continue the analysis:

(1) The area of reality of which we are speaking is the existential tension toward the ground, the participation of man in the divine, the *metalepsis* in Aristotle's sense. Regardless of whether the phenomena of this area of reality are expressed in the symbols of epic poets or tragedians, of the Orphics or the philosophers, whenever they are seen as cases of participation, participation becomes the genus under which phenomena of that kind are to be subsumed. "Participation," however, is a term with the help of which the noetic experience interprets itself. The participation of the philosopher, therefore, would be a species that comes under itself as the genus.

(2) In order to escape this aporia, the participation of the philosopher falling as a species under itself as the genus might be dissociated from the other cases by attributing to it cognitive quality. In that case all non-noetic experiences and symbols would become objects, while noesis would become the science of these objects. The attempt encounters the difficulty that the symbols of the noetic exegesis in fact are not developed as concepts relating to non-noetic objects; rather they are developed as terms in the process of meditation, in which the noetic experience interprets itself. The symbols of noesis relate, objective-wise, to the experience which they are interpreting.

(3) We dissolve these aporias as we acknowledge that the logic of objects and their classification does not apply to an area of reality in which the species is structured by the same kind of knowledge as the supposed generic knowledge and in which, reversely, the supposed generic knowledge has the same material content of participation as the phenomena which it supposedly subsumes.

(4) This decision leads us into another aporia, for the non-noetic phenomena are indeed maneuvered into a kind of object position, by the analysis and classification of the noesis.

(5) In order to resolve this further aporia, one must consider that all participation also contains the component of knowledge about itself and its character—on the scale of compactness and differentiation, direction and misdirection, openness and closing, acquiescence and revolt, etc. On this scale of knowledge, participation has degrees of transparence for itself, up to the optimum clarity of the noetic consciousness, so from each respectively higher position of transparence the respectively preceding position, from which the higher one emerged, appears as a phenomenon of lower ranking truth.

(6) The "objectivization" thus does not refer to participation itself but rather to the difference of truth that arises in the longing search for insight into the right relation to the ground. When Jeremiah scolds the people for having "false" gods, he wavers between the two suppositions that the false gods are nongods (question of truth) and that, though false, they are gods nevertheless (question of participation). Participation with a low grade of transparency is still participation; and the noetic illumination of consciousness in the tension to the ground is not anything more than participation. There is no Archimedean point from which participation itself could be seen as an object.

(7) Participation is a process of consciousness over which we cannot jump into an objective beyond. The relation of knowledge and object is a relation immanent to the process between degrees of truth of participation. The reality of participation has an immanent structure of different levels of truth, in which even the present knowledge, seen from the vantage point of a future presence, turns into a phenomenon of the past, and it is of this structure we speak as the field of history.

(8) The dropping down of a participation of inferior truth to a phenomenon of the past occurs in the consciousness of concrete persons who look for truth and find it. The consciousness that out of this process emerges a "new man" is old, even though the urge to describe the process produces the symbolic form of autobiography only in later times. The origin of history is human consciousness, which moves a phase of its quest for the truth of the ground into the distance of the past. The quest, however, occurs in a society, and the starting point can always be only a traditional knowledge that is experienced as unsatisfactory. Thus the personal field of history generates a social one. Such fields, generated by new participation, are structured

by the characteristic human types that Plato has developed in the *Symposium*. For the man of mythical participation Plato, following the vocabulary of the epics, uses the term mortal (*thnetos*), the man who stands over against the immortal gods. The man who lives in the erotic tension to his ground of being is called *daimonios aner*, i.e., a man who consciously exists in the tension of the in-between (*metaxy*), in which the divine and the human partake of each other. Insofar as the call of the new humanity is not heard at all or even rejected, the man whom the call addresses sinks down to the status of spiritually dull being, the *amathes*. The past world, the new world, and the resisting environment are the core of the field of history as constituted respectively through a new truth that experiences itself as epochal.

The noetic experience, interpreting itself, illuminates the logos of participation. Our own analysis, linking up with that of Aristotle, has by now progressed to the point where we can distinguish three dimensions of the exegesis. First, consciousness discovers as its material structure the direction-giving *ratio*, i.e., the tension of the knowing questioning about the ground. Further, it discovers itself as the luminosity of knowledge about the tension toward the ground. Finally, it discovers itself as a process of quest that puts behind itself phases of less luminosity, as the past. I shall now characterize the three dimensions as well as their relation to each other, again beginning with the Aristotelian analyses, insofar as this is possible:

(1) The direction-giving *ratio* is the material content of consciousness, even when it is not known in the luminosity of noetic consciousness. *Ratio,* in the sense of questioning about the ground, also provides the structure of the myth from which noesis differentiates consciousness as the center of order. This was known to Aristotle, who further knew that myth and noesis do not immediately confront each other but that there are transitional forms, like the Ionic speculation in which the elements supplant the gods as the *arche* of things. His own analysis therefore assumes the form of a criticism of the Ionic speculation. One cannot simply posit something as the ground, he says, so that man derives from earth, the earth from air, the air from fire, and so on, ad indefinitum (*apeiron*). Indefinite series

(*euthoria*) he deems inadmissible since they contain merely intermediate causes (*meson*) but not a first cause (*proton*); and if the series has no limit (*peras*) in a first cause (*arche*), there is no *aition* at all (*Met.* 994a1 ss). More particularly, series of this kind are inadmissible in a theory of human action. For man is a being having reason (*nous echon*); and a rational being is not content with intermediate goals in a theory of action; only a goal (*telos*) having the character of a limit (*peras*) can be rational (994b ss). Furthermore, precisely for this reason the *aition* cannot have material character, for wood does not make a bed and bronze a statue (984a25). The *aition* that is the origin of movement can therefore be only the *nous*.

(2) While the above argument endeavors to isolate the truth concerning the ground, it still takes into account the other dimensions of consciousness, i.e., the luminosity and the historicity of the process. Especially the decisive point of the argument, *viz.*, that man is noetically open and therefore can recognize his ground in the *nous*, is not itself an argument or the result of an argument, but rather the premise that alone makes the argument possible. Let us look at it from the premise of the luminosity of consciousness: On the one hand, Aristotle knows that in his noetic experience the *nous* is the adequate symbol for the ground, and therefore he has no need to prove this truth by an argument. On the other hand, though, he requires the argument in order socially to establish the material structure of consciousness vis-à-vis rival interpretations of the ground. The traditional knowledge of participation, expressing itself in the form of aetiological series without an adequate *arche*, is given, and the new knowledge of the ground must justify itself by means of a criticism of the traditional knowledge. That justification, however, is possible only when one isolates the question of the ground as the tension of consciousness, a tension that creates symbols even where the symbols of reality to be expressed are not yet adequately differentiated. The isolation of the aetiological dimensions thus reveals the field of history as the field of endeavors to grasp and symbolize the truth of the ground. This essential character of the historical field is not revealed by the aetiological argument itself but through the light thrown on the prenoetic past by the luminosity of the noetic experience. Only because the noetically open man (*nous echon*) knows about his ground can he enter into a critical con-

tention with a knowledge of participation that has inferior transparency. By entering into this contention, however, the Aristotelian argument is pushed to the limits of the aporias that we examined above. Is the Ionic speculation a proposition about the object "ground," which the argument proves to be false? And is the assertion that the *nous* is the ground a proposition about the same object, which one can prove right by an argument? With regard to these questions of "objectivization," Aristotle's analysis still is not as exact as might be desirable, even though there can be no doubt about its intentions. The reasons for this shortcoming of exactness are still to be discussed. One can, however, exactly fix the point at which the argument arrives at the limit of aporia, if we recall the previously mentioned case of Jeremiah and his suppositions concerning the "false" gods: In his aetiological argument, Aristotle concentrates so exclusively on the question of truth that the dimension of the question of participation is momentarily obscured. The critical speculations are not altogether as "false" as they appear in Aristotle's description, for they, too, have their meaning in the context of a knowledge of participation, even though a more compact one. One can corroborate that on the basis of the extant pre-Socratic texts. On the other hand, Aristotle's identification of the ground with the *nous* is not altogether as "right" if he relies on arguments rather than on the context of the noetic knowledge of participation. Let us, therefore, repeat once again: The tension toward the ground is the material structure of consciousness but not an object for propositions; rather it is a process of consciousness having degrees of transparency for itself. In the noetic experience, consciousness attains its optimum luminosity in which the tension toward the ground can interpret its own logos. And from the presence of the luminous exegesis of its logos, it can constitute the field of past history as the field of the less transparent phases of the same endeavor to know the truth of the ground. Without the dimension of consciousness's luminosity, there is no aetiological dimension of consciousness; and without these two, there is no historico-critical dimension of the knowledge of participation.

(3) It is only on the occasion of the aetiological argument that Aristotle pushes his analysis so close to the limit of objectivization, that the relation of the truth of the ground to the dimensions of luminosity and of history remains not wholly

clear. A contributing factor may have been his assumption that there is a continuum of philosophy comprising both the Ionic transitional form and noetic philosophy. On this assumption, he would conceive his criticism of the aetiological series as an intraphilosophical contention about the truth of the ground, a contention in which the problem of two different types of experiences, a non-noetic and a noetic one, would not be a factor. This assumption of a continuum of the type of experience, beginning with the Ionians, continues even today as the unshakable convention of philosophy's history, but I still doubt its correctness. The type of experience that produces material *archai* as well as aetiological series as its symbol seems to me to differ from the noetic one. At this point I shall not dwell on the character of this type of experience. The question must be touched only because the difficulties that arise on occasion of the aetiological argument disappear as soon as Aristotle confronts noetic philosophy with the myth—in other words, with a type of experience and symbol about the non-noetic character of which he has no doubt. In the confrontation of philosophy with the myth, out of which it has grown, the historical dimension of participation becomes the theme; through its analysis, Aristotle has gained insights the textual formulation of which are well known to every classical philologist and historian of philosophy, while their character as insights into the historicity of consciousness has hardly been noticed. Fortunately these insights are not only important but also formulated simply and tersely.

All people are equally excited by *thaumazein* (wondering), but they can express their wonderment either through the myth or through philosophy. Side by side with the *philosophos* there is, therefore, the *philomythos*—a neologism that the philosophical language unfortunately has not retained—and that "*philomythos* is, in a sense, a *philosophos*, for the myth consists of wonders (*thaumasion*)" (982b18 ss). The linguistic thread tying the wonders of the myth with man's general wondering, from which also philosophy arises, is then spun further in that the philosopher, while not disposing of the *thaumasia* of the myth, has a *thaumasion* in the divine *nous* (1072b26). Even though myth and philosophy, as symbolic expressions for the experience of wondering and participation in the ground, are equivalent, they nevertheless do not achieve equal knowledge of truth

concerning the ground. The philosopher, therefore, cannot accept the *thaumasia* of the *philomythos*, or at least not all of them.
For Aristotle holds the belief of the fathers (*patrios doxa*)—that
the heavenly bodies are divine—to be divinely inspired and
true, and embodies it in his own symbol of the Prime Mover of
the cosmos. On the other hand, he considers the tradition that
gods have human or animal form an invention for the edifica-
tion of the people, a tradition that must not be accepted
(1074b1-15). The philosopher thus eliminates the *thaumasia* of
the polytheistic myth but retains the knowledge of the
philomythoi about the divinity of the ground. He clearly grasps
the difference of the grades of truth between the primary experience of a cosmos full of gods and the noetic experience for
which the divine is the ground of the cosmos and of man. In
spite of his recognition about this difference of truth, the myth
still so fascinates the philosopher that the late Aristotle confes-
ses: "The more solitary and retired I become, the more I love
the myth" (*philomytheros*).

Aristotle's name does not conjure up in our time the figure of
a philosopher of history. And yet his analysis of the temporal
flow in consciousness as the dimension in which noesis recognizes itself as the presence of truth and, at the same time, the
myth as the past, is a philosophical accomplishment about history that has not been surpassed until today. Let us recapitulate
the essential points.

Above all, history is not a field of indifferently objective materials from which we may select some according to arbitrary
criteria, in order to "construct" a tableau of history. Rather,
history is constituted by consciousness, so the logos of consciousness decides what is and what is not historically relevant.
Be it noted especially that the time in which history constitutes
itself is not that of the external world, in which the somatically
founded life of man leaves its traces, but rather the inner dimension of consciousness of desire and search after the
ground. Since, regarding this dimension, all men are equal, the
field of history is always universally human, even if only a relatively small sector of the philosophers' position would be materially known. The human universality of the desiring and
searching participation in the ground results further in the
equivalence of the symbolisms in which the consciousness of the
ground is expressed. By equivalence I mean the fact that all

experiences of the ground are in like manner experiences of participation, even though they may considerably differ from each other on the scales of compactness and differentiation, of finding and missing the ground. The equivalence of the symbols thrown up in the stream of participation, finally, leads to the loving turning back to the symbols belonging to the past, since they express phases of that same consciousness in the presence of which the thinker finds himself.

Our own analysis has followed that of Aristotle as far as possible. We now have to determine at which point a noetic exegesis in the historical situation of our time must diverge from Aristotle.

The insight of the noetic experience dissolves reality's image of the cosmic primary experience. The place of a cosmos full of gods is taken up by a dedivinized world, and, correlative to it, the divine is concentrated into the transcending ground of being. Immanent and transcendent are spatio-metaphorical indices attributed, in the postnoetic dispensation, to the areas of reality that have become, respectively, the world of things in space and time, and the divine being of the ground beyond space and time. Aristotle was fully aware of this restructuring of reality, from the image of a cosmos to that of a world, as a result of the noetic experience, even though the older images of the divine stars (*phanera*) or the geocentric, spheric cosmos still linger on. The residue of *patrios doxa* in the cosmology strictly speaking does not constitute the big obstacle for the further development of Aristotle's philosophy. Natural science, especially, was successfully pursued in the Peripatos; and Aristotle's geocentric concept did not prevent the emergence of a heliocentric image in his school. It was the dogmatic-geocentric resistance of the Stoics against the heliocentric liberty which the Peripatetics had taken, which seems to have caused the stagnation after Aristarchus. The obstacle must rather be seen in the unfinished state in which Aristotle left the noetic part of his work, as well as in the lack of interest of his immediate successors in the unfinished problems. For the restructuring of the image of reality required a philosophical vocabulary that expressed most precisely the new truth of the structure of being. If "being" was to remain the term for reality in general, as Aristotle intended, then he needed a differentiated vocabulary for the modes of being. Obviously, the existence of things in space and time is a mode of being different from the mode of divine being beyond space and time, and this latter, in turn, is a mode different from that of the nonobjective reality of consciousness together with its tensions and dimensions which we have here analyzed. This kind of vocabulary, however, was not developed, possibly because Aristotle was still too close to the myth so that he did not feel handicapped by the technical deficiency of his own analyses.

The deficiencies of Aristotle's vocabulary was one of the factors that pushed the post-Aristotelian philosophy into the direction of dogmatic metaphysics. The specific point of departure for the development was the symbolism of *ousia*.[1]

In the cosmic primary experience, there are no terms for being and its modes. All "things" are called directly by their names: heaven and earth, gods and men, country and ruler. All of them are "real" and "true" in a way not precisely determined. All of them are themselves and yet at the same time consubstantial, so they can be related to each other through genesis, which in its turn is expressed in the mythical narrative of their generation. This background is so much alive for Aristotle that the one term *ousia* suffices him for all modes of being; his glance always passes through the *ousiai* correctly to the "things" of the primary experience. "The question that has always been asked and is still being asked today, the ever-puzzling question 'What is being?' amounts to this: 'What is primary being (*ousia*)?'" (1028b3–5). It does not make sense to translate *ousia* in this sentence with "substance," as is conventionally done, for one would thereby only get involved, anachronistically, in the problems of later dogmatic metaphysics. The meaning of this *ousia* is the undoubted, unquestionable, and convincing reality of "things" in the primary experience. If one is looking, in Aristotle's language, for an explanatory synonym for *ousia*, the closest would be *aletheia* in its double meaning of reality and truth. For

---

1. The symbolism of *ousia* is not the only point at which the post-Aristotelian *parekbasis* of "metaphysics" could have been engendered. The language of the literary corpus that falls under the general title of "metaphysics" reflects a number of cases of experiences that, not always clearly recognizable, offer various opportunities for dogmatization. Regarding the dogmatism that stems from the works of Aristotle, cf. Philip Merlan, *From Platonism to Neoplatonism* (The Hague, 1960).

Aristotle, everything that is convincingly real falls under the title *ousia*. Form and matter are *ousia* and also the thing that is composed of form and matter. Beyond that the soul, or at least its noetic part, is *ousia*, inasmuch as it is the form (*eidos*) of man. Furthermore the constitution is such a real form (*eidos*) of the polis—a mishap the consequences of which still plague us today as the doctrine of state forms in political science. Finally the divine *nous*, the Prime Mover, has the status of *ousia*.

Obviously great misunderstandings must arise when the term *ousia* loses its transparence for the reality of the primary experience. Under the pressure of the noetic experience, which dissociates the cosmos into the world and its ground, all "things" that Aristotle calls *ousia* are then objectivized according to the model of things in the world, composed as they are of form and matter in space and time. When the transparency vanishes and the *ousiai* become objects of speculation, then there originate the millenial controversies of dogmatics about the soul—its existence, pre- and post-existence—about the existence of God and its proofs, about the finality or infinity of the world in time, and so on. Finally, when the criticism of Enlightenment and Positivism removes the dogmatisms of theology and metaphysics from the intellectual discourse, the mistaken treatment of the problems is not replaced by a better one, but together with the misunderstandings the entire mistreated reality is thrown out. The residual mode of world-immanent existence alone still carries the title being and *ousia*. At this point, however, the intellectual grotesque, which originates in the misunderstanding of Aristotle's symbols, enters into a phase that materially must be recognized as its final phase, inasmuch as the reality of reality, about the truth of which man historically is concerned, is simply denied. The characteristic result is the appearance of symbols like "the end of history" and "the point of existence," in which the experience of existence without reality is groping for an expression. The horrid consequences of the denial of reality for the order of society in the age of ideology are well known to everybody.

I have used the word *grotesque*. It offers itself readily because since the nineteenth century the grotesque has become a literary form that is best able to express the phenomena resulting from the cleavage of language and reality. The great experimenter and also master in this area was Flaubert. In his *Tenta-*

tion de Saint Antoine, he has grasped the phenomena of intellectual decay on the level of the spirit; in *Bouvard et Pécuchet,* the vulgar level of a middle-class farce of cliché, prefiguring the middle-class ambiance in which Hitler would come to power. If one wishes to see, as a whole, the crescendo of decay down to the catastrophe, one need only put side by side with each other Flaubert's *Dictionnaire des idées recues* and the pages in Karl Kraus's *Dritte Walpurgisnacht,* in which he characterizes Goebbels through his cliché language. With Flaubert we are still in the phase in which the language loses its grip on reality and begins to have a life of its own as cliché; with Karl Kraus it has come to the phase in which the cliché asserts the claim to realize itself; but since reality cannot be produced out of nonreality, its place must be taken by bloody grotesque.[2] Among the more recent attempts to comprehend the phenomenon of National Socialism in the form of the grotesque, I should like to mention Doderer's *Die Merowinger* and Frisch's *Biedermann und die Brandstifter.* In his prologue to the latter, Frisch has formulated the problem of the grotesque: "Just because it happened, nonsense (madness) never deserves to be called reality." Doderer, with the same intention as Frisch, also uses the term "nonsense" (or madness) in the *Merowinger.*[3] For as a result of the loss of reality, human action turns into a phenomenon that can no longer be understood by means of such reality-charged categories as "destiny." Even the term *action* misses its mark, since action in the sense of classical ethics is oriented by means of the existential tension toward the ground, while action minus this orientation becomes nonaction. The social advancement of symbols like "activism," "decisionism," "terrorism," and "behavior" is symptomatic for the need to find adequate words for the experience of reality-forsaken, world-immanent conduct in its active and passive varieties. Insofar as political events drop down to the level of unhistorical "nonsense" (madness), it can indeed no longer be interpreted by symbols that have originated in consciousness' center of order and its exegesis; new terms are required in order adequately to describe the

2. Gustave Flaubert, *Le Dictionnaire des idées reçues* (*Oeuvres* vol. II, Pleiade). Karl Kraus, *Die dritte Walpurgisnacht* (Munich 1955), p. 41 ff.

3. Max Frisch, *Biedermann und die Brandstifter* (Frankfurt 1958), p. 9. Heimito von Doderer, *Die Merowinger* (Munich 1962), p. 363.

pneumopathological phenomena of the "loss of reality," which we prefer to the accurate, but fuzzy "nonsense" (madness).

The misunderstanding and dogmatization of a noetic exegesis as a proposition about things cannot be prevented; but it is possible to differentiate the reality represented compactly by the symbol *ousia* to such an extent that the analysis offers few inducements to the dogmatizing disposition.

I refer back to the sentence of Aristotle that the question "What is being?" merges into the question "What is *ousia*?" and to my comment that the "*ousia*" is a matter of reality of "things" that matter-of-factly and convincingly confronts us in the cosmic primary experience. Let us then talk about reality and articulate the area to be covered by the term: Reality (*a*) is not a thing that man confronts but the encompassing reality in which he himself is real as he participates; real (*b*) are the "things" that can be distinguished in the encompassing reality—the gods, men, and so on; real (*c*) is also the participation of things in each other within the encompassing reality. Further, in the case of man—if we for the moment leave aside the questions of bodily reality—participation has the structure of consciousness, so we can speak of consciousness as the sensorium of human participation. In the experiences, recollections, phantasmata, and symbolizations of consciousness arise the images of reality, in which the poles of participation, i.e., the realities of god and world, of other people and of the concretely participating man, find their place. Among the experiences of participation, finally, the noetic one has its special place, in that it elevates to clarity the tension toward the divine ground not merely as the material structure of consciousness but as the fundamental structure of all reality that is not the divine ground itself. As a result, the mythical image of reality that operates with intracosmic things as the ultimate ground must be changed into the philosophical image of the order of being.

Let us pursue the resulting problems in more detail.

Following the language of the preceding paragraph, we must formulate the sentence: A reality, called man, relates itself, within an encompassing reality, through the reality of participation—called consciousness—to the terms of participation as reality. The ambiguity of Aristotle's expression "*ousia*," which we criticized above, seems to return in this sentence as the ambiguity of "reality." And that is no mere appearance; it does indeed return. What, then, have we gained? One could answer that this sentence, in its differentiation, makes it clear why the analysis of existence can express a certain phase of its process only through an ambiguous symbol. The symbol must be ambiguous because every attempt to limit it to one or the other unambiguous meaning would destroy the insight in the structure of reality that the philosopher, within reality, has gained through participation in its process. That insight would be lost if he were to make reality into an object of knowledge from a standpoint outside of reality. Insight into reality is insight from the perspective of man who participates in reality. The term *perspective* must not be understood, or rather misunderstood, in a subjective sense. There is not a multitude of perspectives, but only the one perspective that is determined by the place of man in reality. Insight as reality of consciousness determines the content of the insight as the reality of human participation, as the poles of participation and as the encompassing reality. In a real sense the noetic exegesis thus arrives at the point at which its insight in reality can be expressed adequately only through a symbol referring ambiguously to all dimensions and aspects of reality, in which the exegesis itself, knowing in perspective, really moves. The ambiguity is not the result of sloppy language but rather is required by the noetic insight. The symbol, therefore, though couched in ambiguous language, is noetically unambiguous. It is unambiguous insofar as it is a symbol through which the reality of the exegesis, which produces it, attains transparency of itself for itself. As the expression of a phase of the exegesis, the symbol does not refer to a reality outside of itself; it itself is reality. The Aristotelian symbol *ousia* thus is not objectionable on account of its ambiguity, which rather proves the noetic self-assurance of Aristotle in the treatment of his problem. It is objectionable only insofar as it tends (*a*) to limit reality to the terms of participation and (*b*) within this limited meaning to suggest the mode of being of things in spatio-temporal existence as the model of reality so that it tends to lose the occasion of experience which (*a*) gives noetic unambiguity to the linguistic ambiguity and (*b*) exhaustively determines the content of the perspectival ambiguity.

It is obvious that a situation that is linguistically and noetically so complex can give rise to a number of misunderstandings. It is advisable to anticipate the historically and practically most important of them, two in number:

(1) As we contrast the philosophical image of being to the mythical one of reality, we obviously do not wish to say that it is reality that has changed but rather only our image of reality. In the context of this statement, "reality" becomes a kind of constant given, the structure of which is seen better by the philosopher than by the philomyther. This idea has a solid core, inasmuch as there is indeed a difference of truth between the compact-cosmic and the noetically differentiating experience, in relation to which difference reality appears as a constant. The idea is misunderstood, however, if one makes the metaphor of an "image" too literal, forgetting that "images" are the symbols with the help of which men express their respective experiences of participation. The images are not more or less correct representations of a reality existing as a datum independently of the experience of participation; rather they are more or less adequate expressions of the experiences. Participation is also reality. The difference in truth between two sets of images is immanent to the historical dimension of consciousness. If one overlooks the reality of consciousness, then the following results occur: (*a*) the terms of knowing participation turn into data independent of participation, (*b*) the images and the differential of truth between them turn into events in the time of the world (most suitable for materials of a history of philosophy), and (*c*) participating man turns into a subject of knowledge beyond participation (which is capable of progressing most delightfully from theology to metaphysics to positive science). When the symbols become detached from the experience for the exegesis of which they were created, they become images in a mistaken sense. Then there develop the secondary phenomena of philosophy, e.g., the manipulation of noetic symbols as if they were propositions (this being called metaphysics), also the eternal truths found by philosophy, or the idea of a *philosophia perennis* (sixteenth century), or the quarrel of the isms about the correctness of the images.

(2) Reality is constant in relation to the differential of truths in consciousness. Consciousness, however, is reality of human participation, and this reality is characterized by a presence of experience that puts phases of lower grades of truth behind itself, as the past. Reality, then, is not constant. Just as one can

forget the changeability of reality—we call it history—because of its constancy, so one can forget the constancy of reality because of its experienced changeability. The differentiating experience, either noetic or pneumatic, can be so intensive that the man to whom it occurs feels transformed into a new being. The new image of the world resulting from the experience can be misunderstood as a new world; and the process of change itself can turn into a structural datum of reality that can be extrapolated into the future. As that changeability that is experienced in participation mutates into images of a changeable reality comprising the poles of participation, we have the roots of the phenomena of metastatic beliefs: The gradualistic idea of infinite progress in the time of the world, the apocalyptic visions of the catastrophe of an old world and its *metastasis* into a new one resulting from divine intervention; the revolutionary ideas of a *metastasis* manipulated by human action; and so on. Since, in spite of the changeability within the realm of participation, reality does remain constant, the metastatic outbursts are followed by disillusionment: The social dwindling away and dying out of metastatic beliefs; the turning from metastatic exuberance to the necessities of everyday life; the retreat of the adepts from the stubborn, unchanging world into underground sectarianism; Isaiah's "remnant"; pietistic communities that remain aloof from the corrupted world; the disappointment of the expectation of *parousia;* the decline of the revolutionary momentum aiming at world conquest to co-existence; and so on.

The reality of consciousness is not unconscious, but through symbolic expressions in various degrees of illumination it relates to reality, either to its own reality of participation, or the poles of participation. The images themselves thus are reality, the reality of consciousness, but they are not the reality to which they relate themselves in knowledge. Consciousness is always consciousness of something. There would be no possibility for misunderstood, imaginary, or intentionally false images if consciousness were not a process of relating itself to reality through images. We are here touching the origin of all objectivizations of consciousness itself.

The problem arises at the beginning of the noetic experience and its symbolization. The intentional character of participating consciousness becomes a central theme in the generation of the philosophers about 500 B.C. Parmenides says it is the same thing to think (*noein*) and to be (*einai*) (B 3); and Heraclitus uses the term *logos* in a double meaning of exegetic thinking and explained reality (B 1). A trias of being-thinking-symbol is a reality identical with itself and, at the same time, analytically kept distinct as being, thought of being, and expression of thinking as well as of being. Noetic consciousness is the luminosity in which thinking about reality finds its language, and in this linguistic expression it again relates itself to reality. The enthusiasm of the newly experienced tension of man toward his ground, and the will to knowledge about the divine ground, which lightens up reality as a convincing "Is!" (*esti*) also effaces a good many things that should have been distinguished,—above all the limit between the reality of participation and the reality of its poles. Precisely this exuberance of Parmenides is characteristic also for the treatment of noesis in Aristotle, even though Plato had already progressed further in the differentiation of the area of erotic tension. For in Aristotle we find this sentence: "Thought (*nous*) thinks (*noei*) about itself because it shares the nature (*metalepsis*) of the object of thought (*noeton*); for it becomes an object of thought in coming into contact (*thigannon*) with and thinking (*noon*) its objects, so that thought and object of thought are the same. For that which is capable of receiving (*dektikon*) the object of thought, i.e., the essence (*ousia*), is thought (*nous*)" (*Met.* 1972b20–22). The existential tension in Parmenides is already a differentiated reality as it is for Aristotle: the trip from night to light, the tensions of desire and being-led, which Parmenides describes at the beginning of his poem, correspond strictly to Aristotle's analysis of existence in *Metaphysics* I and II. In Aristotle, however, the will to knowledge is so exuberant that consciousness is in danger of drawing into itself the reality of the ground, a reality to which consciousness in its participation relates itself and that, for that reason, it also keeps at objective distance. The boundary between image and reality becomes fuzzy. Aristotle does indeed push his image of participation in the divine, through what in man is divine, to the point where he maintains that the activity (*energeia*) of participation, which man, tied down by his body, attains only in rare moments of the highest bliss, is a perpetual happiness in God's reality. It is no accident that we find the above-mentioned quotation from Aristotle in Hegel's gnostic-dialectical speculation as the great peroration of the *Encyclopedia*. The occasion on which the intentionality of consciousness becomes a theme in the classical noesis is also the occasion for saying something more about the reality of the divine ground than a strict exegesis of the existential tension would permit.

The intentionality of consciousness as such would not conduce to the fallacious images of reality if man's participation were an automatism that produced in consciousness infallibly correct pictures of reality and nothing but correct pictures. Consciousness, however, has a dimension of freedom in the design of images of reality in which are found such disparate phenomena as mythopoeic freedom, artistic creation, gnostic and alchemistic speculation, the private world view of liberal citizens, and the constructions of ideological systems. What concerns us in this wide range of problems is only the possibility of a disparity between form and content of reality. In this disparity the phenomena of the loss of reality originate.

From the knowing anxiety of ignorance, through the desiring knowledge and knowing questioning, man can advance to the optimum consciousness of his existential tension toward the ground and thereby to an understanding of the structure of his consciousness. He is, however, free either to enter this quest with but little interest, or to be content with partial success, or to accept falsehood as truth, or to refuse the quest and even resist it, without ceasing to be participating man and as such to have consciousness. There are easy-going people like the couple whom Doderer describes in his *Merowinger:* "They belonged to the multitude of the happy-without-history endowed with the well-being of born atheists, who do not necessarily conduct themselves without piety, and mostly also go to church."[4] They, too, are human; they, too, have consciousness; they, too, design images of reality—even if of questionable quality. Human consciousness—let us definitely state this point—has reality in the form of participation and the material structure of *ratio* even when the existential tension is low and the reality realized

4. Doderer, *Merowinger*, p. 353.

by consciousness correspondingly small. By reality we mean, in this context, the previously outlined perspective that is determined by man's place in reality. This perspective is the form intended by the images, regardless of whether the content is rich or sparse, whether compact-oblique or differentiated-clear, whether it stems from man's experienced tension toward the ground, from the experienced revolt against the ground, or from the velleities of the passions. Whenever the desire of knowledge is sufficiently intensive to elaborate somewhat comprehensive images of reality there occurs a filling-in of the perspective form of reality. This relation between images and form of reality exists in fact, as has been implicitly found in situations in which comparisons are unavoidable. Such discoveries have been made, sometimes with chagrin, as when Christians discovered pagan parallels to their own verities of faith and their cults; sometimes with pleasure, as when secularist interpreters of the Qumran texts thought it possible to diminish the importance of Christ through the earlier figure of the "teacher of righteousness"; sometimes with the erudite apparatus of cultural diffusion, as when astonishingly similar images appear in different civilizations; sometimes with psychological cleverness, as when parallels are explained by way of archetypes of the collective unconscious. As one can see, the insight into the form of reality is not without importance for the economy of science, for it eliminates the element of astonishment and renders superfluous occasional theories for the explanation of parallels. Further, the insight provides general rules for the investigation of image-designs, like the following: Images of reality must be examined for their form of reality; when the pattern of form has become clear, the contents must be examined; schemes of reality that present themselves as systems must be examined for the intellectual tricks with the help of which the nonsystematic form of reality is closed to make up a system; particularly one must not accept the demand of adherents of a system that their premises are the condition for understanding the system, for precisely systems can be understood only by interpretations "from without," i.e., interpretations beginning with the form of reality; when the investigation deals with a cosmological society expressing its compact experience of reality through myths, the myths about the different areas of reality must be carefully collected and classified in order to gain a somewhat correct idea of the image of reality of that society; and so on. Finally, the insight makes it possible to formulate more precisely the problem of the loss of reality: There is no other reality than that of which we have experience. When a person refuses to live in existential tension toward the ground, or if he rebels against the ground, refusing to participate in reality and in this way to experience his own reality as man, it is not the "world" that is thereby changed but rather he who loses contact with reality and in his own person suffers a loss of reality. Since that does not make him cease to be man, and since his consciousness continues to function within the form of reality, he will generate *ersatz* images of reality in order to obtain order and direction for his existence and action in the world. He then lives in a "second reality," as this phenomenon is called, since Musil's *Man without Qualities*. The *ersatz* images can draw their content from various sources, the most important ones being the lust for wealth, power, or sex, as well as the *superbia vitae* positing the autonomous Ego in place of the ground. The effects of a loss of reality are pneumopathological disturbances in the existential order of the respective person, and, if life in the "second reality" becomes socially dominant, such massive disturbances of social order as we have witnessed.

In our time the loss of reality is not only registered by revolutionary violence, noisy propaganda, bloody executions, indifferent complacence, or dull apathy. It is also experienced and suffered as loss. The awareness of suffering a shadowy life, however, is the low point of turning around, the *periagoge,* from where the ascent from the cave to the light can begin. Our time is characterized not only by extreme losses of reality but also by efforts to fill the form of reality again with the reality of existential tension. The indications—and more than indications—of this movement are the insights into the nature of the second reality, the grotesque and imbecility of this time, into the fraud of systems and intellectual swindle, into the *ersatz* character of images of reality without reality, with their origin in the refusal to apperceive reality. Let us add to this list a reference to Albert Camus, whose work is a prototype of existential catharsis. *The Myth of Sisyphus* (1942) is still governed by an experience of the absurdity of existence that comes from the area of Dostoevsky's psychology of the revolutionary. Suicide appears as the only possible response to absurdity. In *The Rebel* (1951) Camus accomplished a second phase of the ascent, as he accepts the

endurance in uncertainty about the meaning of life as his burden and seeks to keep the tension free from dogmatic *ersatz*
realities, be they theological, metaphysical, or ideological. The
third phase of his meditative *progressus*, of which he hoped to
gain the freedom of creation,[5] was shortened by his untimely
death. More than one of his formulations, however, indicate
the goal toward which he was moving. On the concluding pages
of his work on rebellion, he made clear its character in such
clarity that it had to collapse: The rebel cannot cope with the
order of his life and thus replaces the presence of life by his
dream of the future. These men "despair of personal freedom
and dream of a strange freedom of the species; reject solitary
death and give the name of immortality to a vast collective
agony. They no longer believe in the things that exist in the
world and in living man; the secret of Europe is that it no
longer loves life." Instead of the man who lives here and now in
the tension toward the ground, there is the Ego without a present arrogating to himself power over life and death of his
fellow beings, under the pretense of justice and politics. "For
want of something better to do, they deified themselves and
their misfortunes began; these gods have their eyes put out."
The vision of healing: Rebellion has attained its meridian of
thought—men refuse to be gods and thus relinquish the unlimited power to inflict death. The new rule of ethics, the sole
"original rule of life today": "to learn to live and to die and, in
order to be a man, to refuse to be a god."[6] In other words, the
murder of God, the preoccupation of the European intellectual
from the Marquis de Sade to Hegel and Nietzsche, and which
logically led to the murder of man, is reversed. A contemporary
note in the *Carnets* makes clear that Camus's self-analysis had
already gone beyond the formulations of *The Rebel:* "Not
morality but fulfillment. And there is no fulfillment other than
that of love, meaning the renunciation of self and dying to the
world. Going on to the end. Disappear. To dissolve oneself in
love. It will be the power of love which then creates, rather than
myself. To lose oneself. To dismember oneself. To deny oneself in the fulfillment and the passion of truth."[7] It seems to
have been more difficult, although understandable for

5. Albert Camus, *Carnets* II (Paris 1964), p. 324 ff.
6. Albert Camus, *L'Homme révolté* (Paris 1951), p. 376 ff.
7. Camus, *Carnets* II, p. 309 ff.

everyone who knows the milieu of intellectual terror, to have courage for the theoretical consequences of the new insight from love. I quote a touching remark from *The Rebel:* "The analysis of rebellion leads at least to a suspicion that there is a human nature, as the Greeks thought, and contrary to the postulates of modern thought."[8] If one does not take "human nature" in this sentence to mean that kind of information that textbooks on philosophy always offer, but rather take it to mean active life, ordered by the loving tension of existence to the divine ground, in which tension the autonomous self dissolves itself, one would not miss the direction of the progressus. It is remarkable how young people understand Camus, taking him as model and guide in the analysis of existence that today is the burden of everybody who, resisting the time, seeks to regain his reality as man. At more than one American university, I could observe that the imitation of Camus's meditation has become, for numerous students, the method of catharsis. In this way they rid themselves of the intellectual pressure of either the leftist ideologues or the neo-Thomists or existentialist theologians, according to their respective milieu. The great effect of Camus's work seems to stem from his inexorability in the endeavor for purity as he divests himself of *ersatz* realities.

The analysis of consciousness could start from the classical noesis, following it to an insight into (*a*) the material structure that we called *ratio,* (*b*) luminosity of consciousness and (*c*) the historical gradation of truth. At that point it had to go beyond Aristotle in order to introduce the further problems (*d*) of the perspective of reality, (*e*) the form of the intentional object, and (*f*) the form of reality of consciousness, as well as that of the content of reality and the loss of reality. The two phases of the analysis were required by the historical change of the noetic situation from antiquity to modernity. In the classical noesis the point was to differentiate consciousness as the center of human order, in opposition to the cosmic primary experience and to the compact symbolism of the myth. In the modern noesis the point is to re-establish consciousness in opposition to a dogmatism bare of reality. The two efforts are phases in the histori-

8. Camus, *L'Homme révolté,* p. 28.

cal continuum of consciousness, inasmuch as (1) the incomplete condition of the classical noesis set up the development of post-classical dogmatism to which we are in opposition today, and (2) we can struggle out of the misery of dogmatism only by returning to the classical noesis and to try to solve its unfinished problems. Let us, then, formulate the unfinished problem as it presents itself now, at the end of our own efforts.

The classical attempt was essentially successful but was not followed through to the end required by its own beginnings. The noetic experience led to the dissociation of the cosmos of primary experience, "full of gods," into the dedivinized world and the divine ground of being. In the same process human consciousness comes into view as the reality of experience and the source of the images of reality. The insight of the noetic experience thus encompasses all at once two areas of reality, that of consciousness and that of the poles of participation, that can be distinguished from each other but combine in the reality of noetic experience to the one truth of the perspective of reality. The difficulties arise from the "all at once." For the consciousness of the ground cannot attain the optimum clarity of insight into its logos without gaining insight into the poles of participation and their relation to each other, in which process the mythical image of reality changes into the philosophical image of being. On the other hand, there is the danger that the new truth about the poles turns into propositions about a reality supposedly independent of the perspective of noetic experience. These propositions, in turn, would induce alternative propositions unmotivated by the noetic experience, propositions concerning the supposedly same reality. If propositions about the poles of noetic participation, i.e., about man, his divine ground, and the world, are detached from the perspective of reality of the noetic experience, they come out not only as false propositions about the poles but also destroy the existential tension of consciousness and thus the center of human order. There then ensue the phenomena of the loss of reality and spiritual disorder. In the classical noesis, as it was just detaching itself from the myth, the truth of the perspective of reality was so much taken for granted that the problem, as we have here sketched it, did not become a theme. The speculations about *ousia* and *nous* set up the postclassical dogmatism not because they themselves had left behind the noetic experience and lost its reality but because the analysis of the desire for knowledge developed directly into the knowledge of man and of the divine ground itself. The areas of participation and of its poles were neither adequately distinguished from each other, nor was their connection adequately clarified. Thus it was possible to forget the noetic experience and to make the symbols it had produced into instruments of intellectual games in the context of utterly different contents of reality, just because the experience itself as the ordering reality of man had not become a central theme. It is therefore incumbent on us to secure the reality and function of the experience by clarifying the connection between it and the symbolism relating to the poles of noetic participation.

CHAPTER NINE

Linguistic Indices and Type-Concepts

Consciousness is reality, but it is not one of the realities that the cosmic primary experience discerned in the encompassing reality. Consciousness is the experience of participation, participation of man in his ground of being. In the optimum luminosity of the noetic experience it is, then, knowledge of a relation between the things of the primary experience; and in its full meaning, it is a knowledge of order concerning reality. The noetic knowledge of relationship, however, is not the type of knowledge of the natural sciences, observing things "from without," but the experience of a relation "from within." The relationship is experienced through the reality of living within it. Since "things," in this case man, do not cease to be what they are as they experience life within the relationship, life within the relationship belongs also to the objective reality of the thing. More yet: Since the relationship is participation in the ground of being, the ground of being, insofar as it can be experienced, extends into the reality of man. As we move in the relationship in meditation, and linguistically express our movements, we speak also of the realities that participate in each other and express insights into them. Knowledge of participation becomes knowledge of man and of his ground.

There is no need, at this point, to continue the meditation. What has been said is sufficient to make clear what was meant by our expression "nonobjective reality." We are compelled to speak in terms of objects because consciousness intends the form of objects, but the linguistic terms do not have the character of concepts or definitions relating to things. They have no meaning apart from the movement in the area of participation. In order to avoid misunderstandings, it is therefore preferable to call them linguistic indices of the meditative movement. The terms we used in our analysis are examples of such linguistic indices: consciousness of the ground; openness to the ground;

existential tension toward the ground; poles of the tension; participation from within, from without, reality; perspective of reality; and so on. To the class of indices there also belong certain terms that in vulgar discussion play a considerable role as "concepts." For instance, neither an immanent world nor a transcendent being "exist"; rather these terms are indices that we assign to areas of reality of the primary experience, as the noetic experience dissociates the cosmos into existing things and their divine ground of being. The two indices are correlated in the meditative movement; they do not designate "things" about the "existence" of which one could dispute, but they designate the relation of order between the divine and nondivine areas of reality that in the light of noetic experience is seen as "truth." The term *man* also belongs to the indices, insofar as by "man" we mean the immanent pole of the existential tension toward the ground. For this reason there are no "philosophical anthropologies" through which man could be understood "correctly" as a world-immanent being. For "philosophy" itself is a linguistic index of the meditative movement toward the ground, so that to speak philosophically of man means to understand him as a reality that in participation transcends toward the ground. There are experiences of "loss of reality" and "alienation," but we have no experience of a man who has not the form of reality of a transcending consciousness. Philosophical anthropologies construing man as a non-transcending, world-immanent being thus belong to the class of dogmatic derailments with the help of which "second realities" are constructed.

The symbols of noesis are the linguistic indices of a movement of participation. They primarily illuminate this movement as such, but they cannot illuminate it without also expressing insights into the participating realities. We are in the "in-between," Plato's *metaxy*, which is not an empty space between immanent and transcendent objects, but rather the area of mutual participation of divine and human reality. In contradistinction to the cosmic primary experience, the noetic experience renders conscious the tension toward the ground of being as the core of the quest for the origin of order. The insights of the noesis should therefore be characterized as follows: The noetic experience does not yield knowledge of a reality hitherto unknown but makes possible differentiating insight into the reality that hitherto has been experienced as compact. Moreover, the new insight does not quantitatively increase our knowledge about objects abiding unchanged in themselves but introduces a change in the mode of knowledge. Finally, this change originates in changes in the reality of participation. The insights of the noesis concerning the realities of God, man, and world arise from an event in the stream of participation; they cannot be made into a "truth" independent of the event. The event, however, is the new intelligibility of participation for itself; it is the event in the history of being through which the logos of participation appears in the luminosity of consciousness.

Some corollaries of the characterization are required:

(1) The noetic experience brings about a change in the mode of knowledge insofar as (*a*) it makes transparent the material structure of consciousness which we have called *ratio* and thereby provides (*b*) rational criteria for the correct symbolization of the poles of participation, i.e., man and the divine ground of being. By contrast to the truths of non-noetic participation, the truth of noesis has the character of rationality and science. This sentence does not open a debate on what is science, and whether the noetic indices can rightfully claim the title of science for themselves, but rather establishes the historical fact that the Platonic-Aristotelian noesis has developed the indices science (*episteme*) and theory (*theoria*) in order to express the character of their mode of knowledge and to distinguish it from the non-noetic modes of knowledge as the *doxai*, beliefs or opinions. "Science" is not determined by the mystery of a preexistent definition, it rather discovers itself as the knowledge of the structure of reality, when consciousness historically attains the illumination of itself and its ratio. Particularly one should also note that "world" is also an index of consciousness and that noesis was the first to free the autonomous structure of the world for scientific investigation, as it critically removed mythical, revelatory, and ideological hypotheses of truth. Modern natural science, having freed itself well-nigh completely of such mortgages, is science not because we recognize it as such by convention but because the methods it uses to investigate the structure of the world are compatible with the *ratio* of noesis. This relation between the measure and that which is to be measured, by virtue of which the claim of an enterprise to be sci-

ence must be adjudicated in the light of the *ratio* of noesis, is not reversible. The popular assumption, for instance, that mathematical natural science is *the* model of science and that an enterprise not using its methods cannot have the character of science, is not a proposition of natural science or of any science but merely an ideological dogma stemming from modern scientism.

(2) The area of reality of participation is the area of the changes in being that we call history; in the area of these changes the noetic experience is the event through which we have become conscious of the history of participation as such. Just as the new mode of knowledge of noesis frees "the world" for the investigation of its autonomous structure, it also assigns the index of "history" as a field of rational structure. For when consciousness gains insight into the *ratio* as its material structure, it shows that all experiences, even the non-noetic ones, are attempts to gain true insight into the existential tension toward the ground. When the conscious criterion of *ratio* makes it possible to characterize the degree of rationality of the other truths and to judge them critically, history, until then only imperfectly transparent, becomes radically transparent with a view to its *ratio*. In order to meet the requirements of the new tasks of knowledge, concepts of types are formed, of the kind mentioned in the course of our analysis. I refer to Plato's analysis of the field of history by means of the types of *daimonios aner, thnetos,* and *amathes,* further to Plato's concepts of *philodoxos* and *sophistes,* Aristotle's *philosophos* and *philomythos,* and finally the series of such modern concepts of types as compact and differentiated experience, the cosmic primary experience, the noetic and revelatory experience of transcendence, the *parekbasis,* or derailment, into dogmatism, the metastatic, apocalyptic, and gnostic experiences, the revolutionary experiences, and so on.

(3) The symbols of this list should preferably be called "concepts" in order to distinguish them from the indices of the exegesis, in which the noetic movement of participation attained transparency for itself and became linguistically communicable. For although type-concepts can be developed only in consequence of the exegesis, they do not interpret the noetic experience itself but refer to phenomena beyond its area. Here we again encounter the problem that occupied us at the begin-

ning, of the noetic interpretation pushing all other interpretations of order into the role of "objects." Since it now comes up again, we are in a position to distinguish more precisely the several meanings of "object" that are involved when we talk of these tensions in political reality. The first meaning of "object" is given by the reality of consciousness and its need to express itself through objects. The second meaning is given by the historical dimension of consciousness in which the desire for knowledge advances and leaves behind it superseded truths that become "objects" in the past. The temporal dimension of the differentiation of truth, in which history constitutes itself, takes place within the consciousness of a concrete person. Therefore this second layer of meaning cannot fully cover the phenomena to which the type concepts refer. For while these concepts refer to phenomena pertaining to the historical differences of truths in the consciousness, the phenomena are spread over the consciousness of a multitude of men. The third meaning of "object," which we must now add, stems from the spreading of consciousness to a multitude of men in discrete physical existences. The experienced phenomena, which we apprehend by the means of type-concepts, may be characterized as follows: The phenomena pertain to the nonobjective area of participation, but they do not belong to the reality of the noetic consciousness that interprets itself in objective form; while they do not belong to the things of the spatio-temporal world, they are related to that world because they are experienced by men in spatio-temporal existence. The peculiar "objective" quality of the phenomena, their specific distance to the noetic consciousness that apperceives them as if they were objects, stems from the fact that consciousness is not *intellectus unus,* i.e., not a single cosmic, divine, or human consciousness, but the discrete consciousness of concrete men.

(4) In order to avoid misunderstandings, it should be noted that consciousness is real discretely but that the field of history does not for that reason dissolve into a field of persons of whom everyone has a private consciousness for himself, in the classical sense of *idiotes.* For consciousness is the existential tension toward the ground, and the ground is for all men the one and only divine ground of being. History becomes a structurally intelligible field of reality by virtue of the presence of the one ground in which all men participate, no matter how different

may be their experiences of participation. The structure of the field is the structure of reality. It cannot be dissolved psychologically into opinions, views, "projections," "legitimizing values," of particular people. Finally, may it be noted that any construction of history as the unfolding of *the* consciousness—whether it be a consciousness of humanity, God's consciousness, history's consciousness, or an absolute mind—is incompatible with the discrete reality of consciousness. Dialectic constructions of an *eidos* of history using this or similar tricks to establish a system are noetically without meaning, even though they may have their place as symbols in the experiential complex of the *libido dominandi*. Since we are human beings and not disembodied consciousness, the field of history has no other meaning for us except the one recognizable through the *ratio* of *noesis* and the development of type-concepts relating to the phenomena of participation. Should we attempt to transcend our own transcending toward the ground and to outstrip our perspectival knowledge of reality in the endeavor to possess reality in a kind of absolute knowledge, we derail into gnosticism.

(5) The previous passages have dealt with the analysis of the object-quality in the dimension of history. Each of the three meanings, or layers of meaning, that we had to distinguish is additionally complicated by the problems of the existential tension and its poles. For consciousness is a reality in which divine and human reality participate in each other without merging into one, so consciousness relates to the participating realities, the poles of tension, as objects. We already mentioned the possible misunderstandings arising from the objectivization of the poles into things existing independently of the tension of participation. At this point we should further clarify, by means of examples, the interaction of the two dimensions of the matter, i.e., the historical and the material, in the development of type-concepts. (*a*) Regarding the interaction within the area of the noetic exegesis, let us recall Aristotle's analysis: His quest for the truth of the areas of reality, the *ousiai*, had such a momentum that the exegesis of the noetic experience itself became something like an "introduction" to the main part, i.e., to the truth of the divine ground and man's relation to it, which incompleteness provided the occasions for a later dogmatization. (*b*) The interest in the truth of the ground was still more dominant in Aristotle's criticism of the aetiological series,

which, compared to his own knowledge of participation, appeared as untruth that was about to fall away into the past. Again, the problem of the ground as object intrudes to such an extent that the criticism of past truth as untruth could appear as a matter of logical argument, causing the motivation of the two symbolisms by two experiences of participation to disappear from view. (*c*) Regarding the interaction in the area of discrete consciousness, I refer only briefly to the polemics of our time in which the adherents of different dogmatisms berate each other for the untruth of their differing truths without giving any attention to the motivating experiences or even without having ever heard about the problem of experiences.

(6) Other examples could be mentioned, in which the reality of experience and the truth of the realities to which experience relates are better balanced. In the case of Aristotle, for instance, one might remember not so much his criticism of the aetiological series but rather his understanding of the experience of the *philomythos*. Still, the cases in which the interest in the truth of the poles of participation predominates seem to be most valuable. While they do not obscure the problem of objects, they represent the dominant form of conceptualizing types, in the struggle about the truth of political reality. Thus they point to a problem that has been repeatedly touched but not yet treated thoroughly: The formation of type-concepts, on the part of rival truths in the process of history, is not a privilege of noesis alone. In the introduction to this part we mentioned that while noesis pushed the non-noetic interpretations into the role of objects, that procedure could also be reversed. Every symbol expressing an experience can become the premise of a "position" entailing the classification of other truths. This can go as far as the grotesque "general suspicion of ideology," for consciousness has the form of reality-intention as well as the form of object-intention even when the perspective of reality has not been adequately differentiated or when the consciousness' content of reality is defective. Phenomena of history will be typified as forms of reality even when history has not come into the full light of consciousness as the real dimension of participation. We must therefore distinguish between noetic and nonnoetic types and may speak of type-concepts in the strict sense only where the historical phenomenon of participation is fully typified. This requires not only the fullness of symbols but also

of the experiences for the expression of which the symbols were created. For history is the history of participation, and the symbols referring to the poles of participation are the indices of experience. When the indices of experiences are made into an autonomous object of history, the result is the *parekbasis* of doxography, or the "history of ideas."

CHAPTER TEN

The Tensions in the Reality of Knowledge

The noetic exegesis lifts the logos of participation into the light of consciousness by interpreting the noetic experience of participation. Noetic knowledge, therefore, is not abstract knowledge obtained by gathering cases of participation and examining them for general characteristics. Rather, it is concrete knowledge of participation in which a man's desire for knowledge is experienced as a movement toward the ground that is being moved by the ground. In this movement the divine ground of being is illuminated as the ground of man and world. With this sentence, the accent of our analysis shifts from reality to knowledge.

We mentioned before the trias of being-thought-symbol as a single identity and yet as distinct in itself. As we interpret this trias, there results not only the equation "thought and symbol is being" but also the equation "being is thought and symbol." While we have up to now insisted that the noetic exegesis is the reality of participation, we now emphasize that the reality of participation is knowledge. Noesis lifts a reality that is knowledge into the light of consciousness. This reality is knowledge even when it is not fully conscious of its own character, i.e., even when it is not knowledge about knowledge. The desire for knowledge is the reality not only of the noesis but of every experience of participation, as Aristotle already observed. In every case it engenders symbols that express the truth of the divine, the human, and the world, as well as the relations of the areas of reality to each other. It is always man's existential transcending toward the ground, even when the ground does not become conscious as the transcendent pole of the desire. Noesis, then, contributes no more than its rendering intelligible the logos of consciousness, which belongs to the reality of participating knowledge even in the absence of noesis.

This is not said to belittle the contribution of noesis. But we must now analyze the reality of knowledge, and the reality of participating knowledge is historically so rich that it goes far beyond the *ratio*. I am thinking particularly about the experience of faith, love, and hope, which already Heraclitus recognized and distinguished as sources of knowledge. It is thus in order to speak not only of a *cognitio rationis* but also of *cognitiones fidei, amoris, et spei*. Furthermore, the *cognitiones* in the reality of knowledge are woven into a complex that is knowledge only as a whole. Neither is there a *ratio* independent of the other modes of knowledge nor the latter without the former. In the case of Plato's and Aristotle's noesis, we have noted the background of the cosmic primary experience and of the mystery cults. On the basis of the extant texts, we can be more specific, beyond those general remarks: Out of a comprehensive complex of knowledge, the classical noesis differentiates the consciousness of the ground by way of love of God, of being moved by grace of the ground to the point of feeling compelled to "turn around" from being lost in the world toward inclination to the ground, of experiences of the shadow-like character of worldly existence, of the world as a prison and foreign land, of experiences of light shining in darkness, of being-led on the right way, and so on. This complex of knowledge is effective as a whole, even though noesis isolates the component of *ratio*, differentiating it from the whole. This rich spectrum of modalities of knowledge, in which the rational modality is only one among several, unfolds its living insight as it is encompassed and penetrated by the experience of death. Plato characterized the whole of this knowledge in the three symbols of *eros, dike,* and *thanatos:* the searching and knowing love for the divine ground, the right order of life, and death as the widest of all perspectives in which the art of measure, the *techne metretike,* must weigh the rightness of action.

Man's existence thus is ordered by knowledge—even by rational knowledge, since the *ratio* is one of the threads in the web of knowledge—even when noesis has not differentiated the logos of consciousness. As long as the knowledge of order contains the *ratio* only in a compact manner, it is lacking the explicitly rational control. Wherever noesis happens, it therefore appears with the authority of *ratio,* which criticizes the conventional symbols and truths, either the symbols of the cosmic primary experience that drop away into the past, or the symbols of revelation insofar as they are not kept under rational control by the pneumatics themselves, or the respectively personal experience of a philosopher in which the *ratio* is merely a component, or the derailments in the wake of the noesis. On the one hand, then, *ratio* is but a component in the reality of knowledge of participation, while noesis, as it interprets consciousness, is an important area of differentiated knowledge of reality but no substitute for its full richness. On the other hand, *ratio* illuminates the structure of reality and thus turns into an instrument of criticism as soon as noetic experience has differentiated it, the criticism being able to examine the truths of the non-noetic experiences for their compatibility with the knowledge of structure that is proper to noesis.

The last sentence formulated the crux of the tension between noetic and non-noetic interpretations of order, as we remarked at the outset. We said there that the noetic experience arises late in history so that, wherever it happens, it runs into the non-noetic knowledge of social order. The non-noetic interpretations remain the form of society's self-interpretation even after the rise of noesis, and there are no societies whose self-interpretation is exclusively noetic. We must deal in more detail with some of the problems of this tension in the field of political reality, which we recognize as tension in the field of knowing participation.

In order to clarify the premises of the problems, we first recall the three main phases in the process of tension which we have mentioned repeatedly but so far only incidentally:

(1) The first phase is the Hellenic one. Vis-à-vis the declining myth and the *parekbasis* of sophism, the classical noesis appears with the double claim, on the one hand, of having filled the existential tension again with the content of reality, and, on the other hand, of having drawn a differentiated and true image of the realities God, man, and world, and their relations to each other. The attempt to restore and save the reality of order in the framework of the polis and, beyond it, of an Hellenic federation, failed and was superseded by imperialistic expansion. After Aristotle there was no great flowering of philosophy or a new noetic order of the polis; rather the city states were drawn into the power sphere of the ecumenic empires, while on the spiritual plane Alexander's cosmic imperial religion expressed

the order intended by his conquests. Noesis then derailed into the dogmatism of the schools, and that dogmatism in turn provoked the phenomenon of skepticism, with Sextus Empiricus collecting its arsenal of arguments.

(2) The dogmatism of the schools is the *parekbasis* of a noesis that in turn had differentiated itself vis-à-vis the myth. This phenomenon became the representative of noesis in the second phase of tensions, the Judaeo-Christian tension to the pneumatic experiences of revelation. The noetic experience differentiates the consciousness of the ground vis-à-vis the cosmic primary experience and thereby lifts into the light of consciousness not only the logos of consciousness but also the transcending of man. In the presence of revelation, however, it only needs to stress thematically the logos of a very intensive consciousness of transcendence fed by pneumatic sources of knowledge. In the Hellenic complex, noesis finds itself in opposition to the compact myth and the derailment of sophism. In the Christian phase, it enters into an amalgamate with the Hebrew and Christian truth of revelation, an amalgamate that, as theology, was socially and historically most successful. On the Hebrew side, this was accomplished by Philo of Alexandria; on the Christian side, by the Church Fathers. This combination with revelation has had unfortunate results for noesis. Since Philo, the theologians sought to assign to philosophy the role of theology's handmaiden. That was understandable, for the theologians saw the fullness of truth about God, man, and the world given by revelation, so philosophy needed to perform only the service of constructing the framework of *ratio* for revealed truth. In this relationship, the critical function of noesis in radically freeing the areas of the world and history could not become fully effective, since the transformation of noetic symbols into concepts of dogmatic metaphysics had weakened the authenticity of noetic insight as it is given only in the process of the exegesis. Not that noesis was deprived of any function; but its most significant achievement was the development of an optimum-rational *doctrina Christiana,* in opposition to pneumatic truths of lower rationality, the so-called heresies. The limitations of its critical effectiveness, however, became obvious where the freeing of the realities of world and history was concerned. One can observe these limitations in the conflict of modern natural science with ecclesiastical authorities and also

in the conflicts of the historians with the socially dominant orthodoxy. Hegel still was compelled to be cautious when his dates of oriental history threatened to outstrip the orthodox date of the world's creation.

(3) As philosophy struggled to maintain itself in opposition to theology in the second phase, it retained the form of dogmatism in which philosophy had entered the Judaeo-Christian realm of truth. This play of dogmatic position and opposition has remained the dominant form of self-understanding for the order of Western civilization into the modern period. When skepticism, enlightenment, and positivism rebelled against the older dogmatism, attention was again drawn to the experiences for the expression of which the symbols of the truth of order were created, but the process did not lead to a decisive renewal of noesis. After dogmatic theology there came dogmatic metaphysics, and, following that, the equally dogmatic ideology. Comte's "three phases of history" have something to be said for them, if one remembers that the *philosophie positive* is a case of the third dogmatism. Unlike the classical noesis, today's noesis does not find itself in opposition to myth and sophism, but in quite another situation of resistance against the dogmatisms, especially the ideological ones. This situation determines the questions of the tension of reality which must now be discussed.

Noesis cannot do more than lift into the light of consciousness the material structure of *ratio* contained in the reality of the knowledge of participation. Where there is no active participation, there can be no rational consciousness that could be differentiated. This sentence aims at the crux of the situation that has arisen in hundreds of years of dogmatomachy. I shall try to lay bare the layers of the problem.

(1) The symbols of ideological dogmatism dominating the contemporary thought of Western societies do not express the reality of knowledge but the rebellion against it. They do not attempt to draw men into participation by persuasion; rather, they constitute a language of obsession designed to prevent the contact with reality, a language developed by men who have closed themselves against the ground. The access to consciousness as man's center of order is blocked massively by the ideologies of Positivism, Marxism, historism, scientism, behaviorism, also by means of psychologizing and sociologizing,

by world-intentionalistic methodologies and phenomenologies. For in the symbolism of the rebellions one cannot find the logos of the reality of knowledge, unless it be in the mode of second reality which is present even in the rebellion and its symbols, but which can be recognized as such only from the reality of knowledge. The nihilistic rebellion cannot be overcome on its own level of experiences and symbols, for instance, by means of a criticism of ideology, culture, or the times, as attempted by intellectuals who no longer feel easy in their situation. Such attempts can lead only to a confused stirring around in the nothingness of lost reality. The non-noetic thought about order of the kind that rebellion produces offers no point of contact to the noesis.

(2) This formulation of the problem seems to show the way to a solution: Whoever has had enough of rebellion against the ground and wishes again to think rationally needs only to turn around and toward that reality against which the symbols of rebellion aggress. It seems that the rebellion itself can become the guideline for the seeker, inasmuch as that against which it rebels is precisely that which he is seeking. The turning away and turning around is indeed the *sine qua non* for finding the way from rebellion to reality; the *periagoge* must in any case be performed. If one, however, simply follows rebellion as a guideline, one finds the desire for knowledge again blocked, for the rebellion aims not directly at the reality of knowledge but rather at its forms of decay, i.e., against the theological and metaphysical dogmatisms. These older dogmatisms, which we first encounter as we turn around, are closer to reality than the rebellion against the ground, even though they have the character of a *parekbasis*. We must not forget, though, that they, too, suffer from a kind of loss of reality which has provoked the ideological rebellion since the eighteenth century, and that, on the other hand, the rebellion has freed socially effective areas of the world, society, and history that the social oppression of orthodoxy sought to keep under cover. The rebellion was a historical accomplishment in the service of noesis even though its *hybris* has buried the source of noesis in the tension to the ground underneath ideological rubble; the accomplishment, though, cannot be undone. There have been attempts of return, motivated by the totalitarian climax of the rebellion, but

these attempts could not go beyond the older dogmatism, to the reality of knowledge itself. They therefore have produced a curious gray zone of thought about order that is as characteristic a phenomenon of the time as the ideologies themselves, to which it is opposed. One might speak of an area of secondary ideologies. The phenomenon first could be observed in the wake of the Russian Revolution after the First World War, and gained further strength in connection with National Socialism and the Second World War. Its most important linguistic symbols are the "traditions" and "conservatisms." We have Judaeo-Christian and classical traditions, which, especially in English, roll majestically off the tongue. There are liberals who are conservative and conservatives who are liberal and in any case have understanding for the problems of the time. We discover the City of Man and the *Civitas Humana,* as well as the Brotherhood of Man (*la recherche de la paternité est interdite*); there is a new enthusiasm for the church which already Max Scheler declared to be a special case of "sociological catholicism"; we have a continental-European movement of Christian Democracy drawing its strength chiefly from the odium of Communism, Fascism, or National Socialism that is the burden of their opponents; we have a *démocratie des principes,* a pluralistic democracy, and unceasing renewals of natural law. Thus we are richly supplied with *ordo,* but what is lacking is the noetic clarification that renders conscious the origin of the *ordo* in the existential tension toward the ground. For this reason, there is no strength of conviction of the *ratio* in the debate with ideologies.

(3) Whoever wishes not to get stuck in the secondary ideologies must push on, beyond the traditions, to the predogmatic reality of knowledge. Apart from the mystery of participation that is hidden between God and man, where in the dimension of history of consciousness can we find the hidden reality? And where can we find, together with the reality, the men with whom we can live and die in the community of knowledge? Let us ask concretely: From where did Albert Camus get the strength that sustained him for decades in the tension of his meditation and enabled him to look through the perversion of rebellion and to overcome it? For Camus it came from the myth. "We shall choose Ithaca, the faithful land,

frugal and audacious thought, lucid action, and the generosity of the man who understands."[1] The "madness" of the time is no home for man; he must choose the home in which he, living, will again create a home in time. Camus chooses the myth: "The world where I feel most at ease: the Greek myth."[2] The course of his meditation is the course of his life in which he comes to be "the man who understands." Yet what bends at the end is the beginning. The "understanding man," who gains insight, is the "knowing man" of Parmenides who permits himself to be led to truth. In the *Carnets* one finds the plan of his work in three phases: I. The Myth of Sisyphus (the absurd).—II. The Myth of Prometheus (rebellion).—III. The Myth of Nemesis.[3] From the very first the work was deliberately designed with a view to a meditation in the medium of the myth. In the degree in which his quest through knowledge is illumined, the mood of existence changes. "Now there rises the strange joy which helps us to live and to die and which we shall henceforth refuse to send back until later."[4] The rebellion aims at the presence of life in the tension to the divine ground; it manifests itself in the ideological apocalpyse of the futuristic utopias; when the futuristic alienation from the presence subsides, the joy of the here and now of existence can stir again; the *kakodaimony* gives way to the *eudaimony*.

(4) Conscious-rational orientation of man in the relation to God and world, society and history is possible only when in the knowledge of active participation the *ratio* of this participation is experienced and differentiated. When the desire for knowledge cannot use the dominant symbolisms of society, it must look for the home of the reality of knowledge in the dimension of history. The quest for the "faithful land," which we have exemplified by the meditation of Camus, is just as characteristic of the situation of dogmatomachy as the dogmatisms themselves. The ideologies suppress the *ratio;* the secondary ideologies preserve it in the form of tradition, underneath the crust of the older dogmatisms. Therefore the regeneration of noetic knowledge of order is possible only by the

1. Camus, *L'Homme révolté*, p. 377.
2. Camus, *Carnets* II, p. 317.
3. Camus, *Carnets* II, p. 328.
4. Camus, *L'Homme révolté*, p. 377.

roundabout way of investigating societies whose constitutive self-understanding occurred before or beyond the area of dogmatisms. This third phenomenon of the configuration, the study of the predogmatic realities of knowledge, has grown, parallel with the furor of the ideologies and the return to the traditions. Since the Second World War it has become a movement with strong momentun. It has as yet no center in the sense that the contacts with reality might have conduced to a deliberately undertaken noetic interpretation of order. Rational thinking requires training and the mastery of the materials to which it refers. Even if one does know where the problems lie, one cannot overnight undo a social work of destruction that has gone on for centuries. Since that movement occurs as yet below the threshold of noetic differentiation, it has still but a small effect on political science in the academic sense, at that place where one might expect the major impact. For political science as an academic discipline focuses, with pragmatic intention, primarily on the institutions of national societies and the international organizations. These institutions are precisely the area of ideological and secondary-ideological self-interpretation of order. The same applies to the churches as social organizations, which historically did everything that could provoke the ideological rebellion, under the pressure of which they suffer today. In a material sense our contemporary institutions, therefore, offer only minimal opportunities of an access to the reality of knowledge. If, for instance, one wishes to inform oneself about the great problems of thinking about order in Germany, one would do better to read the literary works of Robert Musil, Hermann Broch, Thomas Mann, Heimito von Doderer, or the dramas of Frisch and Dürrenmatt, rather than the professional literature of politics. Today the most important contributions to a political science—not in the academic but in the noetic sense—come from archaeology, the research on myths and ethnic cultures, the history of the ancient Orient, of classical antiquity and the Far East, from classical philology, the history of Judaism and Christianity, of patristic and scholasticism, from the sciences of comparative religion and comparative literature. For when the symbols of order of a society express a predogmatic reality of knowledge, they impose on the researcher at the very least a motion toward noesis, even though he may not reach the goal. Reversely, the historical materials attract those people in whom the desire for knowledge is alive, since it is in those materials that they find the reality of knowledge. Since the movement has as yet no center, it is preferable to speak of the noetic convergence of its particular phenomena. The material massiveness of the movement is overwhelming. As one makes the round of an American college bookstore, one can come away with a library of predogmatic knowledge in the form of inexpensive paperbacks: monographies of the religious phenomenology of primitives, about sacred kingship and the myth, critical text editions of the Vedas and the Upanishads, the speeches of the Buddha, Lao-tzu, the Qumran texts and most recent passages of the Nag-Hammadi discoveries, documents of Zen-Buddhism, selections of Christian mystics, sources of Chinese, Japanese, and Indian tradition, a covey of new translations of the New Testament and especially of the Gospels, critically revised editions of the Old Testament, histories of Israel, of the apocalypses, of Gnosticism and early Christianity, the religious movement of the megalithicum, and so on. On the other hand, Plato and Aristotle, the great noetics, are still misunderstood as if they were metaphysicians, and their works, even though they are also available as paperbacks, still are overshadowed by the antimetaphysical taboo. This situation has resulted, in America, in certain much-discussed displacements in the departmental structure of the universities: On the one hand, philosophy, under the ban of the antimetaphysical resentment, dries up into logic, while education in "the humanities" is shifting to the departments of history, literature, and religious science, which are correspondingly growing in strength. There is no way of predicting how the here-mentioned phenomena will develop and where the chances for a breakthrough to noesis can be found. At any rate, however, the Western societies of today, compared with the situation fifty years ago, have accumulated an area of latent *ratio* which would make such breakthroughs possible.

The classical noesis and mysticism are the two predogmatic realities of knowledge in which the logos of consciousness was differentiated in a paradigmatic way. They have special importance for any attempt to bring *ratio* once again into the luminosity of consciousness in the struggle against dogmatism. Let us therefore characterize the relation of these two areas for dogmatomachy, as it has developed in the centuries of modernity, even though we cannot do more than give the barest hints of the problem, in the context of this investigation.

(1) I have mentioned the antimetaphysical taboo, in the shadow of which contemporary philosophy is still laboring. The taboo is still so strong that hardly any distinction is made between predogmatic philosophizing and its dogmatic *parekbasis*, or derailment. It is therefore useful to recall some historical dates that, it is true, one can find in any good dictionary of philosophy,[5] the importance of which has nonetheless not penetrated into the publicly shared notions of thought about order. Let us state, first, that neither Plato nor Aristotle were "metaphysicians" and that Aristotle, in particular, never wrote a "metaphysics." The term "Metaphysics," contracted from *meta ta physica*, did not appear until the high Middle Ages. It seems to have had a brief Arab prehistory and then was introduced into Western thought by Thomas, in the *prooemium* of his commentary to Aristotle's metaphysics, as a concept for a philosophical science founded on natural reason. The *prooemium*, however, contains no analysis of the noetic problem but rather proceeds by way of definitions. Thomas defined "metaphysics" summarily as a science of *primae causae*, of *principia maxime universalia*, and of substances *quae sunt maxime a materia separatae*. By way of examples for such causes, principles, and substances, he mentions *ens* and *Deus*. The classical noesis, as I mentioned before, does indeed offer many points at which dogmatic misunderstandings could arise, and since the misunderstandings actually developed immediately after Aristotle in the dogmatism of the schools, the *parekbasis* of dogmatism existed already through fifteen centuries before Thomas. But only Thomas crystallized the misunderstanding into "metaphysics" and brought about the perversion of noetic exegesis by hardening its terms into a propositional science of principles, universals, and substances.

This conception of Thomas has determined the further destinies of "metaphysics." Descartes, in the *Preface* to his *Principles of Philosophy*, defines it as that science "which contains the principles of knowledge, between which is the explanation of the main attributes of God, of the immateriality of our souls,

5. I used André Lalande, *Vocabulaire technique et critique de la philosophie* (Paris, 1962).

and of all the clear and simple ideas which are in us," and puts those over against the principles of natural science and the applied sciences. In the eighteenth century—the "barbaric age of philosophy" (Lachelier)—the philosophes thus had no trouble in throwing overboard the doubtful science of doubtful principles and substances. Voltaire's article, *"métaphysique,"* in his *Dictionnaire Philosophique,* is the decisive document of the time. The antiphilosophical resentment of the ideologist thus is not directed against the classical noesis, of which they know nothing, but against Thomas's design of a propositional "metaphysics" treating of universals, principles, and substances. The ideological rebellion, as I already said, was indeed strongly provoked.

This sympathy with the rebellion, however, has its limit, when rebellion includes the predogmatic noesis into the taboo that was meant for the dogmatic "metaphysics." For when noesis is put into the same basket as "metaphysics," we lose the reality of knowledge of the noetic experience and also the differentiated material structure of the *ratio,* which means that we have no noetic science of order any more. This loss did indeed occur and has become the problem of all attempts of rational thought since the eighteenth century. When Kant wanted to put "metaphysics" again on the path of science, he rebelled both against Baumgarten's *Metaphysica* and the form which Christian Wolff gave to "metaphysics" his voluminous work, but he did not return to the classical philosophers but rather became a critic of "pure reason," who had to contend with the "transcendental appearance." When Hegel wanted to tear philosophy from dogmatic metaphysics and re-establish the right of "experience," he also thought of Wolff's *Metaphysics* as his opponent; his "experience" is not that of classical noesis, either, but a gnostic experience with a strong affinity to Jacob Böhme so that in Hegel *metaphysic* is turned into the new derailment of the *dialectic.* That loss has not been made up to this day. Even Heidegger's remarkable attempt, in his "fundamental philosophy," to regain for his feet the firm ground of the reality of knowledge, was heavily inhibited by his orientation to eighteenth century "metaphysics" as his philosophical antagonist, as well as by the analytical inadequacy of his return to classical philosophy.

(2) Mysticism's reality of knowledge has twice in modern

times become the source of attempts to find the way back from dogmatism to the rationality of thought: once through Bodin, in the sixteenth-century theological dogmatomachy; the other through Bergson, in the situation of the twentieth-century ideological dogmatomachy. Both French spiritualists go back to the neo-Platonic reality of knowledge; in the case of Bodin it is mediated through Pseudo-Dionysius Areopagitica, while Bergson returns directly to Plotinus. For our present purposes it will suffice to characterize these attempts by a reference to Bodin's problem of *conversio*.

In its early form, the problem arises in Bodin's *Letter to Jean Bautru*, of 1563. In this letter Bodin speaks of the confusion of the soul as it is exposed to the pressure of contending religions. He admonishes his friend not to be carried away by the opinions about them (*variae de religionibus sententiae*) but always to remain conscious of "true religion being nothing else than the turning (*conversio*) of a purified spirit to the true God."[6] This definition of the true religion remains constant in Bodin's work. In the *Methodus* of 1566 the formula runs like this: *Religio vero ipsa, id est purgatae mentis in Deum recta conversio.*[7] The term *conversio* has represented, since Eriugena, the *epistrophe* of Pseudo-Dionysius; it is widely used in the literature of the Renaissance, for instance, in the *Oratio Joannis Trithemii de vera conversione mentis ad deum* (1500). The fascination of the Renaissance thinkers by the mysticism of Pseudo-Dionysius seems to have stemmed from the latter's proximity to Plato's noesis, with its emphasis on *eros* in the tension toward the ground. Pico della Mirandola, in his *Heptaplus*—which title probably suggested Bodin's *Heptaplomeres*—investigates the *conversio* of the angels and in this context speaks of the "movement of the *conversio*" as a *motus amoris*.[8] Marsilio Ficino, in his commentary to the *Theologia Mystica* of Pseudo-Dionysius, speaks of the *fruitio Dei* and emphasizes that it is less a movement of self to God but rather a being-moved by him. To this almost Aristotelian

6. Jean Bodin, *Lettre à Jean Bautru de Matras*, in Colomiès' *Gallia Orientalis* (1665), p. 76 ff.; reproduced in Roger Chauvire, *Jean Bodin, Auteur de la république* (Paris, 1914), p. 522 ff. About the letter, cf. Pierre Mesnard, *La Pensée réligieuse de Bodin, Revue du Seizième Siècle*, vol. 16 (1929).

7. Jean Bodin, *Methodus*, p. 32 in the edition of 1566. Now: *Jean Bodin*, (Paris: Edition Pierre Mesnard, 1951), p. 121.

8. Pico della Mirandola, *Heptaplus* III, 2 and 5. *Opera* (Basle, 1601).

understanding of the movement he adds, in the imagery of the *Symposium,* the remark that *fruitio* is not like being emptied but rather like being filled. Finally, it is not a movement of the intellect to the *bonum* but rather a being-carried in by love: *non est per intellectum versari circa bonum, sed amore transferri.*[9]

Pico della Mirandola and Ficino seem to have resorted to mysticism as a method by which they could find and lift into the light of consciousness the existential tension toward the ground, behind the theologico-metaphysical dogmatism. Two generations later, it became Bodin's method to understand the time dimension of consciousness and the structure of history. The *Letter to Jean Bautru* contrasts the solitude of the *conversio* to the sociality of the historical religions. Men do not all have the same spiritual rank. There are the select ones—*selecti vitae puriores homines*—to whom revelations occur, and there is the great mass of mortals who would grope in eternal darkness if God did not from time to time stir up the "highest virtues" in some particular persons so that they can point out the right road to their fellow-beings. The fate of the select ones, both in the *historia sacra* and the *historia pagana,* is pathetic. They are slandered, exiled, killed, and punished as subverters. Even when their message becomes socially effective, it soon is distorted by superstition, when the historical-human form of revelation is taken for its essence, and fanatical literalists obscure its function, i.e., the purification of the spirit and the turning of the soul to God. Mankind is understood as a society in the mode of existence of history, and history as divided into periods and regions of civilization, in each of which there occurs the inevitable drama of the spirit: the appearance of the prophet—the transformation of *vera religio* of the solitary soul into the historical religion of the people—finally a return form the historical religion to the solitude of the prophetic soul. In Bodin's later work this image of history is subject to several changes and supplementations but remains constant in its fundamental features. It is closely related to the image of history of Bergson: the opening of the soul, the rigidification on the new level, and the renewed opening, in his *Two Sources of Morality and Religion* (1932).

Bodin is no utopian. Neither the different levels of spiritual

---

9. Marsilio Ficino, *Dionysii Areopagitae, de Mystica Theologia, ad Timotheum Liber, Opera* (Basle, 1576), vol. II, p. 1019f.

rank of various men nor the pluralism of the historical religions will disappear from history. In his later years, his insight into the problem seems to have penetrated deeper, as he sees pluralism no longer as a consequence of the differentiations of spiritual rank but as a necessary result of the sociality of symbolic expressions. The symbols are described as means that are essentially inadequate to express fully the reality of knowing participation. Behind the knowledge, which enters into the symbol, there is always the ineffability of the knowledge about the inexhaustibility of the ground. While the *conversio* remains the way to escape the dogmatomachy of the literalists, it does not remove the tension between the symbol and the ineffability. As soon as the knowledge of participation is communicated, it enters into the realm of symbolism, and enters only as far as it can enter into symbolic expressions. The *parekbasis* into literalist dogma, therefore, can be avoided only by maintaining the balance between symbols and the knowledge back of it. That is Bodin's position in his late work, the *Colloquium Heptaplomeres* of 1593. The participants in the great religious conversation take leave from each other with embraces and assurances of friendship. "Never again did they dispute about religions," but each one remained active within his own.[10] Symbolism is no more than the last word of each historical religion; the reality of faith through *conversio* lies beyond the symbols.[11]

Bodin's insight into the essence of tolerance, as a balance between silence and the expression of a reality of knowledge, has employed insights of the *Theologica Mystica* of Pseudo-Dionysius for the area of noesis. Further fruitions of the same source are few and far between in modern centuries. One cannot escape the difficulty of communicating the insight into the balance of tolerance, precisely because one of the areas to be balanced is that of silence. Thus there is no language other than the existential tension toward the ground that could express the depth of the ground. Pseudo-Dionysius tried to find a way out by putting the preposition *hyper* before the philosophical and

10. Jean Bodin, *Colloquium Heptaplomeres de Rerum sublimium arcanis abditis,* ed. L. Noack (1857), *in fine.*

11. Joseph Lecler, S. J., in his *Histoire de la tolérance au siècle de la reforme* (Paris 1955), vol. II, p. 154 ff., inclines to define the position of Bodin as that of a deist. Even though I do not consider this view as correct, it still has its value, for in the mysticism of Jean Bodin I see indeed the possibility of dogmatic derailment into the deism of the seventeenth century.

revelatory symbols of the ground; thus he arrives at such compound words as *hypertheos, hypersophos, hyperagathos, hyperkalos, hyperousios, hyperagnostos, hyperarchios,* and so on.[12] Even were one to extend this series further, one still does not gain more than the insights that we (1) experience, in the tension to the ground, reality transcending incomprehensibly everything that we experience in participation, and that we (2) can speak of the ineffable only by characterizing it as going beyond the symbolic language of participation. In his discussion of Pseudo-Dionysius's *De divinis nominibus,* Thomas Aquinas has brought the problem of the depth of the ground to the following formulation: The name HE WHO IS is most proper for God because it goes beyond the particular forms of mundane life. Beyond that name, there is the name GOD, because it signifies the divine character of the ground; and beyond that there is the name Tetragrammaton, since it expressed the incommunicability of the divine substance. (*ST* I, XIII, 11) Thus Thomas identifies three areas that we also have encountered in our analysis of the existential tension toward the ground: (*a*) the area of noetic exegesis that cannot go beyond the symbol of the ground of being; (*b*) the area of the comprehensive pneumatic reality of knowledge to which belongs also the experience of being personally addressed by God; and (*c*) the area of the incomprehensible, of which we know only that it is the area which we touch by the symbolic terms of noetic and pneumatic experiences. Insofar, however, as we know about the ineffable beyond the expressions of experience by means of such symbols as the Ineffable or the Silence, this knowledge, too, belongs to the consciousness of the ground as one of the dimensions of its logos.

The insight into the knowledge of the Ineffable is most important for the understanding of a large class of phenomena of order. Tolerance, understood as balance between the areas of silence and of symbolic expressions that we just mentioned, is one of the phenomena of this class. Tolerance is only one part in an area the scope of which becomes clear when we consider

12. About the terminology of Pseudo-Dionysius, cf. the terminological table in P. G. Théry, *Etudes Dionysiennes* II (Paris, 1937), s.v. *épistrophe.* Further the Index Terminologique in: Maurice de Gandillac, *Oeuvres complètes du Pseudo-Denys l'Aréopagite* (Paris, 1943).

that the dimension of the Ineffable appears not only in the noetic consciousness but similarly also in the experiential modalities of compactness, differentiation, and the *parekbasis*. The phenomena of this class cannot be more than intimated here: When the experience of the Ineffable remains compact, the respective symbolic expressions for the consciousness of the divine ground receive a specifically sacred character. In them the divine ground appears completely and definitely incarnated, so alternative symbolic expressions of the knowledge of participation are inadmissible and must not be replaced by new symbols of a differentiated experience. If, historically, the experiences become differentiated nonetheless, they must assume the form of a commentary on the sacred text. Among the examples of such sacred texts that impose on subsequent differentiated experiences the character of commentaries are the Vedas or the classical Chinese writings. In the Judaeo-Christian area, we find the similar phenomena of the canonization of scriptures, the Torah and scriptural commentary, the interpretative change of the meaning of the sacred texts by allegoresis and theologizing. When the Ineffable, on the other hand, is differentiated vis-à-vis the sphere of historico-human symbolism, the new expression for the differentiated experiences appears as the phenomenon of mysticism. In the Christian area, the new type of symbol of Pseudo-Dionysius's *Theologica Mystica* (about 500) is added to the affirmative and negative theology. From there the main line of Western mysticism runs down to our own time. Finally, when the balance between the differentiated Ineffable and symbolic expression is lost again, the spiritual discussion may then sink down to the level of contentions about correct theologies. The situation of dogmatomachy is at hand. The symbolism of theological dogma, which obtains its differentiated meaning from the balance to the differentiated Ineffable, can derail into an unbalanced and rigid dogmatism; and the type of the derailed dogma in turn may become the prototype of "the truth," becoming the orientation not only for the theologians but also for the ideologists following thereafter. In the area of the ideological *parekbasis* there then arise the well-known phenomena of the ideological classics and the ensuing literature of commentaries and apologetics, a phenomenon closely akin to that of compact sacred texts and their commentaries.

CHAPTER ELEVEN

The Concrete Consciousness

Human consciousness is not a free-floating something but always the concrete consciousness of concrete persons. The consciousness of the existential tension toward the ground, therefore, while constituting the specific human nature that distinguishes man from other beings, is not the whole of his nature, for consciousness is always concretely founded on man's bodily existence, through which he belongs to all levels of being, from the anorganic to the animalic. Following Aristotle, we call the character of man, as an epitome of all levels of being, his synthetic nature. Concrete man orders his existence from the level of his consciousness, but that which is to be ordered is not only his consciousness but his entire existence in the world.

Man's bodily existence is also the basis for his social existence. This may grow quantitatively from the family, to the labor-dividing small society, to that size in which ordering consciousness finds the material basis for the unfolding of the *eu zen,* the good life, Aristotle's criterion of the *eunomia,* the good social order. No matter how well ordered society may be, its corporeality, compelling it to provide material care and the control of the passions, requires an existence in the form of organized rulership. The organization of society through representatives charged with care for the social order within and for defense against external dangers is the *conditio sine qua non* of society to such an extent that the investigation and description of the various pragmatic organizations is a main part of political science. A theory of politics cannot stop there, however, since this part deals only with that aspect of political reality that is founded in man's corporeality.

The implications of the concreteness of consciousness for the structure of political reality as well as for the interpretation of its order must be clarified by means of a series of corollaries:

(1) A theory of politics must cover the problem of the order of man's entire existence. In actuality, however, the title theory also covers attempts to interpret order that postulate either a

free-flowing consciousness without corporeal foundation or a corporeal foundation without ordering consciousness. Such attempts are symptoms of a disease that indicate the pneumopathic phenomenon of the loss of reality, the obscuring of sectors of reality—the *skotosis*, to use the *terminus technicus* that Lonergan has recently coined for this phenomenon.[1]

(a) When a theorist is inclined to liberate consciousness from man's corporeality, there arise symbols of order like the realm of the spirits, or the perfect realm of reason to which mankind is approaching, or the withering away of the state and the coming of the *Third Reich* of the Spirit, or the realms of perfection that are expected as the result of a metastasis of man to a *homo novus* or a superman, be it that of Marx or that of Nietzsche. One can speak of this class of symbols as utopian, if one means by utopia, in Thomas More's sense, a fantasy of order in the construction of which an essential factor of the corporeal basis has been omitted. Utopian thinking dominates the arguments of our daily political debate: Those who subjugate their fellow-beings by the terror of violence in order to enter into the perfect realm of utopia are heroes of liberty and peace; those who are not fooled by ideologies but rather defend themselves as long as it is still possible are militarists, imperialists, aggressors, or at least belong to a *Wall Street Circle*.

(b) When *skotosis* extends to the ordering consciousness, then there remains only man in his corporeality and his lusts. If the phenomenon of organic society is to be interpreted from the point of this residual reality, order must be construed as an artifact generated by contract. The appearance of the so-called contractarian theories is heuristically valuable for the theorist, since it points to the wider syndrome of spiritual disturbances in a society, of which disturbance the contract theories are only a part. There is no need to discuss the contract theories further at this point, since the essential remarks have already been made by Plato in Book II of the *Republic*.

(2) The concrete consciousness of concrete man is the only consciousness given in our experience. Such constructions as a collective consciousness—either the consciousness of a society or the consciousness of mankind in history—are hypostases that

---

1. Bernard J. F. Lonergan, *Insight. A Study of Human Understanding* (1957), (New York, 1958), pp. 191–203.

have no standing in theory. For instance, when we said that each society produces the symbols through which it expresses its experience of order, we did not mean that the society is a subject having a consciousness that could interpret itself through symbols. Such statements are, rather, an abbreviated way of talking about the process by which concrete persons create a social field, i.e., a field in which their experiences of order are understood by other concrete men who accept them as their own and make them into the motive of their habitual actions. Fields of this kind are called societies if their size and relative stability in time allows us to identify them. Since such fields are processes and not objects given once and for all, they manifest not only the processual characteristics of their founding and preservation but also those of resistance and mutation, of tradition and differentiating development, of ensuing rigidity and revolt, and so on, until their final decomposition and disappearance.

(3) The social fields of concrete consciousness are not identical with organized societies, even though the ideologists of power like to assume that social organization exhausts all political reality. We are in the realm of freedom of the concrete consciousness. True, every organized society is sustained by a social field of consciousness expressed in the respective civil theology, but that sustaining consciousness is not the only social field in society and many of the other fields far transcend the area of social power. One may refer to the danger to the national consciousness constituted by the ideological social fields in our time and also to the precarious compromise of pluralistic democracy, by means of which one hopes to maintain a balance between the potentially disruptive fields and the sustaining field of an organized society. Furthermore, the fields of consciousness are not personally and mutually exclusive, as they must be in organized societies with their basis in corporeality; rather a concrete consciousness may belong to several fields at the same time. A Greek living in the fourth century B.C., for instance, can be simultaneously an Athenian and a Hellene, a Sophist or philosopher, and a member of a mystery cult.

(4) The theorist should give special attention to the much neglected problem that Toynbee has raised in his *Study of History*. In addition to the organized societies typified, for instance, by the Sumeric city states, the Greek polis, the Chinese *kuo,* or

Western national states, there are the civilizations or cultures. They are doubtlessly identifiable as social fields; and they doubtlessly extend far beyond the listed types of organized units. According to Toynbee's theory, however, they are related to these units in the way that they furnish the framework for historical power struggles. In the process of a civilization, the above mentioned types of units are therefore subdivisions which characterize one phase of the process, while a later phase brings forth the imperial organization of the entire civilization into a so-called universal state. Beyond the subunits of organization Toynbee introduces the historical process of power and the civilization as its framework in order to determine the *intelligible field of study*, which through this expansion of the temporal dimension does not cease to be a study of political reality. I see no theoretical objection against the inclusion of the time dimension into the study of the organizational units. And if Toynbee's massive empirical materials have secured anything, then it is the thesis that the organized units of the type of national states cannot be the last units of historical studies but that, rather, civilizations are the minimum field.

(5) I am speaking somewhat cautiously of the civilizations as the minimum field of the study, for one may object to Toynbee's concept of the *intelligible field of study* that it has been too narrowly drawn by its identification with civilizations. There are, of course, universal states that constitute indeed the late imperial organization of a civilization, for instance, the empire of the Han Dynasty in China. But there are also multicivilizational empires, like the Persian Empire, the intended empire of Alexander's conquest, or the Roman Empire. Toynbee's theory of civilizations has in principle raised a problem that should be further investigated, for the just mentioned examples indicate that beyond civilizations there are still more comprehensive fields of the process of power. These wider fields have been well observed and theorized at the time of their creation. To Herodotus we owe the concept of the ecumene, meaning the entire known world of culture that potentially might be organized. He mentions it in the context of the Persians. The concept of the ecumene then appears again in Polybius as a designation of the *telos* of Roman expansion. Finally it figures both in Christianity and Manichaeism as the term for the *telos* of missionary expansion. The ecumene, meaning the respectively

contemporaneous cultured humanity as a field of potential organization, seems to be a social field of consciousness that belongs to the structure of political reality. The problem deserves
special attention because in our time the global ecumene has
become just as much a potential field of organization by
ideological empires as the smaller ecumene of the Persians was
in Herodotus' time.

(6) Careful distinction must be made between the ecumene
as a field of contemporaneous cultured humanity and humanity in the sense of the universal field of history. When the consciousness of order, moved by the existential tension toward the
ground, attains the luminosity of the noetic and pneumatic experiences, it is attended by its knowledge of humankind. The
knowledge of humankind interprets itself by the symbols of
man and of humanity. Man and humanity thus are not objects
of the external world about which one could make empirically
certain propositions; rather they are symbols found by concrete
men, with ascertainable historical dates, as an expression for
the universally representative character of their experience of
the ground. It is only by means of this symbolism that a field of
universal history is interpretatively constituted, into which we
try to order all human events in time. To this universal field, by
virtue of retrospective interpretation, belong all men and social
fields, even though they may not themselves have attained the
optimum luminosity of experience that would enable them to
articulate consciously their being part of this field. When we use
this concept without qualifying attributes, we therefore mean
by "history" the interpretative field of a consciousness that experiences its essential humanity.

(7) Universal humanity is a symbol rather than a field of
potential organization. Further, it is not a framework of a process of power, as are the civilizations and ecumenes, for besides
the now living persons it also embraces all men of the past and
the future. The experience of essential humanity rather is the
point at which concrete men experience their concrete consciousness as the place at which man, even though existing in
time, participates in the eternal being of the ground. The consciousness of the existential tension toward the ground, i.e.,
man's center of order, ontically rises above all immanent-
temporal processes of history.

(8) History is a field of interpretation. The origin of the

symbol in the knowledge of essential humanity determines the material principle of the interpretation, in so far as men and social fields of the past must be interpreted for the order of their existence. Since a society expresses its experience of order by corresponding symbols, every study of order must concentrate on the acts of self-understanding and then pursue from this center the ramifications into the order of the collective existence—in other words, into the government and administration, the economy, the social hierarchy, the educational system, and so on. With this we have again returned to the non-noetic self-understanding of society, the point from which we set out. Whatever structures of the universal field are discovered in the course of such an investigation belong to empirical research rather than to speculative construction. At any rate, these structures can be no more than lines of meaning in the past of the field. The total structure of the universal field, which conventionally is called "the meaning of history" is no possible object of knowledge. The interpretations of the total meaning, as represented since the middle of the eighteenth century under the title "philosophy of history," are therefore to be seen as acts of the self-interpretation of ideological social fields rather than as noetic interpretation of history and its order. There is no need further to elaborate on the pragmatic meaning of these "philosophies of history," since all of us know that they are dominant in the contemporary political scene.

(9) In the optimum luminosity of consciousness man experiences himself both as existing in time and as participating in the eternity of the ground. The tension toward the eternity of the ground therefore belongs to the structure of the universal field. Nothing more than has been said here can be remarked about the participation of the universal field in the eternity of the ground on the basis of noetic analysis, but it is possible to symbolize this participation on the basis of pneumatic experiences. The symbolisms of this class are usually called eschatologies. When using this term, we need not necessarily think of the revelatory eschatologies of Christianity. Eschatological symbolisms are found also in the context of the classical noesis, especially in Plato's dialogues. But Plato was a philosopher who knew how to philosophize. His eschatological interpretations never raise the claim to be noetic analysis or empirical propositions; he always dressed them in the mantle of the myth.

CHAPTER TWELVE

About the Function of Noesis

Noetic exegesis differentiates the *ratio* as the material structure of consciousness. The authoritative knowledge of the *ratio* is the basis for the critical function of noesis in the relation to the non-noetic interpretations of order as formulated in the course of our study: Noesis frees the structure of the world in a radical way by removing mythical, revelatory, ideological, and other mortgages on truth (p. 177) and it can remove these mortgages by examining the truths of the non-noetic experiences with a view to their compatibility with the properly noetic knowledge of the logos of consciousness (p. 184f.). Numerous examples in the course of this investigation have made clear how these general formulations are to be applied concretely. All the same, it is useful, by way of conclusion, to sketch the entire structure of noetic interpretation, for thereby we obtain a model of theory that elucidates the criteria with the help of which topical symbols of order in our time are to be examined.

Our study set out from the classical noesis but went considerably further. In order to sketch the entire structure of noetic interpretation in the sense of our results, we therefore need a more differentiated language than that of classical philosophy. No longer can we speak, without qualification, of "human nature," "the nature of society," or of "the essence of history," as if "man," "society," and "history" were things unconnected with each other, of which each had a "nature" or "essence" by itself. For symbols of this type, although they belong to the area of classical noesis, are characterized by the fact that experienced realities are expressed, through them, with the still compact immediacy of prenoetic, cosmic primary experience. Noetic experience, however, brings into view the relations between the ground of being and man, ground of being and world, man and world, as well as the relations between things in the world, so that the reality-image of being replaces the reality-image of the cosmic primary experience. That does not mean that the primarily experienced reality—gods and men, cosmos and society—turns out to have been no reality. It means that the noetic experience differentiates structures that change the image of reality as a whole. These changes, in the wake of the noetic experience, are not brought about all at once but are the result of a thousand-year process. In the area of classical noesis, the investigation of political reality is still predominantly an investigation of organized society in which the thinkers are living, i.e., of the polis. Such empires as that of the Persians remain at the margin, even though their political reality can hardly be denied. The question of a society of spiritual substance detaching itself from the decaying organized society is not pushed to the point of a theory of spiritual revolution and social, new foundation, although the tension between the two social fields is the central theme of Plato's and Aristotle's politics, and the new society finds some expression in the foundation of philosophical schools. The experience of universal humankind is not embodied in suitable symbolic expressions, although the fulfillment of human existence through the *bios theoretikos*, beyond the fulfillment through one's existence as citizen, continues to press toward such expression. The problems of civilization as framework of power processes do not shake the confidence in the polis as the exclusive field of study, even though Aristotle was a witness of the conquests of Philip and Alexander. In addition to the organized society in which we live and which we experience compactly as *the* reality of society, there are also the further experiences of man and society, which we have just adumbrated. Beyond them there are the pneumatic experiences of order as expressed in prophesy, metastatic faith, apocalypse, and gnosis; further, the in-depth differentiations of the ground of being by mysticism on which are based tolerance and the balancing of the symbolism of order by the ineffability; further still the experiences of rebellion with the corresponding "philosophies of history" and their mass movements, and so on. Horizons of experience thus open vistas of human existence and its order, which compel us to place the compact units of primary experience in wider contexts. This context of human experiences and order, which is much more comprehensive than the compactly experienced ambiance of one's respective organized society, we call the *realm of man.*

The *realm of man* is not an object of empirical perception but a function of the participating consciousness. If we posit the existential tension toward the ground as the center of man's order, the realm of man comprises "objectively" all phenomena of human order that originate in the reality of knowledge of participation. Phenomena of order become "objective" in the noetic sense only insofar as the noetic exegesis differentiates the logos of consciousness, so they become recognizable as phenomena originating in the center of order of consciousness. The realm of man, then, is empirically determined (a) by the history of the knowledge of participation and of the phenomena of order derived therefrom and (b) by the historically respective level of noetic exegesis. This strict, empirical determination forbids any deviation in the name of arbitrary images of reality that present themselves under the title of "theory."

As the noetic consciousness of the flowing presence intends "objectively" the realm of man, there unfolds a nexus of problems the structure of which is determined by the noetic movement. The movement originates in the existential tension that drives toward the noetic exegesis of consciousness. When the movement transcends the concrete, self-interpreting consciousness and expands toward the interpretation of order in the realm of man, it must move along certain objective lines; along these lines there are found certain objective areas; and the areas, in turn, are related to each other in intelligible ways. The objective lines, objective areas, and their relations are the parts of the model, with the help of which noesis discharges its critical function.

The objective lines, along which the exegesis expands toward interpretation, are, first, the line from man to humankind and, second, the line from consciousness to the corporeal foundation. Let us characterize the model that is engendered by the movement of the noetic consciousness along these lines:

(1) The existential tension toward the ground is man's center of order. Starting from this center and moving along the line toward humankind, three objective areas can be distinguished: (a) In the first place, the order of the concrete-human consciousness from which the movement originates; following, (b) the order of human existence in organized society, as well as the order of nonorganized social fields; further (c) the order of human and social existence in history. The following relations

link these areas to each other: (*a*) the series is neither reversible, nor can (*b*) an objective area exchanges its place with another, nor can (*c*) any of these areas become an object independent of the two others.

(2) Moving on from the consciousness of existential tension into the corporeal basis, we run, in the realm of man, into the synthetic nature of man, in Aristotle's sense, with its realms of human-psychic, animalic, vegetative, and inanimate being. These tiers of the hierarchy of being are related to each other in (*a*) the material dependence of the higher on the lower and (*b*) the organization of the lower by the higher ones. The relations are not reversible. On the one hand, there is no *eu zen,* no good life in Aristotle's meaning, without the basis of *zen;* on the other hand, the order of the good life does not emerge from the corporeal foundation but originates only when the entire existence is ordered from the center of the existential tension.

(3) Inasmuch as neither man, nor society, nor history occur without a corporeal foundation, the objective areas overlap and fit together into a comprehensive structure of the realm of man. The relations and the rule of their irreversibility apply to the model as a whole.

The model does not concretize the multitude of problems that were mentioned in our investigation by way of examples, but rather the model is confined to the two great objective lines in the realm of man. In spite of this simplifying limitation, it is of considerable value, given the state of science in our time, because it draws attention to violations of the model in the socially dominant ideologies. The violations occur either against the rules of the relationships within the model or against the structure of the model as a whole.

An example of a violation against the rules of relations is the conception of order of the ideological mass movements. The series man-society-history is reversed so that, under the title "philosophy of history," history itself becomes the dominant factor of interpretation which dislodges the existential center of order as well as the organized society. In his study, *L'Angoisse du temps présent et les devoirs de l'esprit* (1953), Paul Ricœur has dealt with the violation and its consequences. He mentions a "new level" of the sense of existence that has been attained by the "philosophers of history." He calls it "historical" because in this new conception of order man "figures as the protagonist—the maker and the sufferer—of the history of men taken at its collective level. It is by a remarkable leap, which we can attribute to Hegelianism and to French sociology, that we pass from the concerns of mental health to the destiny of groups, peoples and classes." The consequence of this violation, when the false theory is taken for a right interpretation of order, is the opening up of a new source of anxiety. Suppose the ratio of speculation and the meaning of existence do not correspond to each other? "A terrifying possibility is discovered by anxiety: what if the effective history has no meaning? what if Hegel's mediation is nothing but a philosopher's invention? The nothingness the threat of which is announced is a nothingness of meaning, on the very level of the spirit, a nothingness of meaning at the heart of this presumed meaning which should give both purpose and task to mental hygiene and should cure Narcissus."[1]

A violation against the structure as a whole is implied in the question about principles that was put at the beginning of our investigation. We said then that there are no principles of political science, because there are no propositions. Rather, the "propositions" of political science are common-sense insights into correct modes of action concerning man's existence in society, from insights concerning the organization of government, to insights into the requirements of domestic and foreign policy, finance and military policy, down to concrete decisions. We know, for instance, the tendency of power to be abused by its possessor and we consider it expedient, in the interest of order, to attach to the possessor of power advisory, controlling, or vetoing instances; we know that cabinets should have no more than a certain number of members because beyond the number of twenty consultations and decisions become most difficult. Especially in the area peripheral to the person, e.g., the organization of administration, those insights have conduced to types of order of great stability so that a study of bureaucracy, like that of Max Weber, could become a "classic" of political science. In areas that are closer to the human person, however, commonsense insights seem disposed to sway with the winds of history. The present Basic Law of the Federal Republic of Germany, for instance, has weakened the presidential executive power as compared with the stronger position of the president

1. Paul Ricoeur, *Histoire et Verité* (Paris, 1955), p. 252 ff.

in the Weimar Constitution because that stronger position made possible the rise of Hitler. The constitution of the Fifth Republic of France, however, has strengthened the position of the president, as compared with the constitutions of the Third and Fourth Republic, in order to avoid the frequent crises of government. Proportional representation is considered unfavorably by a number of German political scientists, again because it was a factor in the rise of Hitler; in America, however, it is looked upon with favor because it has often helped to break the power of a political machine on the municipal level. Probably there will never be "classical" studies about the presidency or proportional representation because the situations contains too many historical variables to admit typification. Commonsense insights, even the most tried and stable ones, are no "propositions" beyond which there could be found principles. If we go beyond the commonsense level we get to the insights into order of consciousness, by which commonsense insights receive their direction. These insights, however, do not have the character of higher generality vis-à-vis common sense but that of the lowest propositions which directly interpret a concrete experience. The insights of noesis owe their "height" not to their generality but to the level of the participating consciousness in the hierarchy of levels of being. The existential tension toward the ground orders the entire existence of man, the corporeal foundation included. Every attempt to construe the commonsense insights, which refer to the order of the entire existence, as scientific "propositions" according to the model of the natural sciences, and to find beyond them "principles" that could take the place of the real source of order, is a violation against the structure of the realm of man. Furthermore, every attempt of this kind is not only a symptom of existential disturbance but also a source of social disorder insofar as it can induce disturbances of the rational consciousness in other people.

The term *common sense*, which we have just used, must be understood in the sense of the Scottish School, especially of Thomas Reid. For Reid, man is *rationis particeps*, in Cicero's sense; and common sense is a compact type of rationality. "There is a certain degree of it which is necessary to our being subjects of law and government, capable of managing our own affairs, and answerable for our conduct towards others: This is called common sense, because it is common to all men with whom we can transact business, or call to account for their conduct." Common sense means the same as "a branch or degree of *ratio*" for which a separate name is justifiable in "that in the greatest part of mankind no other degree of reason is to be found. It is this degree that entitles them to the denomination of reasonable creatures." Common sense, therefore, does not connote a social deadweight of vulgar ideas, nor any *idées reçues* or "relatively natural world view," but rather it is the habit of judgment and conduct of a man formed by *ratio:* one could say, the habit of an Aristotelian *spoudaios* minus the luminosity of his knowledge of the *ratio* as the source of his rational judgment and conduct. Common sense is a civilizational habit that presupposes noetic experience, without the man of this habit having himself a differentiated knowledge of *noesis*. The civilized *homo politicus* need not be a philosopher, but he must have common sense.[2]

The reference to the common sense is meant to make clear once more that and why there can be no "theory of politics" in the sense of principles rising above the propositions of an "empirical" science of politics. For the "empiry" of politics is the habit of common sense which, although compact, has been formed by the *ratio* as the material structure of consciousness. As we characterized this habit as that of the *spoudaios* minus the luminosity of consciousness, we also could reverse the statement and say that Aristotle's *Politics,* insofar as it does not deal with the logos of consciousness itself, is a commonsense study of typical situations that arise in society and history when man attempts to order his collective existence. Not without reason did Aristotle identify the *episteme politike* with the virtue of *phronesis*.

The reflection about the close relation between common sense and classical politics was meant to call attention to the limits of common sense as well as to its importance. As far as the importance is concerned, the phenomenon of common sense as

2. Thomas Reid, *Essays on the Intellectual Powers of Man* (1785) and *Essays on the Active Powers of the Human Mind* (1788). For the passages quoted, cf. *Intellectual Powers,* Essay VI, ch. 11 "Of Common Sense"; for the context also *Active Powers,* Essay III/3 "Of the Rational Principles of Actions". *The Works of Thomas Reid,* ed. Hamilton, 8th ed. (Edinburgh, 1895).

a refuge of *ratio* in the modern crisis of order can hardly be overestimated. Commonsense philosophy arose in the eighteenth century as resistance both against theologico-metaphysical dogmatism and skepticism—just in time not to be broken by the ideological dogmatism. It is not a secondary ideology like the "traditions" but a genuine residue of noesis. The remarkable strength of the Anglo-American cultural area in resisting the ideologies could be traced to the strong social field of common sense. As far as the limitations are concerned, they are given by the noetic compactness of common sense. We are living in the time of ideological dogmatomachy. The ideologies, in spite of their dogmatic derailments, constitute an explicit coming-to-grips with the order of consciousness. Common sense may insist on its self-assuredness "to judge of things self-evident" but it cannot meet the ideologies on their level of argumentation, since it does not have an explicit noesis. The remarkable power of resistance of the Anglo-American social field against the ideologies, of which we just spoke, must not obscure the just as remarkable sterility of the philosophical contention with the ideologies. If common sense, thus, is a pragmatic factor of highest importance for the stability of political order in the West, it still is no substitute for differentiated noesis, in our historical situation. The desire for "principle" of political science, however, which I characterized above as a potential source of social disorder, seems to me also to express a genuine desire to go beyond the relative inadequacy of common sense and to attain again the luminosity of noetic consciousness.

Index